OPEN FIRE

OPEN FIRE

THE OPEN MAGAZINE PAMPHLET SERIES ANTHOLOGY

Number 1

Edited by
Greg Ruggiero and Stuart Sahulka

THE NEW PRESS
New York

An earlier version of "U.S. Politics and Global Warming"by Tom Athanasiou appeared in the April 1991 issue of *The Socialist Review*.
"Los Angeles Was Just the Beginning" by Mike Davis is an expanded version of two articles originally published in *The Nation*, © *The Nation* 1992

Published in the United States by The New Press, New York
Distributed by W. W. Norton & Company, Inc.
500 Fifth Avenue, New York, NY 10110

The editors wish to thank the authors, who permitted us to publish their work for little or no pay; Joe Albanese for his invaluable friendship, energy, and ideas; Noreen Carver, Flora Martins, John Schwartz, and Tracey Cooper for their friendship and support; the South End Press collective for their camaraderie and encouragement; and Yvette Tillema for all her help managing things in Amsterdam.

LIBRARY OF CONGRESS CATALOGING-IN-PUBLICATION DATA

Open fire / edited by Greg Ruggiero and Stuart Sahulka. — 1st ed.
p. cm. — (The Open magazine pamphlet series anthology ; no. 1)
ISBN 1-56584-056-9 :
1. United States—Politics and government—1989–1993.
2. United States—Social conditions—1980–
3. Radicalism—United States.
I. Ruggiero, Greg. II. Sahulka, Stuart. III. Series.
E881.064 1993
973.928—dc20 92-50758

First Edition

Book design by Laura Lindgren

Established in 1990 as a major alternative to the large, commercial publishing houses, The New Press is intended to be the first full-scale nonprofit American book publisher outside of the university presses. The Press is operated editorially in the public interest, rather than for private gain; it is committed to publishing in innovative ways works of educational, cultural, and community value, which, despite their intellectual merits, might not normally be "commercially viable."

——THIS BOOK IS DEDICATED TO——

David Barsamian of Alternative Radio, whose constant camaraderie, encouragement, and friendship has made the Open Magazine Pamphlet Series a reality;

Camille and Robert Ruggiero for their generosity and support in allowing a portion of their home to become the Pamphlet Series headquarters for its first year;

Everyone at Falcon Printing in Westfield, New Jersey, for their excellent work and lightning speed in printing all of our pamphlets.

CONTENTS

THE NEW WORLD ORDER

SILENCE=DEATH
The Body As Battleground

GREENING AMERICA

A THOUSAND POINTS OF LIGHT

Race, Repression, and Resistance

STORMING OZ

PREFACE

Greg Ruggiero and Stuart Sahulka

Let your life be a counter-friction to stop the machine.
—Henry David Thoreau

Broadcast = Attack.
—Radio Patapoe, Amsterdam

The *Open Magazine Pamphlet Series* was created as an emergency broadcast effort in resistance to the Gulf War and the sickening incest between the media and state that supported it.

While Iraqi people were being devastated by 42 days of round-the-clock bombing, people in the United States and Europe received nothing more than a spectacle of pro-war propaganda, dubious poll results, and commercial programming. Little authentic information, dialogue, or debate flowed through the tourniquet of yellow ribbons that Washington, CNN, and the major media tightened around the pulse of public intelligence.

The Gulf War grimly illustrates how thoroughly media diversions corrupt the information base necessary for a functional democracy. Now, more than two years and two dozen pamphlets later, we are still protesting—but instead of one war, we are protesting many wars, instead of questioning the power and actions of one administration, we are questioning why only two parties and a handful of commercial media networks dominate the entirety of political discourse in this country.

A functional democracy is a progression of ongoing struggles and open debates. So long as we do not control our own government, our government will continue to control *us*. The question is, what new strategies can we employ to build a more democratically empowered citizenry? With the twelve-year curse of right-wing control temporarily lifted, glasnost, if not perestroika, is possible in America. Instead of relaxing, we must now bridge our differences, raise our voices, organize, and act.

The wars being waged today, like past wars, will eventually pass. The president in office today will join the others in the Disney wax museum. What will never pass is our determination to continually exert our freedom, define our own cultures, and achieve the highest attainable standards of health, education, and welfare.

The quality of our democracy depends on the degree of public intelligence exercised on a day-to-day basis—in the press, in our homes and places of work, and in our schools. However, in an age so much defined by characters like George Bush, Charles Keating, David Duke, and Jesse Helms, public intelligence itself is a subversive activity. Such is the state of our democracy.

This book gathers the work of one dozen insurgent scholars, activists, and historians whose analysis and opinion call for radical change in almost every sector of American society. These are voices from the frontlines of contemporary activism, from the grass roots of American culture.

As a record of dissidence in America, however, *Open Fire* is far from complete. The voices of Native American resistance and the imperatives of urban restructuring and economic rebuilding are but a few of the glaring omissions. These and other urgent concerns will be addressed in our next anthology.

In the meantime, our work with the *Open Magazine Pamphlet Series* aims not just to publish dissident perspectives and trigger debate, but to disseminate information as an act of social empowerment. Whether we connect over the airwaves or in the streets, through pamphlets or in the flesh, until there is open freedom there will continue to be open fire.

HOWARD ZINN

Introduction
ON PAMPHLETEERING IN AMERICA

Perhaps the most important publication in the history of the United States was neither a book nor a periodical, but a pamphlet. It was Tom Paine's *Common Sense,* which appeared in the English colonies of North America early in 1776, and emblazoned across the sky the bold, exciting idea that was in the mind of more and more colonists: Independence from England!

Paine's words were simple, his logic powerful, his message provocative: "Society in every state is a blessing, but Government even in its best state is but a necessary evil."

And the English monarchy, he went on to say, was far from the "best state." So why endure its rule? "I challenge the warmest advocate of reconciliation to show a single advantage that this continent can reap by being connected with Great Britain."

England had involved the colonists in war after war. There was no practical economic advantage to remain an English colony.

Paine laid on argument after argument, like a master bricklayer, and then came to an emotional climax: "Everything that is right or reasonable pleads for separation. The blood of the slain, the weeping voice of nature cries, 'TIS TIME TO PART."

Common Sense went through twenty-five editions and sold hundreds of thousands of copies. It was the best of best sellers. Considering that the population of the country then was about three million, and if just 100,000 were sold, that would be the equivalent of 8 million copies of a pamphlet sold today in the United States.

The thought leads to flights of fancy: What if someone today were to write a pamphlet—eloquent, persuasive, powerful—explaining why the American people should declare their independence of the government and set up their own decision-making bodies, more democratic, more responsive to their needs? And what if the country were in such a state of desperation, going through such a crisis of confidence in our political leaders, that eight million Americans bought such a pamphlet? Might that not be a unifying force for a Second American Revolution, or some radical change approximating a revolution?

Pamphlets are almost as old as printing itself, and became popular because they met an urgent need. Printing a book was always costly, and time-consuming. Newspapers were cheaper and quicker, but fleeting in their impact. A pamphlet, bound but with paper covers, combined the advantages of both: it was low-priced, produced in no time, but something that could be kept, pored over, passed on to others.

Furthermore, pamphlets have been especially useful to express the ideas of dissidents, being short (from five pages to a hundred or so), written in language that ordinary people could understand, and easy to conceal from the authorities when that was necessary.

In the mid-1600s, in England, the anarchist ideas of "The Diggers," arguing against private property and tyrannical government, were disseminated in pamphlets. The Diggers got their name by their insistence that they could take over unused land—even if it "belonged" to someone legally—if it were needed by someone without a place to live, or a plot of land to till. A pamphlet by Gerard Winstanley, one of the Diggers, argued their case to the English public, at a time when England was going through the turmoil of the Puritan Revolution against monarchical power.

Tom Paine's *Common Sense* was the most widely read pamphlet of the Revolutionary period, but it was not alone. Over four hundred pamphlets appeared in the twenty-five years preceding the Declaration of Independence, arguing one side or another of the conflict between the English crown and the colonists, discussing questions of disobedience to law, loyalty to authority, the rights and obligations of citizens in a society.

Early in the new government of the United States, Congress passed and President John Adams signed the Sedition Act, which made it a crime to say anything "false, scandalous, or malicious" against the government, Congress, or the President, with intent to "bring them into disrepute." Ironically, it came seven years after the First Amendment was added to the Constitution, as if to state the lesson early on, that in the real world, constitutional promises are one thing and political realities are another.

The Act, despite its intimidating language (and the jailing of a number of dissenters) led to newspaper columns and pamphlets denouncing it. George Hay, a member of the Virginia House of Delegates, produced a pamphlet, *An Essay on the Liberty of the Press,* arguing: "A man may say every thing which his passions suggest . . ."—and not be prosecuted.

Hay's pamphlet influenced a pamphlet that appeared in 1800, shortly after his, which was *The Report of the Virginia House of Delegates,* written by James Madison, and which therefore carried the prestige of the "Father of the Constitution." In that Report, Madison argued brilliantly against the reasoning, used by the Justices of the Supreme Court, that allowed the Sedition Act to stand.

In this same period, the grievances of the French people, which led to their great Revolution of 1789, were being expressed throughout the nation in pamphlets, or *cahiers* (literally, notebooks, actually petitions or statements in pamphlet form). One pamphlet, *Patriotic Reflections,* by a law professor in Rennes, put the resistance to change of the Old Regime in a universal context:

"Negro slaves—you are reduced to the condition of brutes—but no innovations! Children of Asiatic kings—the custom is that the eldest of you strangle his brothers—but no innovations!" And similarly, the nobility were causing the French people to suffer, but, "no innovations!"

The two privileged estates in France before the Revolution were the nobility and the clergy. The Third Estate—everyone else—was subordinate. And so the pamphlets of the Revolution expressed a new class consciousness. The Abbe Sieyès wrote, in a famous pamphlet, *What is the Third Estate?,* that the Third Estate was the nation, and compared the nobility and clergy to "a malignant disease which preys upon and tortures the body of a sick man."

The French Revolution, however, in its *Declaration of the Rights of Man,* and in its restriction of the right to vote to male taxpayers, did not fulfill its promise of universal democracy. And so, in 1791, the French actress Olympe de Gouges wrote the pamphlet, *Declaration of the Rights of Women and Citizenesses,* which protested the exclusion of women from the promises of the Revolution.

In England at this time, Mary Wollstonecraft was writing her powerful argument for the equality of women, *A Vindication of the Rights of Women,* saying that men were themselves degraded by the subordination of women.

And in the United States, the first half of the 19th century saw a burst of female protest, with pamphleteering a principal way of communicating with the nation. The sisters Sarah and Angelina Grimke, from a family of slaveowners in South Carolina, became abolitionists and feminists, and the first women to speak publicly to mixed audiences. Sarah Grimke's pamphlet, *Letters on the Condition of Woman and the Equality of the Sexes,* was published in Boston in 1838, and gained wide attention. A small sample of it:

"Man has inflicted an unspeakable injury upon woman, by holding up to her view her animal nature, and placing in the background her moral and intellectual being. Woman has inflicted an injury upon herself by submitting to be thus regarded . . ."

Later on in the century, when the right of women to vote became an issue, there appeared a pamphlet, *"Common Sense" Applied to Woman Suffrage,* which became a classic in the literature of the suffrage movement. It was by Dr. Mary Putnam-Jacobi, who was the first woman physician elected to the New York Academy of Medicine. She pointed to the changed nature of "women's work," which was so frequently nondomestic, and thus there was no basis any more for man's control over his wife's property and earnings.

In the movement for the abolition of slavery in the United States, pamphleteering was an essential weapon. One of the earliest and most powerful was *Walker's Appeal,* written in 1829 by David Walker, son of a slave, who now lived as a free man in Boston, where he sold old clothes. Walker was an early militant, and his language has a Malcolm X ring to it:

"Let our enemies go on with their butcheries, and at once fill up their cup. Never make an attempt to gain our freedom or natural right from under our cruel oppressors and murders, until you see your way clear—when that hour arrives and you move, be not afraid or dismayed.

. . . God has been pleased to give us two eyes, two hands, two feet, and some sense in our heads as well as they. They have no more right to hold us in slavery than we have to hold them. . . . Our sufferings will come to an end, in spite of all the Americans this side of eternity. . . .'Every dog must have its day,' the American's is coming to an end."

The pamphlet infuriated Southern slaveholders. Rewards were offered by the State of Georgia to kill him or deliver him alive. The following year, David Walker was found dead near the doorway of his shop in Boston.

It was common to transcribe lectures and speeches and distribute them in pamphlet form. Henry David Thoreau, who had expressed his opposition to the Mexican war and to slavery by refusing to pay his tax, and going to jail, later gave a lecture, "Resistance to Civil Government." This was then printed as a pamphlet, *Civil Disobedience:* "It is not desirable to cultivate a respect for the law, so much as for the right."

In the late 19th century, farmers in the United States organized the Populist movement, to defend themselves against the powerful corporations that were squeezing them into poverty ("Wall Street owns the country," one of their leaders told a Populist convention in Kansas). The movement set out to create an independent culture for farmers, to reeducate millions of farm families in politics, economics, law, philosophy. It set up a Lecture Bureau, with 35,000 lecturers traveling through the country, and distributed thousands of pamphlets to carry on this re-education.

The anti-imperialist movement that rose up in the nation around the time of the Spanish-American War and the conquest of the Philippines also produced a considerable pamphlet literature to inform the American people of the atrocities being committed overseas against people, for the sake of creating an American empire.

While the labor movement of this period, dominated by the American Federation of Labor, was conservative in many ways, it expressed itself strongly against American overseas expansion. One pamphlet, written by Bolton Hall, treasurer of the American Longshoremen's Union, called *A Peace Appeal to Labor,* declared:

"If there is a war, you will furnish the corpses and the taxes, and others will get the glory."

The great radical union of the early 20th century, the Industrial Workers of the World, representing the poorest, the least skilled, the most exploited of American workers, found the newspaper and the pamphlet natural forms of expression. After the IWW was formed in 1905, the *Preamble to its Constitution,* a defiant call for class struggle, was printed in hundreds of thousands of copies and distributed all over the country and abroad. It began: "The working class and the employing class have nothing in common. There can be no peace so long as hunger and want are found among millions of working people and the few, who make up the employing class, have all the good things of life. Between these two classes a struggle must go on until the workers of the world organize as a class, take possession of the earth and the machinery of production, and abolish the wage system. . . ."

In the decade before the first World War, countless pamphlets were produced during the labor struggles and battles for free speech of the IWW. That war gave the government an excuse to prosecute, and effectively destroy the IWW. But there were exultant moments of solidarity even in defeat, and exultation in occasional victories.

One of the high points in the history of the IWW was its leadership in the strike of 25,000 textile workers in Lawrence, Massachusetts, in 1912. Many of the strikers were recent European immigrants, a majority of them women and children. A woman physician in Lawrence reported that a third of the men and women working in the mill died before they reached the age of twenty-five.

Two extraordinary Italians became important to the strike, Joseph Ettor, an IWW leader who could speak English, Italian, and Polish, and Arturo Giovanitti, a poet and orator, who took charge of the relief operation for the strikers. When a striker was shot and killed, the two were arrested and jailed for "inciting" murder, though neither was at the scene. At their trial, they made closing statements which were printed as a pamphlet. Ettor told the jury:

"Does the District Attorney believe . . . that the gallows or guillotine ever settled an idea? If an idea can live, it lives because history adjudges it right. I ask only for justice. . . . An idea consisting of a social crime in one age becomes the very religion of humanity in the next. . . ."

After a long trial, during which they were kept in cages in the courtroom, they were acquitted.

Radicalism and pamphleteering have always been natural partners. Surely the most influential piece of political literature in modern history was the hundred-page *Communist Manifesto* of Karl Marx and Frederick Engels. And all over the world, socialist, communist, anarchist movements have depended on the power of such writing: concise analyses, passionate arguments, inspiring visions of a new society.

Of the many pamphlets produced in the course of the Russian Revolution, those of Lenin (*What Is To Be Done?*, *Left-Wing Communism: An Infantile Disorder*, *State and Revolution*, and many more) are the best-known. But we should also take note of the writings of Alexandra Kollontai, Bolshevik and feminist. As one who criticized the Soviet bureaucracy from within for distancing itself from the people (in her pamphlet, *The Workers Opposition*) she was writing in the same vein as Rosa Luxemburg, who protested the limitations on democracy in the new Soviet state.

In her 1914 pamphlet, *Working Woman and Mother*, Kollontai wrote in plain language about the problems of women in Tsarist Russia. One of her statements struck a special chord in the United States in 1992 when conservative opponents of a woman's right to choose spoke of defending "family values." She wrote: "The humbugs and hypocrites of the bourgeoisie maintain that the expectant mother is sacred to them. But is that really in fact the case?"

As for anarchism, no one expressed its ideas with greater simplicity and clarity than Alexander Berkman, whose *The ABC of Anarchism* was printed as a cheap pamphlet by a group of English libertarians. And we can find no more colorful and daring presentation of the feminist viewpoint (which landed her in jail dozens of times) than Emma Goldman, whose speeches (like the infamous one deriding marriage as "an insurance contract" and declaring that marriage had "nothing in common" with love) were reprinted as pamphlets in the early years of this century.

It is times of social crisis that has brought the greatest outpouring of pamphlet literature. We are not surprised, then, to find that in the year 1991, in the United States, there appeared with dramatic suddenness and remarkable success, a series of pamphlets put out by two young men, Greg Ruggiero and Stuart Sahulka. They were barely out of college, working out of their parents' homes, with very little money and very little equipment—exactly the historic conditions for radical pamphleteering.

The time was right because the United States government was just waging a swift and devastating war in the Middle East. Presumably the war had been waged to restore the independence of Kuwait against Iraqi aggression. But it was surrounded with suspicious facts which suggested that the motives had more to do with control of oil, with assertion of American military power, and with the political fortunes of the Bush administration.

There was another motive: a determination to wipe out the ugly memory of that long, corpse-ridden, unpopular war in Vietnam and replace it with images of military glory in a quick overwhelming victory, a "a splendid little war" (as an American official had characterized the war against Spain in 1898).

It was possible to accomplish this, during the January-March war against Iraq, by something close to a totalitarian control of information, against which the major media raised feeble cries of protest while cooperating with obsequious magnanimity. In this way, the polled public that was divided half and half on a military solution to the invasion of Kuwait was converted into a 90 percent majority cheering the President on as Iraq was bombed into submission. A few hundred American lives were lost, but perhaps one hundred thousand Iraqis, including tens of thousands of children, died as a result of the bombing and the destruction of food and water sources.

This was a situation which called for voices to bring the truth about the war to the attention of the American people, evading the orthodox, money-controlled lines of communication. There were speeches made at rallies and gatherings around the country, mostly unreported in the press and on television. But a number of these talks were picked up by small radio stations around the country, and broadcast and rebroadcast in an attempt to break through to the American people. Whereupon Ruggiero and Sahulka turned to someone in Boulder, Colorado, an ingenious and apparently tireless "radio person" named David Barsamian, who was interviewing what might be called "American refuseniks" and sending the cassettes to other community radio stations throughout the country.

Barsamian had recorded a talk on the war that Noam Chomsky had given at Harvard. Chomsky, world-famous as a linguistic philosopher, became, during the Vietnam War, the nation's leading intellectual critic of the war. He had now turned his cool, sharp analytical skills to the war in the Gulf, and was one of the most persistent speakers on the close-to-underground circuit of antiwar people. Barsamian sent a transcript of this talk to Ruggiero and Sahulka.

They entered this into their computer, laid it out, and had 250 copies printed on cheap paper, as a long, narrow pamphlet which, if opened, was exactly 8½ by 11 inches, and so could be easily duplicated. They were not interested in copyright privileges or profits—they wanted to spread the word about the war as quickly as possible. The demand for the pamphlet quickly exhausted the supply, and printing after printing brought the number of distributed copies to more than ten thousand. Before long, bookstores and newsstands around the country were carrying this and other pamphlets of what was now the Open Magazine Pamphlet Series.

The war was over, but in 1992 the country was in a severe economic crisis. For forty million people—working mothers, single mothers, elderly people, sick people, black and Hispanic families, perhaps a third of the nation's children—the crisis was permanent. But now, the middle class too was feeling the effects of that long, post-war drain of the nation's wealth into military budgets, the corporate rush to profit, ignoring the most basic needs of the population. It showed in the deterioration of the cities and the natural environment, the hopelessness of the young, and the rise in the crimes of the poor, met by the counter-crimes of the justice system. It showed in the neglect of health, represented most dramatically by the AIDS epidemic. When there was a rebellion in the ghettoes of Los Angeles, it spoke of something larger, long-term.

In this situation, there was a need for fresh voices, unsparing analyses, new information, bold ideas. More pamphlets came off the presses of Falcon Printing, the Westfield-based printer responsible for turning Ruggiero and Sahulka's handiwork into finished pamphlets overnight. They were now being distributed in Amsterdam, London, and Paris. Orders were coming from Australia and islands in the Pacific Ocean.

And so, a collection of these pamphlets in, horror of horrors, a real book! But put out by a new, open-minded, vibrant, nonprofit publisher. And the pamphleteering, we are assured, will go on. Let us hope so. The need is great.

PART I

THE NEW WORLD ORDER

NOAM CHOMSKY

ON U.S. GULF POLICY

AN EXCERPT FROM A LECTURE:
HARVARD UNIVERSITY—NOVEMBER 19, 1991

A LITTLE BACKGROUND

Just take a look at the logic of the situation as it is evolving in the Gulf. After the Iraqi invasion of Kuwait there were two responses by the international community to try to force Saddam Hussein out of Kuwait. One was the 1990s economic sanctions and the embargo. A second was the U.S. response, which was quite different. That involved installing a huge invasion force in Saudi Arabia. None of that has anything to do with the United Nations. That was made very clear by the European Community in mid-August when they were asked to support it and refused, saying, as Germany had said a couple of days earlier, that this was a bilateral arrangement between the United States and Saudi Arabia not mandated by the Security Council and therefore having no status and no legality. There has been a major attempt to try to obscure this difference and to make it look as if the entire world is marching steadfastly behind our banner. But the difference is quite real and very significant. Since August, the United States has been virtually alone, apart from Great Britain, which has its own special interests in the oil and investments in Kuwait, but apart from Great Britain the United States has been essentially alone in driving toward war. There have been major efforts to threaten and cajole and plead with the rest of the world to make token contributions to this, or at least provide a cover for it, and they have so far been almost completely unsuccessful. That's important to bear in mind.

The first approach to reversing the aggression was the U.N. approach, i.e., sanctions, but the thinking was that the effect could be slow and over time. On the other hand, the invasion force can't be sustained over time. The bigger it gets, the harder it is to keep there. It's very hard to keep a major military force, an invasion force, in place in the Saudi desert. It's going to be impossible after a couple of months. That means that there are two choices coming up: either you withdraw them or you use them. Withdrawal is virtually impossible politically because of the high moral principles and posturing with which all of this is presented and the tremendous cosmic significance of driving Saddam Hussein out of Kuwait by force with which the whole story is invested. Given that kind of high pinnacle, it's going to be impossible to withdraw. That means the forces will be used, which means we'll have a war. That's the logic of the situation, and it's been pretty clear since early August.

SETTLEMENT FEATURES

There is an alternative that's also been pretty clear since early August. The alternative is negotiations and a diplomatic settlement. That's really the only alternative. But the United States has shot down every hint that there might be a diplomatic track ever since the beginning. If Washington succeeds to bar any diplomatic track, then we can pretty confidently expect that there will be a war. As to a settlement, its contours have also been pretty clear since August. Proposals of this nature have been floated repeatedly by Iraq and proposed by Jordan, the PLO, France, and others who are trying to find a way out of this catastrophe. The major features of a settlement would involve some form of guaranteed access of Iraq to the Gulf, which everybody agrees is not an unreasonable request. Kuwait was partially set up in the British imperial settlement to block that access. Access would involve something quite insignificant, something like the lease of a couple of uninhabited islands. A second feature of a negotiated settlement would be some decision about the Rumaila oil field, (95 percent of which is inside Iraq, 5 percent inside Kuwait,) over an unsettled and disputed border. There are various charges and countercharges about overdrilling. That's again the kind of issue that certainly seems as though it could be subject to negotiation. Harder map conflicts than that have been negotiated. Third, there has to be some kind of regional security arrangement, done within a regional framework. Fourth, some of the proposals also call for a plebescite or other expression of popular will inside Kuwait. That has wide support in Europe, but is strenuously opposed and denounced in the United States. Those are the basic contours of a possible settlement, coupled with Iraqi withdrawal from Kuwait.

Are these proposals serious? When these proposals were floated by Iraq, for example, were they serious? That you don't know. You never know whether proposals are serious until you pursue them. That's what diplomacy is about. You try to pursue the proposals and see if they mean anything. But they can't be pursued, because the United States refuses totally, and has shot down every hint that there might be a way out. And therefore we're going to have a war with the consequences that I will not bother to discuss, but which will be very bad.

AGGRESSION, INTERNATIONAL LAW, LINKAGE

To continue with the logic of the situation, why is the United States refusing any possibility of negotiation? There is an answer to that, too. The answer is that we stand on high principles, and when you stand on high principles you don't compromise. There are a couple of catchwords that express the high principles. One, which you hear over and over again, is that aggressors cannot be rewarded. International law is sacred, and we've got to uphold that principle. Second is that a regional settlement, for which the technical term is "linkage," is a bad thing. You're supposed to understand that linkage is a bad thing, in this case; in other cases it's a good thing, but in this case linkage is a bad thing, and therefore we have to prevent it because it rewards aggressors. Furthermore, all of this is of just transcendent importance right now because we're entering a potential new world order. The United Nations is finally acting in the way it was supposed to act but never could in the past, because of Russian intransigence and various third-world psychotics with their shrill anti-Western rhetoric. But now that the United States has won the Cold War and the Russians are no longer obstructing, we can disregard these third-world types and the United Nations can actually function in its peacekeeping role, as it was intended 40 years ago but never could. That's very significant. James Baker says we are living in one of those "rare, transforming moments of history, an era full of promise," a vision that will be shattered if Saddam Hussein's aggression is not punished by the sword of the righteous avengers. The proof of all of this is the way the United Nations is functioning.

That's the basic story, and now we have a question. If indeed the United States is standing on high moral principle, then there's an argument that you really shouldn't have diplomacy and negotiations. You don't compromise high principles, no matter what the cost, in particular when you have this auspicious moment, this new era of the U.N. finally functioning. If we're going to destroy all the hopes for peace and justice by compromise, then you don't compromise. That's not an implausible argument. On the other hand, if the whole business is just cynical and hypocritical pretense and posturing, then there's no barrier whatsoever to diplomacy and negotiations, and there may actually be a way out short of disaster, as in any other case. For example, take South Africa and Namibia. The United Nations declared the South African occupation of Namibia illegal back in the early 1960s. The World Court had a judgment in which it declared it illegal. Nobody called for an invasion of South Africa. There was no big invasion force set up on its borders. Rather, the United States pursued what it called "quiet diplomacy" and "constructive engagement" for 20 years while South Africa robbed and looted and terrorized Namibia and left it a total wreck and used it as a base for murderous attacks and aggression against its neighbors, leaving them a total ruin, while we carried out constructive engagement. That's supposed to be a great triumph of American diplomacy, that finally, after all of this, the shreds were turned over to the Namibians in some form. The same was true with regard to the racist regime in Rhodesia. There were U.N. sanctions. The United States reacted to the sanctions, at once passing legislation that permitted violation of the sanctions because we needed Rhodesian minerals. That went on for six or seven years and then you had some sort of diplomacy and it was resolved in some fashion.

But this case is somehow supposed to be different. Here, somehow, quiet diplomacy is not right. We've got to have quick vengeance because of the high principles upon which we have always stood and the universal values that are at the core of our culture. It becomes quite important within this framework to answer the question of whether this is just cynical posturing or whether there indeed is high principle and a new world order. When you have a question like that, you turn to the people who are supposed to know about such things, the people who are responsible for giving the answers, and you have a look at what they say: the intellectual community. Have a look at what they say, and you'll find it interesting. There is no exception that I can find to a completely uncritical support for the posturing—and it indeed is posturing. Try to find some critical analysis or account of the position that's taken, that the United States is standing on high principle. You can by now find articles saying it's not wise to stand on high principle, you should do something else, but try to find an evaluation and an analysis of any of the claims that lie behind this. It's worth doing, because if those claims are indeed totally fraudulent, then: a) there's a way out of this crisis, and b) we learn a lot about ourselves, about the nature of Western culture and its core values and its standard-bearers. So let's proceed.

U.S. HISTORY OF VETOING U.N. RESOLUTIONS

Let's begin with the evidence that's offered universally for the new era that we're entering, namely, the sudden change in the behavior of the United Nations, the "wondrous sea change" in the United Nations, as the *New York Times* calls it. There have been hundreds of articles about this in the press. They are basically all the same. I'll take the most recent just to illustrate, but there are many, many others that are virtually identical. This one is in the current issue of the *New York Review of Books*. There's an article called "The Gulf Crisis." It starts as follows: "With the end of the Cold War and the onset of the Gulf crisis, the United States can now test the validity of the Wilsonian concept of collective security—a test which an automatic Soviet veto in the Security Council has precluded for the past 40 years." That's standard. Dozens of articles have exactly the same theme.

It's a question of fact whether automatic Soviet veto has precluded any U.N. action in its peacekeeping function for collective security over the past 40 years. You can look at the facts. It's a little work, of course, because nobody writes books about it and very little of it is ever reported in the press, which may already raise some questions in your mind. But with a little effort you can find out the facts. What happened is quite interesting. Let's just take, for example, the latest U.N. session. The United Nations meets every winter, so the latest session was 1989–90. The question of collective security and peacekeeping, Wilsonian ideals, etc., came up a number of times. In fact, there were three Security Council resolutions vetoed at that session. One of them condemned the U.S. invasion of Panama. A second condemned the U.S. break-in and violation of diplomatic immunity at diplomatic missions in Panama, and a third condemned Israeli violations of human rights in the occupied territories. They were all vetoed by the United States. There were also a series of General Assembly resolutions that dealt with issues of international law and collective security and the nice Wilsonian principles. Two General Assembly resolutions called on all states to observe international law. They passed with overwhelming, though not unanimous votes. In both cases there were two votes against, the United States and Israel. One of the resolutions condemned the United States for its illegal contra war against Nicaragua, the second condemned the United States for its illegal economic warfare against Nicaragua. Both were strictly illegal, incidentally, nothing obscure about this. That had already been determined by the International Court of Justice, in a ruling which the United States immediately rejected because of our universal values and our adherence to international law.

There was another relevant General Assembly resolution condemning the acquisition of territory by force. That one passed 151 to 3, the three being the United States, Israel, and in this case Dominica, for reasons I'm not exactly sure of. So this wasn't the usual vote, it was three instead of two. That one had to do with application of U.N. 242, the major U.N. Security Council document concerning the Arab-Israeli conflict. It's understood throughout the world in a particular way, outside of the United States, Israel, and Dominica. It condemns the acquisition of territory by force and calls for a political settlement of the Arab-Israeli conflict, now beyond U.N. 242, as it's been for the last 15 years, and also calling for a Palestinian state in the West Bank and the Gaza Strip and the return of the illegally annexed Golan Heights to Syria, annexed over a unanimous U.N. Security Council resolution in this case, although nothing happened because the United States, in pursuit of its traditional peacekeeping function, vetoed the Security Council resolution calling for sanctions to enforce the resolution, which was therefore rendered null and void.

Those are the cases in the last session that are relevant to the Wilsonian principles of collective security and indeed there was an automatic veto, but it wasn't Russian; it was American. When it came to the General Assembly, where you can't veto, you have the results that I mentioned. I'm not going to run through the record, but it goes back the same way for the last 25 years, on every relevant issue—aggression, annexation, human rights abuses, international terrorism, disarmament, the Middle East, Central America, observance of international law, you pick it—the United States is far ahead of anyone else, nobody's even close, in vetoing Security Council resolutions and in voting against General Assembly resolutions, often alone or sometimes with one or two client states. That's the typical pattern. In fact, the only other country that even comes close is Great Britain. In the course of its protection of the racist regimes of Southern Africa it has vetoed a number of Security Council resolutions. But nobody else is even in the running, and the United States is way ahead in this.

Let me mention again that there have been hundreds of articles in the mass media and the intellectual journals which have exactly the message of that paragraph in the *New York Review of Books* article, namely, that we're entering a new world order, at least there's the hope of it, extolling this wondrous sea change in the United Nations now that the United States has won the Cold War and there's no longer an automatic Soviet veto, the Russians aren't disrupting anymore and we can dismiss the shrill anti-Western rhetoric of the third-world. If you bother to go on and look at the shrill anti-Western rhetoric of the third-world, you find that rather regularly what it amounts to is a call for observance of international law and for adhering to the principles of the United Nations. The third-world has, not entirely, but pretty consistently, pressed for that because international law provides them with a kind of weak defense against the depredations of the violent states, primarily us. Therefore, they typically call for adherence to international law. That's a large part of the shrill anti-Western rhetoric, but try to find these facts somewhere.

THE HISTORY OF U.S. AGGRESSION

If you look at these facts more closely, then you find out more about the current U.S. defense of high principles. Remember there are three major points. One has to do with aggression, the second with linkage, and the third with a new world order. That one I've talked about, so take a look at aggression. There have been numerous cases of aggression in the past years. Saddam Hussein's aggression in Kuwait is bad enough, but it's by no means the worst. Worse than some, not as bad as others. Let's just take the most recent case, the U.S. invasion of Panama. That was denounced by the United Nations. It was in many ways parallel to the Iraqi aggression in Kuwait. If anything, Saddam Hussein has more plausible pretexts than the United States had. The level of casualties was probably more or less on a par. Casualties in Kuwait were estimated at about two hundred over a couple of months. It's now estimated at a couple of thousand. That's approximately what the killings in Panama were, certainly in the hundreds. In fact, six or seven hundred bodies have already been exhumed from mass graves, possibly in the thousands, as many Panamanians who investigated it claim, and also the Central American human rights groups that investigated it. In Panama, the United States installed a puppet regime of its choice with U.S. military advisors running it at every level. Documents have been leaked and published in the Mexican press about this, but not in the United States. In the United States this is called "democracy." In Latin America it's called farce. The Group of Eight, the eight big Latin American democracies, had suspended Panama from membership under Noriega because of his abuses. Last March they expelled Panama permanently because it was a country under military occupation. That was handled in the United States by just not reporting it. The Catholic Church in Panama in August condemned the invasion as one of the most tragic moments in Panama's history. The Panamanian government commission, established by the government we installed to deal with problems of reconstruction, came out with its proposals in August, the most important of which was to terminate the state of military occupation. None of that is discussed anywhere. That's Panama.

What about Kuwait? Saddam Hussein went on to annex Kuwait, but remember that he did that five days after the U.N. sanctions. If the United Nations had not reacted (as in the case of Panama they could not react because the United States was there to veto any action) then it's entirely possible, although you can't be sure of it, that Saddam Hussein would have done to Kuwait exactly what the U.S. did in Panama, that is, install a puppet regime, back it up with Iraqi military force, make sure it does exactly what he wants it to do. That's the efficient way to run another country. It's entirely conceivable that's precisely what he would have done and then the parallel to Panama would have been very close. The big difference is that in the case of Kuwait the United Nations was able to act because for once the automatic veto wasn't working. The United States was against that aggression, and therefore the United Nations could act.

There are other cases, too. Take the Turkish invasion and virtual annexation of northern Cyprus. That killed a couple of thousand people, drove out several hundred thousand. Turkey carried out extensive looting and destruction. They wanted to eliminate any trace of Greek civilization back to classical antiquity. That's Turkey. Nothing happened. That was the invasion and annexation of part of a sovereign republic. The United States was in favor of it, in fact it had been trying to implement that partition back in the early 1960s. It was called the Acheson Plan at the time, when the United States was trying to disrupt U.N. efforts to bring about a peaceful settlement there. That's again rather similar to Saddam Hussein and Kuwait.

Or take the Moroccan invasion of the Western Sahara, also supported by the United States. Morocco is an ally. The Moroccan justification for that was that literally one Kuwait is enough, meaning it's bad enough that there's one place where rich resources are in the hands of just a bunch of tribesmen. There's no reason why there should be another place, Western Sahara. It rings of Saddam Hussein, if you like. The United States backed that one, so the United Nations couldn't do anything.

Take the Israeli invasion of Lebanon, where the United States vetoed a whole series of resolutions in the Security Council trying to terminate the aggression, separate the forces, and stop the bombing of Beirut, (the first time in history that a major capital has been viciously bombed in front of television cameras). That was all fine, the United States approved of it. In this case it was much worse than the invasion of Kuwait, in human terms, there were at least 20,000 people killed in that, 6,000–7,000 right in Beirut alone, mostly civilians.

Or take the Indonesian invasion of East Timor in 1975. That was on a different scale. That was an invasion and annexation as well. That one was near genocidal, a couple hundred thousand people killed. It compares rather closely to the Pol Pot atrocities in the same years. The

United States strongly supported that one. In fact, the "Human Rights Administration" (Carter) provided 90 percent of the armaments for the Indonesian invaders, and as the massacre increased they expanded the flow of arms to ensure that it could be properly consummated. Previously this was handled at home by simply keeping quiet about it, just silence. In this case, Kissinger was sneaking the arms in while pretending there was a temporary embargo. At that time, the United Nations was also functioning and we had a U.N. ambassador whose name was Daniel Patrick Moynihan. He describes in his memoirs with considerable pride how he acted at the time of the aggression. Take a look at his memoirs, *A Dangerous Place.* He has a couple of paragraphs on this. He says the following: "The United States government wanted things to turn out as they did and worked to bring this about. The Department of State desired that the United Nations prove utterly ineffective in whatever measures it undertook. This task was given to me, and I carried it out with no inconsiderable success." He then goes on to say what the success was: within two months, reports indicated that Indonesia had killed about 60,000 people, roughly the proportion of the population that the Nazis had killed in the Soviet Union through World War II. Moynihan is taking great credit, expressing his pride, in having succeeded in blocking any U.N. action and thus having expedited crimes which he, not I, compares to those of the Nazis. Having done that, he goes on to the next topic. It's therefore only natural that in the current series of accolades to the United Nations, Daniel Moynihan should be picked out as the hero, the man to whom the *New York Times* devotes a magazine story while his book is applauded on the front pages and he is interviewed because here is the man who all his life has been standing up for international law and the sanctity of the United Nations, and finally after his heroic struggle for all these years, the world has come around to his position and he can feel vindicated. That's another local boy, a Harvard professor. I suppose all of that is an effort to show that no matter how rich your imagination, you cannot reach levels of cynicism high enough to imagine the way the respectable and civilized intellectual community will act.

The conclusion of all of this, without any further ado, is that the United States has no objection whatsoever to aggression. The idea that aggressors can't be rewarded is ludicrous to consider as a principle of

U.S. policy. This is so obvious that occasionally there's some mention of it. The context is interesting. The context in which it's mentioned on the rare occasions when it is mentioned is that the United States is not consistent in its opposition to aggression. We make mistakes. We're not clear about what we do. We kind of bungle. But, in fact, there is no inconsistency that I can find in this historical record. It seems to me U.S. practice is quite consistent. If aggression is regarded as in U.S. interests, it's benign. If aggression is contrary to U.S. interests, it's nefarious. That's a consistent reaction. If you can think of an exception to that, I'd like to see it. I don't see any inconsistency here. That's a truth that cannot be articulated. Out of the question.

LINKAGE

Let's take linkage, the last of the reasons why we can't permit negotiations to proceed. Linkage is partly a cover term for a regional security settlement that deals with other relevant issues in the region. For example, the Israeli annexation of the Syrian Golan Heights and its occupation of the West Bank and Gaza and 10 percent of Lebanon. That's one of the things that's part of the linkage thing that we oppose. If you're a right-thinking person, you're opposed to linkage, that is, to developing a general security arrangement that will deal with the issues of aggression and violence in the whole region. Why is the U.S. opposed to linkage? Notice that again in that opposition we're pretty isolated. The last vote in the United Nations was 151 to 3 on a political settlement of the Arab-Israeli conflict. There is a history there, too. For the past 20 years the United States has been blocking every effort of the United Nations or anyone else to achieve a peaceful diplomatic settlement of the Arab-Israeli conflict, and the vote 151 to 3 is a pretty accurate picture of how the world has been divided on this issue. In 1976 and again in 1980 the U.S. vetoed Security Council resolutions proposed by the Arab states, Syria, Jordan, Egypt, and with the backing and direct participation of the PLO, calling for a political settlement along the lines of U.N. 242, with security guarantees, demilitarized zones, borders, etc. The United States vetoed it in the Security Council because it called for a Palestinian State and Israeli withdrawal. It has also regularly voted against it at the General Assembly, virtually alone most of the time. This goes back to 1970, when Henry Kissinger succeeded in taking over control of Middle East policy and switched it. There was a conflict then as to how it should go. The United States at that time was pursuing a position in accord with the general international consensus. Kissinger managed to reverse that. He preferred what he called "stalemate." The issue came to a head in February 1971, when President Sadat of Egypt proposed a general peace treaty on the internationally recognized, pre-June 1967 borders, with all the appropriate conditions, treaty, security guarantees, etc. Incidentally, there was no reference to Palestinians at that time, in 1971 nobody was talking about the Palestinians, no Palestinian state or anything like that. Israel rejected it, recognized it to be a "genuine peace offer" but rejected it on the grounds that if they held out they would get better terms for their borders. Under Kissinger's influence, the United States backed Israel in its rejection. He preferred, as he explained in his memoirs, stalemate to settlement. There are a lot of reasons for that, but that was it, and that's the way it's been ever since. From that time the United States has blocked any effort to achieve a political settlement to that conflict, and it has been against virtually the whole world on that, until the last General Assembly resolution, which I just quoted.

How is that treated by the civilized intellectual community? In the media you get articles like one a few months ago by Alan Cowell in the *New York Times* which has the title, "Soviets Trying to Become Team Player in Middle East." The content of the article is this: The Soviets are moving away from confrontation with Washington and are indicating they prefer partnership in the diplomacy of the region. This shift from confrontation brings the Russians closer to the mainstream of Mideast diplomacy, and if they continue with this more civilized behavior, they may become team players within the mainstream. What's going on here? It's very simple. You have to understand things. The team is the United States. That's the mainstream. The rest of the world is off the team. They are out of the mainstream. Now it looks like maybe the Russians are thinking of getting on the team, joining us on the spectrum of world opinion. If so, they'll be on the mainstream of Mideast diplomacy alone with us. Now we're totally alone in the mainstream, but then they'll be with us and the mainstream will have doubled in size.

What's interesting about all of this is that it passes without a comment, without a smile, even a little flicker of amusement. That tells you the way a really disciplined and fanatic intellectual culture operates, at a level of fanaticism that would be pretty hard to duplicate even among the mullahs in Qum. That's our intellectual culture. That's the way it works. Therefore, nobody laughs or even smiles or even notices anything when these things appear. In scholarship appearing in the media, there's a lot of literature about something called the "peace process." What's the peace process? It's a technical term which refers to U.S. efforts to prevent peace in the Middle East for the past twenty years. The vetoes of Security Council resolutions, the barring of the United Nations, the rendering of it null and void; that's the peace process. Again, nobody laughs, nobody smiles. I should add, as advice to the young, unless you internalize these norms you're not on the team either. So you'd better watch out.

Therefore we can't have any linkage. The United States is opposed to a diplomatic settlement of the Gulf conflict and opposed to a diplomatic settlement of the Arab-Israeli conflict, so obviously it's going to be opposed to a linkage of the two, that is, to a general diplomatic settlement that would include both. So we are, therefore, opposed to a regional security arrangement, which would be one of the plausible and intelligent ways to settle this crisis short of slaughter and massacre. Those are the arguments. That's the high moral pinnacle.

You could ask at this point whether it matters at all. Do the facts even matter? Does it matter if the media and the intellectual community do their little pirouettes and preen in front of the mirror and admire their magnificence and tell us how wonderful we are, as distinct from them; does any of that matter? The trouble is it matters a lot. It matters for exactly the reasons I mentioned before. If the pose of high principle has any merit to it at all, then you've got an argument, a plausible argument that you shouldn't pursue a diplomatic option and that we just have to go to war. The sword of the righteous avenger has to destroy the person who's stopping the magnificent new order. On the other hand, if the whole thing is just cynical posturing, then there might be a way to avoid an imminent catastrophe. For that reason it matters how the intellectual community acts. It matters a lot.

I've talked a little about our intellectual standards. What about our moral standards? In a front-page *New York Times* article on November

3, there's an interview with General Schwarzkopf, commanding general in the desert, known as "Stormin' Norman" Schwarzkopf. It starts as follows: "The commander of the American forces facing Iraq said today that his troops could obliterate Iraq, but cautioned that total destruction of that country might not be 'in the interest of the long-term balance of power in the region.'" In other words, we could massacre 17 million people and wipe a country off the face of the earth with no particular difficulty, but that might be tactically unwise; that is, not in our long-term interest. And there's a reaction to this, a conclusion that was drawn in the article and since—"Stormin' Norman" is really a closet dove. There have been a number of reactions; that's the only one I've seen. "Stormin' Norman" is not in favor of, for tactical reasons, murdering 17 million people and wiping out a country. That tells us something about "us" and "them" and our universal values, and I'll leave it to you at this point to see if you can conjure up the proper antecedents.

Does all that matter? Yes, that matters too, just as it mattered to a lot of people who have experienced firsthand our virtue and benevolence as they actually work out in practice. Why is the United States so hell-bent on war, alone, aside from Great Britain, which as I mentioned has its own interests? I think there are two major reasons for this, if you look. I don't think it has anything to do with access to oil or lowering the price of oil or any of these other things. It obviously has nothing to do with principle. Let's put that aside. That's for the intellectuals to worry about.

AXIOM 1 OF U.S. FOREIGN POLICY

What it has to do with is something that is a leading principle of U.S. foreign policy, so dominant that, writing about this 15 years ago, I once called it "Axiom 1 of International Affairs." That states that no indigenous force is permitted to gain substantial influence over the energy resources of the Middle East. That belongs to the United States, its oil companies and loyal clients. Take a look at the Middle East and you'll notice what the imperial settlement was: plenty of people around, but most of the oil is in the hands of tiny families. That's the way it was set up by Britain and later the United States. If those tiny families are in the pocket of the United States and Britain, everything's just fine. We can say they run everything and they go to Harvard Business School and they do what we tell them. That's independence. On the other hand, if any independent nationalist force that might represent segments of the population begins to have an influence, that's out of bounds. For reasons like that, the United States overthrew the conservative nationalist parliamentary regime of Iran in 1953. It destroyed Nasser, a representative of Arab nationalism, threatening that Egypt, the most populous state, might become part of controlling the resources of the region. It opposed Khomeini. It now opposes Saddam Hussein. On August 2, Saddam Hussein became an enemy. On the 1st he was just as much a torturer and a murderer and a gangster as he was on August 2, his crimes were already behind him, but he was an amiable friend, improving. He was a moderate. We had to be nice to him. He was on our side, nothing wrong with him. Gasses Kurds, tortures people, that's great. But on August 2 he violated Axiom 1 of international affairs and suddenly became the latest reincarnation of Genghis Khan and Hitler. Incidentally, this is also a standard pattern, but a respectable intellectual doesn't see it; that is part of the definition of respectability. The pattern is true of our relation to Mussolini and Trujillo and Marcos and Duvalier and Noriega. Same story all along. They can do anything they like: kill, torture, rob, anything, it's all fine, as long as they don't cross us, as long as they look as if they're supporting U.S. interests. If they cross us, then their record of atrocities can immediately be brought up and we become extremely righteous and have to stand on principle. We can't let this terrible thing go on, and we have to intervene to destroy them and to install somebody pretty much like them most of the time, or often worse. That's a very common pattern, and that happened with Saddam Hussein on August 2.

OIL = POWER

Why does the United States want to control the oil? There's a story on that, too. Back in the 1940s it was well understood that the energy resources of that region, the Arabian Peninsula, were extraordinary in scale. In fact, they were described by the State Department in 1944 as "a stupendous source of strategic power, and one of the greatest material prizes in the world history." A couple of years later they were described in some secret documents as the greatest prize in the field of foreign investment. This was clearly a lever of world control. Whoever had control of that could influence a lot of the world. And the United States was intending to become a global power and therefore wanted to have its hand on that spigot and make sure that nobody else did. George Kennan, who was a very far-sighted and influential planner, pointed out in 1949 that if the United States maintained control over the oil, it would have what he called "veto power" over the potential actions way down the road of rivals like Japan and Germany, who weren't rivals then, but they might be some day. That's why the United States wants the oil. We didn't use it. The U.S. and the Western Hemisphere was the biggest oil producer and exporter in the world until the late 1960s, but we followed exactly the same policy. The U.S. has not regularly sought to lower the price of oil. Sometimes it wants it lower, sometimes higher. But it wants to have its hand on the lever, to be in the dominant influential position. Crucially, no indigenous force should have that role. This, incidentally, is the corollary to a much more general principle: that radical nationalism anywhere in the third-world, independent nationalism, doesn't matter what its politics are, right-wing, left-wing, whatever, is intolerable because independence means diversion of resources to domestic purposes, and that's unacceptable. The role of the third-world is to be "exploited," as George Kennan put it. The third world is to "fulfill its major function," as his State Department policy-planning statement put it, as a source of resources and markets for the industrial world. Independent nationalism hurts that. Therefore, we are uniformly opposed to independent nationalism. In the Middle East it's particularly important because of the great significance of that stupendous source of strategic power, that great material prize in influencing what happens in the world. That's Axiom 1 of world affairs. In that context, pretty much everything that's happened in the region can be understood. The strategic alliance with Israel, as it's called, took shape in the late 1950s in precisely this context. In 1958 the National Security Council concluded that a "logical corollary" of opposition to radical Arab nationalism would be support for Israel as the one predictably loyal Western outpost in the region. In the 1960s Israel was regarded by U.S. intelligence as a barrier against Nasserite pressure on the Gulf states. Egypt was virtually at war with Saudi Arabia at the time. Recent documentary evidence shows that

Yemenite Israeli soldiers were actually involved in that war. We knew for 20 years already that U.S. intelligence had considered Israel to be a kind of barrier to Nasserite attempts to unify the Arab world and bring the resources of that world into the use of the people of the region so that they wouldn't fulfill their function anymore.

THE NIXON DOCTRINE

When Israel managed to crush and virtually destroy Nasser in 1967, the strategic alliance with the United States was strengthened. That's when the United States began to pour arms in there. They had done their job and it continued right through the 1970s. Take a look at the context in which Kissinger blocked the peace settlement by the early 1970s. There was a context. It was called the "Nixon Doctrine," meaning at the time of the Vietnam War, which was pretty far along, the United States realized that it could not run the world by force alone. It had to delegate authority. That's the Nixon Doctrine. Regional powers had to pursue their "regional responsibilities" within the "overall framework of order" managed by the United States, as Kissinger put it. Melvin Laird, the Secretary of Defense, who wasn't a big intellectual, put it more simply. He said there had to be local "cops on the beat," taking their orders from Washington. The cops on the beat in the Middle East were Israel and Iran, then under the Shah, having been put into power by the CIA-backed coup. There was a tripartite alliance between Israel, Iran, and Saudi Arabia, tacit but very real. Saudi Arabia means the couple thousand people who run the oil and work for the United States, and Israel and Iran were the guardians who made sure that nobody got in their way, in particular their own populations if they had funny ideas, as they often did. That continued through the 1970s. The Camp David Accords were part of that system. It was recognized after 1973 that Egypt couldn't just be dismissed. They did know how to shoot the rifles. They weren't just incompetent Arabs, so Kissinger went to the fall-back position, which was to remove Egypt from the conflict. You can't dismiss them, so therefore you remove them from the conflict, the biggest Arab deterrent. Then Israel would be free, with massive American support, which shot through the roof at that time, to expand its integration of the occupied territories and to attack its northern neighbor and strengthen the strategic alliance. That's what's been going on since.

With the fall of the Shah, Israel's role became even more important. Furthermore, immediately after the fall of the Shah, within weeks after the Khomeini takeover, the United States began sending arms to Iran via Israel, paid for by Saudi Arabia. The purpose was stated explicitly by the high Israeli officials who were involved, many of whom surfaced years later in the Iran-Contra affair. The purpose was to try to find Iranian officers who would be able to overthrow the government. It's very common, no mystery about this; it's extremely common to provide military aid to a government that you're trying to overthrow. That was done in the case of Chile under Allende, Indonesia under Sukarno, and again in the case of Khomeini. The reason is perfectly obvious. The way to overthrow a government is to find guys in the military who will overthrow it for you. The way to find guys in the military is by establishing relations with them: you send them military aid, you set up training, you have contacts, you manipulate them and find the ones who can meet your conditions. All of this had to be suppressed during the Iran-Contra hearings. That took a lot of work. You had to pretend that the whole thing started in 1985 when there was a mistake about hostages. It happened years before that and had nothing to do with the hostages. There were no hostages. It was all perfectly public. It was standard operating procedure. That's the way you overthrow governments. But again, nobody wants to talk about that. That's the context in which all of this developed. It's the context in which the tilt toward Iraq developed during the Iran-Iraq war, where the U.S. backed and, we may discover some day, impelled the Iraqi invasion. We don't know that now. That's all within the context of Axiom 1 of International Affairs: make sure that the hand on the lever is ours and certainly not any indigenous people. That's one major reason the United States is in the Gulf.

A NEW WORLD ORDER: UNDETERRED U.S. AGGRESSION

Why do we want to win by force? Why not by diplomacy? This is speculation, but my speculation is that it has to do with other features of the new international order, the new world order. Simply ask yourself what's the strength of the United States? What's our leading card in this new world order? Is it moral and ethical force? You can forget about that one. There's no doubt that we don't have the moral and ethical force. What about political and diplomatic force? We've never had that. The policies the United States has pursued in the third-world are very unpopular and consistently have been, and therefore if any confrontation moves to the field of diplomacy, we would probably lose. That's why the United States has been quite consistently opposed to negotiations and diplomacy in the Middle East, Indochina, Central America, where we repeatedly disrupted the peace proposals and succeeded in doing so. That's why the United States has been rendering the United Nations ineffective in any action it might undertake, to quote Daniel Moynihan. Good reason. Diplomacy is bad news for us. We're not going to get what we want out of diplomacy. We're not strong there. What about economic power? Until the early 1970s we had overwhelming economic dominance. That's not true anymore. The United States is still the biggest economy, but not by a lot. After the Reagan years, which did a lot of long-term damage to the U.S. economy, it's relatively weak economically, as compared to its major rivals, Germany and Japan. The world is tripolar economically, to use the fashionable phrase. So economic strength is not very great. There's one thing left: military strength. The United States has a virtual monopoly of force.

Furthermore, in the new world order, one striking thing is that there no longer is a deterrent to the use of force by the United States. In the past there was a deterrent, Soviet power. The United States could use force up to a certain limit, but not beyond, because if it went too far it might run into the Soviet Union and that was dangerous, and we don't do anything that's dangerous to us. That's the moral principle that we follow. So there was always a deterrent to the use of force. Furthermore, the Soviet Union tended to provide assistance to targets of U.S. attack. There's a technical term for that: that's called Soviet aggression. So the Soviet Union was involved in "aggression" in Nicaragua when they were providing support to a government that the United States was trying to overthrow by violence. Now there's no more Soviet aggression and no more Soviet deterrent, so the United States is much more free to use force, and this is completely conscious and recognized. That's one of the features of the post–Cold War era. The first post–Cold War military intervention was Panama, just like everything in the past, except that there was a different excuse. You couldn't call on the Russians to be an excuse. You needed different lies this time. In that sense it was post–Cold War. Also there was no deterrent. That was made explicit by Elliott Abrams, who exulted over it, pointing out that this was the first time that we've been able to use force without any fear that we might get embroiled with the Russians. Well, you don't get embroiled much with the Russians in Latin America anyway, but in the Gulf it's a big point. There the United States can now use military force quite freely for the first time, quite sure, certain as you can be, that you're not going to get involved with the Russians. They're out of the game. No more deterrent. That's the new world order. We're not only dominant in military force, we're undeterred.

If you just think about it in general, when you have a world order of that sort, a victory for force is very much in the interests of the power that intends to rule by force. A victory for diplomacy is not in the interest of that power. I think that factor goes a long way to explain what's happening in the Gulf.

There isn't a lot of time to avert what might be a major tragedy there. I don't think that time should be wasted. However it comes out, the deeper problems are going to remain, that is, the institutional sources of violence and the cultural factors that defend and support it, and they are very close to home.

UNITED NATIONS

THE IMPACT OF WAR ON IRAQ

EXCERPTS FROM THE CHARTER OF THE UNITED NATIONS
AND THE REPORT TO THE SECRETARY GENERAL
ON HUMANITARIAN NEEDS IN IRAQ IN THE IMMEDIATE
POST-CRISIS ENVIRONMENT BY A MISSION TO THE AREA LED BY
MR. MARTTI AHTISAARI, UNDER-SECRETARY GENERAL
FOR ADMINISTRATION AND MANAGEMENT, MARCH 20, 1991

WE THE PEOPLES OF THE UNITED NATIONS DETERMINED . . .

to save succeeding generations from the scourge of war, which twice in our lifetime has brought untold sorrow to mankind, and

to reaffirm faith in fundamental human rights, in the dignity and worth of the human person, in the equal rights of men and women and of nations large and small, and

to establish conditions under which justice and respect for the obligations arising from treaties and other sources of international law can be maintained, and

to promote social progress and better standards of life in larger freedom.

AND FOR THESE ENDS . . .

to practice tolerance and live together in peace with one another as good neighbors, and

to unite our strength to maintain international peace and security, and

to ensure, by the acceptance of principles and the institution of methods, that armed force shall not be used, save in the common interest, and

to employ international machinery for the promotion of the economic and social advancement of all peoples,

HAVE RESOLVED TO COMBINE OUR EFFORTS TO ACCOMPLISH THESE AIMS.

General Remarks

- I and the members of my mission were fully conversant with media reports regarding the situation in Iraq and, of course, with the recent WHO/UNICEF report on water, sanitary and health conditions in the Greater Baghdad area. It should, however, be said at once that nothing that we had seen or read had quite prepared us for the particular form of devastation which has now befallen the country. The recent conflict has wrought near-apocalyptic results upon the economic infrastructure of what had been, until January 1991, a rather highly urbanized and mechanized society. Now, most means of modern life support have been destroyed or rendered tenuous. Iraq has, for some time to come, been relegated to a pre-industrial age, but with all the disabilities of post-industrial dependency on an intensive use of energy and technology.

Food and Agriculture

- Mission members held working sessions with counterparts from the relevant ministries, visited social centres where various vulnerable groups are cared for, and a dairy production unit. The mission noted that Iraq has been heavily dependent on food imports which have amounted to at least 70 percent of consumption needs. Seed was also imported. Sanctions decided upon by the Security Council had already adversely affected the country's ability to feed its people. New measures relating to rationing and enhanced production were introduced in September 1990. These were, however, in turn, negatively affected by the hostilities which impacted upon most areas of agricultural production and distribution.
- Food is currently made available to the population both through government allocation and rations, and through the market. The ministry of trade's monthly allocation to the population of staple food items fell from 343,000 tons in September 1990 to 182,000 tons, when rationing was introduced, and was further reduced to 135,000 tons in January 1991 (39 percent of the pre-sanctions level). While the mission was unable to gauge the precise quantities still held in government warehouses, all evidence

indicates that flour is now at a critically low level, and that supplies of sugar, rice, tea, vegetable oil, powdered milk, and pulses are currently at critically low levels or have been exhausted. Distribution of powdered milk, for instance, is now reserved exclusively for sick children on medical prescription.

- This year's grain harvest in June is seriously compromised for a number of reasons, including failure of irrigation/drainage (no power for pumps, lack of spare parts); lack of pesticides and fertilizers (previously imported); and lack of fuel and spare parts for the highly mechanized and fuel-dependent harvesting machines. Should this harvest fail or be far below average, as is very likely barring a rapid change in the situation, widespread starvation conditions become a real possibility.

Water, Sanitation and Health

- As regards water, prior to the crisis Baghdad received about 450 litres per person supplied by seven treatment stations purifying water from the Tigris River. The rest of the country had about 200–250 litres per person per day, purified and supplied by 238 central water treatment stations and 1,134 smaller water projects. All stations operated on electric power; about 75 percent had stand-by diesel-powered generators. Sewage was treated to an acceptable standard before being returned to the rivers.
- With the destruction of power plants, oil refineries, main oil storage facilities and water-related chemical plants, all electrically operated installations have ceased to function. Diesel-operated generators were reduced to operating on a limited basis, their functioning affected by lack of fuel, lack of maintenance, lack of spare parts and non-attendance of workers. The supply of water in Baghdad dropped to less than 10 litres per day but has now recovered to approximately 30–40 litres in about 70 percent of the area (less than 10 percent of the overall previous use). Stand-by generating capacity is out of order in several pumping stations and cessation of supplies will therefore ensue if current machinery goes out of order for any reason (spare parts are not available owing to sanctions). As regards the quality of water in Baghdad, untreated sewage has now to be

dumped directly into the river—which is the source of the water supply—and all drinking-water plants there and throughout the rest of the country are using river water with high sewage contamination. Recently, the water authority has begun to be able to improve the quality of drinking water by adding more of the remaining stock of alum and chlorine after assurances from UNICEF and ICRC that emergency aid would be provided. Chemical tests are now being conducted at the stations but no bacteriological testing and control is possible because of the lack of electricity necessary for the functioning of laboratories, the shortage of necessary chemicals and reagents and the lack of fuel for the collection of samples. No chlorine tests are being conducted because of the lack of fuel for sampling. While the water authority has warned that water must be boiled, there is little fuel to do this, and what exists is diminishing. Cool winter conditions have prevailed until recently.

- Only limited information is available to authorities regarding the situation in the remainder of the country because all modern communications systems have been destroyed and information is now transmitted and received (in this sector as in all others) by person-to-person contact. In those areas where there are no generators, or generators have broken down, or the fuel supply is exhausted, the population draws its water directly from polluted rivers and trenches. This is widely apparent in rural areas, where women and children can be seen washing and filling water receptacles. The quantity and quality of water produced by treatment centres is very variable and in many locations there are no chemicals available for purification. No quality control—chlorine testing, chemical testing or bacteriological testing—is being conducted.
- The mission identified the various problems mentioned above: heavy sewage-pollution of water intakes; absence or acute shortage of water-treatment chemicals, especially aluminium sulphate (alum) and chlorine; lack of power to operate equipment; lack or shortage of diesel to run generators; inability to repair generators because of lack of spare parts; in some instances a total absence of generators; the destruction of some

stations; absence of water-testing; lack of a health surveillance system in respect of communicable, and, especially, water-borne diseases. A further major problem, now imminent, is the climate. Iraq has long and extremely hot summers, the temperature often reaching 50 degrees Celsius. This has two main implications: (a) the quantity of water must be increased, and a minimum target of 50 litres per person per day has to be attained (this entails a gross output of 65 litres per person at the source); and (b) the heat will accelerate the incubation of bacteria, and thus the health risks ascribable to the water quality (already at an unacceptable level) will be further exacerbated—especially viewed in the overall sanitary circumstances which have already led to a fourfold increase in diarrhoeal disease incidence among children under five years of age, and the impact of this on their precarious nutritional status.

- As regards sanitation, the two main concerns relate to garbage disposal and sewage treatment. In both cases, rapidly rising temperatures will soon accentuate an existing crisis. Heaps of garbage are spread in the urban areas and collection is poor to non-existent. The work of collection vehicles is hampered by lack of fuel, lack of maintenance and spare parts and lack of labour, because workers are unable to come to work. Incinerators are in general not working, for these same reasons, and for lack of electric power. Insecticides, much needed as the weather becomes more torrid, are virtually out of stock because of sanctions and a lack of chemical supplies. As previously stated, Iraqi rivers are heavily polluted by raw sewage, and water levels are unusually low. All sewage treatment and pumping plants have been brought to a virtual standstill by the lack of power supply and the lack of spare parts. Pools of sewage lie in the streets and villages. Health hazards will build in the weeks to come.

Logistics: Transportaion, Communications and Energy

- The mission examined transportation, communications and energy facilities, as it increasingly emerged that adequate logistics and energy would be essential to support and make effective emergency humanitarian assistance.

- As regards transportation, the fact that the country has been on a war footing almost continuously since 1980 has undermined its capacity. At present, Iraq's sole available surface transport link with the outside world is via Amman to Aqaba. (It has been reported that a bridge has recently been destroyed on the Iskenderun/Mersin road to Iraq from Turkey; and the ports of Basrah and Umm Qasr are currently out of use; nor has there for some years been any direct cargo traffic to Iraq via the Syrian Arab Republic.) Internal transportation by road is now severely affected by a lack of spare parts and tires and, above all, by a lack of fuel. Some internal railway capability still exists on the Baghdad-Mosul line. The mission was informed that a total of 83 road bridges had been destroyed and a number were inspected.
- As regards communications, the mission was informed that all internal and external telephone systems had been destroyed, with the exception of a limited local exchange in one town. It had the opportunity to inspect a number of war-damaged or destroyed facilities and experienced for itself the situation in the Greater Baghdad and other urban areas. Communication in Iraq is now on a person-to-person basis, as mail services have also disintegrated.
- The role of energy in Iraq is especially important because of the level of its urbanization (approximately 72 percent of the population lives in towns), its industrialization, and its prolonged, very hot summers. Pre-war energy consumption consisted of oil and refined products (85 percent), electricity (14.8 percent) and other sources (0.2 percent). About 30 per cent of electric power generation was hydro-power. Bombardment has paralysed oil and electricity sectors almost entirely. Power output and refinery production is negligible and will not be resumed until the first repair phase is complete. The limited and sporadic power supply in some residential areas and for health facilities is provided by mobile generators. There have, officially, been virtually no sales of gasoline to private users since February. The

mission was told that the only petrol, oil, and lubricants (POL) products now available are heating oil (rationed to 60 litres per month per family) and liquefied petroleum gas (LPG), which is rationed to one cylinder per month per family. The authorities stated that stocks of these two products are close to exhaustion and that their distribution is expected to cease within the next two to four weeks. While work is under way to clear sites and assess damages, lack of communications and transport is retarding this activity. Initial inspections are said to show that necessary repairs to begin power generation and oil refining at minimal levels may take anywhere from 4 to 13 months. Minimal survival level to undertake humanitarian activities would require approximately 25 percent of pre-war civilian domestic fuel consumption. Its absence, given the proximate onset of hot weather conditions, may have calamitous consequences for food, water supply, and for sanitation; and therefore for health conditions. It seems inescapable that these fuel imports must take place urgently, and units and spare parts will also be required to enable Iraq to meet its own humanitarian needs as soon as possible. Under optimal circumstances it would be difficult or impossible for such needs to be provided from other sources given all the circumstances of that country's economy and social conditions, and bearing also in mind the limited bulk transportation possibilities that are likely to exist for the foreseeable future.

- During my final meetings in Baghdad on 16 March, I made reference to the need to be able to assess the effective utilization of all inputs that might in future be established under the responsibility of the United Nations. The government assured the mission that it would accept a system of monitoring of imports and their utilization.

Observations

- The account given above describes as accurately as the mission has been able, using all sources, including much independent observation, to ascertain the situation, which, within the time available and the travel limitations referred to earlier, was perceived to exist in regard to urgent humanitarian needs in Iraq during the week of 10–17 March. I, together with all my colleagues, am convinced that there needs to be a major mobilization and movement of resources to deal with aspects of this deep crisis in the fields of agriculture and food, water, sanitation and health. Yet the situation raises, in acute form, other questions. For it will be difficult, if not impossible, to remedy these immediate humanitarian needs without dealing with the underlying need for energy, on an equally urgent basis. The need for energy means, initially, emergency oil imports and the rapid patching up of a limited refining and electricity production capacity, with essential supplies from other countries. Otherwise, food that is imported cannot be preserved and distributed; water cannot be purified; sewage cannot be pumped away and cleansed; crops cannot be irrigated; medicaments cannot be conveyed where they are required; needs cannot even be effectively assessed. It is unmistakable that the Iraqi people may soon face a further imminent catastrophe, which could include epidemic and famine, if massive life-supporting needs are not rapidly met. The long summer, with its often 45 or even 50 degree temperatures (113–122 degrees Fahrenheit), is only weeks away. Time is short.

MICHAEL EMERY

HOW MR. BUSH GOT HIS WAR

Deceptions, Double Standards, and Disinformation

REVISED AND UPDATED VERSION OF *VILLAGE VOICE* COVER STORY, "THE WAR THAT DIDN'T HAVE TO HAPPEN," MARCH 5, 1991

THE EMBARRASSING AFTERMATH OF THE GULF WAR

AMMAN, JORDAN—During the embarrassing aftermath of America's Gulf war victory, with U.S. troops scrambling to set up camps for starving Kurds in northern Iraq, Kuwaitis murdering Palestinians and Israelis dictating terms for postwar talks, it became more important than before to question how this war came about.

Many other questions await answers. Was it necessary to destroy Iraq to achieve the stated U.S. goal of "liberating Kuwait"? Did Saddam Hussein withdraw the bulk of his forces prior to the U.S. ground invasion, or was his army never 540,000 strong? Were most of the 100,000 Iraqis slaughtered by U.S. forces only poor conscripts, many fleeing for their lives? Where is the physical evidence of the thousands of destroyed tanks and weapons? Did more than the estimated 15,000 Iraqi civilians die in the U.S. "rain of steel"? What kind of duplicity is linked to the phrase "Israeli restraint"?

Despite the maze of confusion, much of it caused by a massive coalition-financed disinformation campaign, the war's end made four things clear: (1) The United States and Great Britain are free to physically control events in the oil-rich southern Gulf for another decade or so, until the Arab masses finally revolt against their masters from Saudi Arabia to Egypt. Only increased repression will keep the inevitable from happening; (2) no excuse remains for the Arab states and Israel to avoid formal discussions of the Palestinian Question. The war only delayed its rightful spot on the region's formal agenda; (3) the United States will not hesitate to use its overwhelming force again in the Third World if the action falls within the needs of maintaining the new world order; (4) there now is a precedent for wide-ranging censorship of U.S. correspondents and for increased use of the CIA and psychological operations disinformation—in short, the propagandists won their war.

Despite the understandable desire to move ahead with eyes and ears closed to the shameful events that occurred, and to avoid bitterness, it is important for history if for nothing else to probe the origins of the war, to better understand why an Arab solution to the conflict between Iraq and Kuwait was impossible to achieve. Assigning credit and blame for the prosecution of the war has been a primary subject of postwar politics in the region—just ask the Jordanians and Palestinians, who lost the financial and political support of the bulk of the Arab states because of their resistance to supporting the coalition. The second guessing can be found in Saudi Arabia, Syria, and in Egypt as well.

The first recriminations against Arab members of the U.S.-led international coalition are already being heard in the region. Some Arab diplomats charge that the mainline Arab states, led by Hosni Mubarak of Egypt and encouraged by the Saudis and Kuwaitis, fell in with a long-term British-American plan to control the destinies of Iraq and Iran in the wake of their bloody eight-year war. With the willing assistance of the Egyptians and Kuwaitis, two crucial Arab peace initiatives that would have prevented the crisis were sabotaged, paving the way for war with the Western powers.

The evidence shows that the United States had a two-pronged policy, giving economic support to Saddam Hussein on one recently exposed level and conspiring with others to undermine him on another lesser known level. British, U.S., Egyptian, and other Arab officials secretly cooperated on a number of occasions, beginning at least as early as August 1988, to deny Saddam Hussein the economic help he demanded for the reconstruction of his war-torn nation.

In addition, parties to the Arab negotiations say the Kuwaitis—who had actively supported Saddam Hussein in his war with the Shiite fundamentalists of Iran, providing billions of dollars in loans and helping to acquire sophisticated weapons otherwise unavailable to the widely mistrusted Iraqi regime—had enthusiastically participated in a behind-the-scenes economic campaign inspired by Western intelligence agencies against Iraqi interests. The Kuwaitis even went so far as to dump oil for less than the agreed-upon OPEC price, something the Kuwaitis, with their vast holdings in the West, could easily afford but which undercut the oil revenues essential to a cash-hungry Baghdad.

A four-month investigation of the war's beginnings—based on information from diplomats, long-time Middle East observers, and senior officials of several Arab governments and corroborated by documents purportedly seized by the Iraqis as they captured Kuwait City seven months ago—has generally confirmed this account. The basic outline of the diplomatic rush to war in the Gulf was in turn corroborated by Jordan's King Hussein during an extended interview on February 19 in Amman (see "Exclusive Interview with King Hussein," below).

BALANCING POWER IN THE GULF

Since the end of World War I, when the British and French governments abrogated agreements made with leaders of the Arab revolt and arbitrarily drew the current boundaries throughout the Middle East, Western policy has been based on the vulnerability of the oil-rich, population-poor southern Gulf states to outside control. Ensuring that the oil-burning industrialized countries—rather than Iran or Iraq, the poor but populous Muslim states of the northern Gulf—exercised that control became the central preoccupation of first British, then American foreign policy.

Fomenting national and ethnic divisions became standard operating procedure. In the 1970s, the United States and Israel encouraged the shah of Iran in his support for a Kurdish (Barazani) rebellion in the mountains of northeastern Iraq. The Kurds were betrayed, losing their outside support when the shah and Saddam Hussein ended their dispute over the Shatt Al-Arab waterway. Saddam Hussein then unleashed his forces against the hapless Kurds, while the engineers of the revolt, including the ever-present Henry Kissinger, watched with mock horror. Then, after the fall of the shah, the United States encouraged Iraq's 1980 invasion of Iran as a counter to the alarming rise of Khomeini-style fundamentalism there.

As the Iran-Iraq war dragged on into an eight-year slaughter costing over a million casualties, the United States was active on all sides of the conflict. Even as it officially banned arms sales to either combatant, the United States secretly provided weapons to both. As Murray Waas revealed in a series of investigative reports for the *Village Voice* (see "Gulfgate" and "Who Lost Kuwait," *Village Voice*, December 18, 1990, and January 22, 1991), the Iran-Contra arms-for-hostages swap was but one arm of a two-fisted policy that was simultaneously "tilting" toward Iraq, providing Saddam Hussein with financial credits, satellite intelligence, advanced weaponry, and steady domestic political support.

But once the cease-fire was signed on August 20, 1988, leaving the heavily armed Iraqis as the most powerful military force in the Gulf, the poles of American policy in the region were ready to flip once again.

One of the most pressing postwar problems was a long-standing Iraqi-Kuwaiti boundary dispute involving the Rumaila oil fields west of Kuwait City. The Iraqis charged that the Kuwaitis were pumping more than their fair share of the field, which stretched across the disputed boundary; they also claimed that during the war with Iran, Kuwait had developed farms and settlements up to 60 kilometers beyond its legitimate border with Iraq.

As the only sitting Arab ruler whose administration began in the post-colonial 1950s, King Hussein was acutely aware of how the present border had been arbitrarily determined by foreigners. Before the end of the Iran-Iraq War, when the Kuwaitis were still financing Saddam Hussein in his battle with the fanatical Iranians, the king had helped to engineer three diplomatic missions in an effort to resolve the Rumaila dispute. Strangely enough, even though the two countries were close allies in the war raging just east of nearby Basra, all three attempts to get the Kuwaitis and Iraqis to settle their argument failed.

King Hussein said the Iraqi president felt the border problem with Kuwait remained a "very heavy burden on his shoulders." A number of sources said that the Kuwaiti attitude toward Iraq was well known in the Arab world. Kuwait had loaned Iraq about $17 billion for the war and didn't expect to be repaid, but refused to formally forgive the debt. "It is in Iraq's interest to have this as part of their national debt," the Kuwaitis coolly told King Hussein.

Puzzled by the seriousness of the rift, King Hussein began to hear rumors that Saddam Hussein had ambitions of militarily annexing the southern Gulf territories. These stories came from Western visitors to the Gulf who were passing through Amman on their way home from Saudi Arabia, the United Arab Emirates, or Kuwait.

Had relations between the former allies eroded to the point of war? In late 1988 King Hussein confronted all the Arab leaders, including the Saudis and Kuwaitis, who between them held $30 billion in Iraqi war debts. With a touch of exasperation in his voice, the King said he told his fellow Arabs, "Look, had not this country (Iraq) defended you these last many years, the whole situation would be different . . . their strength is for you. So why, why this attitude? If you have any doubts or suspicions, why not bring them out into the open, remove them, dispel them? This is not really something that is worthy of you."

"But unfortunately the seeds were there, there was something there," he continued, suggesting that covert operations were behind the rumors. "I am sure that there were . . . some intelligence agencies that must have given them the impression that this might have been the case."

THE KUWAITI TIE TO THE CIA

Let's jump ahead to August 2 for a moment. As the leading Iraqi tanks drove through downtown Kuwait City, meeting only widely scattered resistance, the emir and most of the rest of the al-Sabah clan were caught by surprise. Hundreds of highly placed Kuwaitis fled south to Saudi Arabia; the emir made off in his private helicopter just ahead of Iraqi attack choppers. In their wake, the Kuwaitis left everything including an irreplaceable collection of ancient Islamic art, fleets of luxury automobiles, and thousands upon thousands of top-secret documents.

Although most of the Kuwaitis' far-flung industrial interests were controlled from their London offices, thus preserving their business records, the state papers left in Kuwait City detailed not only internal policies but also the nature of the al-Sabah's relationship with Western governments and intelligence agencies.

To make matters worse for the al-Sabahs, along with the documents, they had also left behind thousands of non-Kuwaiti bureaucrats, the "guest workers" who had spent their entire lives in the tiny principality but had always been denied citizenship. Many were Palestinians, and the Kuwaitis now believe that these former employees enthusiastically led the Iraqis to the al-Sabahs' most jealously guarded secrets.

(Feelings were running so high that the Desert Storm command refused to allow Kuwaiti soldiers in the first assault wave that liberated Kuwait City, for fear of touching off a massacre of Palestinians.)

In any case, shortly after the invasion, the Iraqis released a document to Reuters press agency that purported to be a 1989 letter from the chief of the emir's security forces, Brigadier General Fahd Ahmad al-Fahd, to the Kuwaiti minister of the interior. In the letter, Brigadier al-Fahd (who was killed when the Iraqis took Kuwait City) announced that, pursuant to the emir's order, he and another Kuwaiti security official had "visited the headquarters of the United States Central Intelligence Agency" from "12 to 18 November 1989." After noting that the U.S. side "emphasized that the visit should be top secret in order not to arouse sensibilities among our brothers in the Gulf Co-operation Council, Iran and Iraq," the General lists eight major points of agreement he took away from a private meeting with CIA chief William Webster on November 14.

The emir had survived an assassination attempt (which he blamed on the Iranians) in May of 1985, and General al-Fahd's first concern was the CIA's agreement to train 128 bodyguards for the emir and the crown prince, Sheikh Saad al-Abdullah al-Sabah. After agreeing to closer ties between the Kuwaiti State Security Department (KSSD) and the CIA—including American help in computerizing the KSSD offices, in return for information about the "armaments and social and political structures of Iran and Iraq"—the Brigadier writes:

> 5. We agreed with the American side that it was important to take advantage of the deteriorating economic situation in Iraq in order to put pressure on that country's Government to delineate our countries' common border. (The CIA said) broad cooperation should be initiated between us . . . (and) coordinated at a high-level.
>
> 6. The United States side is of the opinion that our relations with Iran should be conducted in such a way as, on one hand, to avoid contact with that country and, on the other, to exert all possible economic pressure on it and to concentrate on effectively bolstering its alliance with Syria. The agreement with the United States side provides that Kuwait will avoid negative media statements about Iran and restrict its efforts to influence that country to Arab meetings.

Although admitting that a meeting did take place between Webster and General al-Fahd on November 14, the CIA immediately denounced the letter as a crude forgery when the Iraqis released it, and it received little if any notice in the American press. But it does go a long way toward confirming the account of events leading up to the war given by King Hussein and diplomats from other Arab countries. After reading the letter during the interview on February 19, King Hussein said that he felt it accurately described U.S. policy toward Iraq and Iran.

THE FIRST SABOTAGE AT JIDDA

Meanwhile, throughout much of 1990, U.S. officials visiting Baghdad were sympathizing with Saddam Hussein in his dispute over the Rumaila oil field border. Convinced that serious ties with Iran were all but impossible, much of the American establishment was still publicly tilting toward Saddam, hoping that his regime could be converted into both a bulwark against Iran and a stable trading partner. Throughout the spring and summer of 1990, Saddam Hussein was given several clear signs of honorable U.S. intentions toward Iraq and indifference about Kuwait.

These included Senator Robert Dole's visit to Baghdad of April 12, Secretary of State James Baker's April 25 testimony before a congressional subcommittee, Assistant Secretary of State John Kelly's numerous statements in support of Saddam Hussein's regime, and the much-quoted July 25 "green light" for the invasion given by April Glaspie, U.S. ambassador to Iraq. (See "Who Lost Kuwait," *Village Voice*, January 22, 1991.)

As Glaspie departed for a long-awaited leave in the United States Arab diplomats were preparing for what would later be seen as the first of two crucial opportunities to resolve the crisis. Underlining the seriousness of its purpose, Iraq continued to mass more than 100,000 troops on its border with Kuwait.

Such is the plump and stately progress of Saudi diplomacy that they are known throughout the Arab world for rarely attending a formal negotiation unless an acceptable deal has already been worked out. And such was the case with the first Arab mini-summit, set for July 31 in Jidda, a comfortable resort in western Saudi Arabia. According to a highly placed source with excellent diplomatic and intelligence contacts, Saddam Hussein didn't want to attend the Jidda summit without knowing in advance that the Kuwaitis were ready to meet his demands either, and King Fahd gave him that assurance.

The secret arrangement between President Saddam Hussein of Iraq, King Fahd of Saudi Arabia, and the emir of Kuwait, according to a Middle East source familiar with the communications between Saddam Hussein and King Fahd, was that the Saudis and the Kuwaitis each would pledge an initial $10 billion to assist the war-weary Iraqis, as a down payment on the $30 billion Saddam Hussein demanded last May. The issues of war-debt reduction, the disputed boundary, and secret oil production were all supposed to be on the table.

King Hussein, who admitted that he was increasingly left out of the Saudi-Kuwaiti dealings, said he did not know at the time that the sheikhs had agreed in principle to making payments of that size. But Saddam Hussein was, as always, blunt. Only two months earlier, in a closed session of the Arab League summit in Baghdad in late May, Saddam Hussein had demanded not only the forgiveness of his entire war debt but an additional $30 billion in reparations from the oil-rich states. It should be noted that the Jidda meeting may not have been the first time that the $10 billion figure came into discussions. For example, Judith Miller and Laurie Mylroie reported in their book, *Saddam Hussein and the Crisis in the Gulf* (1990), that in June Iraq's Saddoun Hammadi toured the Gulf states, asking for lower production quotas and $10 billion in aid. The Kuwaiti response, they reported, was to offer $500 million over three years.

A number of other meetings were held throughout the region in July. Although Kuwait and the U.A.E. finally agreed under pressure from Saudia Arabia, Iran and Iraq to hold down production, the Iraqis continued to push for cash, including compensation for the oil allegedly stolen by Kuwait from the Rumaila field

King Hussein said that he had been so concerned about the parlous nature of the Jidda conference that he and his entourage flew to Baghdad on July 30. That's when he first discovered how truly angry Saddam Hussein was.

"I honestly didn't think he would invade," the King recalled. "But I really got quite uncomfortable. (Saddam Hussein) was talking about how, when the Kuwaiti emir was subjected to the (1985) assassination attempt, he decided to retaliate against the (Iranians) and sustained 1500 casualties. He said, 'We took all that . . . and now they are doing this to us.'

"I sensed an anger and so many manifestations of it that I hadn't seen before . . ." the King said. "I got extremely worried."

The King immediately flew from Baghdad to Kuwait to urge the al-Sabahs to soften their attitude toward Iraq (at the time, the King had no idea that a rough agreement had already been sketched out). According to both the King and another participant, despite Saddam Hussein's army on their border, the Kuwaitis were in no mood to listen. Why were the rulers of this tiny city-state so sure of themselves?

Apparently, the Kuwaitis thought they knew something the Iraqis didn't. In their July 30 meeting, Kuwaiti foreign minister Sheikh Sabah al-Ahmed al-Sabah, the emir's brother, began by making sarcastic remarks about the Iraqi soldiers near the border. The Jordanians rebuked him, urging the sheikh to take the Iraqis seriously at the mini-summit scheduled for the next day. Then Sheikh Sabah shocked the Jordanian delegation by saying, "We are not going to respond to (Iraq) . . . if they don't like it, let them occupy our territory . . . we are going to bring in the Americans."

At that moment Sheikh Sabah must have realized he had let something slip because, according to one source, he quickly added, "Well, you know what is embarrassing about this . . . what is embarrassing is the Israeli-American dimension."

He would have been more embarrassed had he known that in 1987 U.S. officials gave an increasingly alarmed Israel the green light to bomb any existing Iraqi chemical, biological, and nuclear facilities, similar to the 1981 Israeli raid that brought worldwide condemnation. The source for this information, who obtained it from U.S. officials in Washington, said Israel was told the bombing could be at a politically convenient time.

However, after the Palestinian intifada broke out in December 1987, U.S. officials reportedly told the Israelis they would have to wait—it wouldn't look good to bomb an Arab country while Israeli soldiers were beating Arabs on television in the streets of the West Bank and Gaza. Denied this opportunity, the Israelis applied heavy pressure on the United States during late July and early August.

The Jordanians, dismayed by what they considered an incredible display of arrogance, had no idea why the Kuwaitis felt so confident of U.S. intervention. But King Hussein said he learned later in that same week, the Kuwaiti crown prince had called senior military officers together and told them their duty—in the event of an invasion—was to hold off the Iraqis for 24 hours. By then, the crown prince told them, "American and foreign forces would land in Kuwait and expel them."

King Hussein left the discussion profoundly worried about the next day's conference in Jidda. As he headed past an honor guard at the Kuwaiti airport, King Hussein sensed tension in the eyes of the youthful soldiers. "I thought how young people like this could be the victims of mistakes of their leaders," he said.

Actually, they had good reason to be tense. Deal or no deal, the sheikhs had no intention of coughing up billions, even with a battle-hardened army at their gates. The initial Jidda session lasted only two hours. According to a source close to the discussion, the next day the Kuwaitis offered an enraged Iraqi Vice President Izzat Ibrahim a mere $500 million, far short of Iraq's demand. The meeting broke up the next day without even a discussion of Iraq's oil production and border complaints. Two days later, Saddam Hussein invaded Kuwait.

PROOF OF A PLANNED BETRAYAL

There is some documentary evidence of a pre-Jidda arrangement between the Iraqis, Kuwaitis, and Saudis. This writer has obtained a copy of the official invitation to the July 31 Jidda meeting sent by King Fahd to the emir of Kuwait. Although the document was published by some Arabic newspapers, it went virtually unnoticed. The text of the translation reads:

> Your Excellency, my dear Sheikh Jaber al-Ahmed al-Sabah, Prince of Kuwait:
>
> Peace be with you and the blessings and mercies of God be with you. I wish you the best of health and happiness. I would like to refer to the brotherly communications that took place with your Excellency and President Saddam Hussein of Iraq and what you agreed upon regarding the meeting of his Excellency Sheikh Saad al-Abdullah al-Sabah and Mr. Izzat Ibrahim in your second country the Kingdom of Saudi Arabia.

It is my pleasure to welcome his Excellency Sheikh Saad al-Abdullah in Jidda on Tuesday, July 31, 1990 according to what we agreed upon.

And I am looking forward to this brotherly meeting. I have full confidence in your judgment and wisdom in fulfilling all that we are looking for and what your Arab brothers are looking for in overcoming all of the obstacles and confirming the love and friendship between the two brotherly countries.

Finally I would like to take the opportunity to express my love and appreciation along with my sincere brotherly wishes to his Excellency for good health and happiness and to our brothers the Kuwaitis' wealth and prosperity.

May God bless you and keep you. Your brother, the servant of the two holy shrines.

—Fahd Ibn Abed al-Aziz al-Saud
The King of the Kingdom of Saudi Arabia

Interestingly, King Fahd's invitation refers twice to pre-conference agreements between Kuwait and Iraq ("I would like to refer to the brotherly communications that took place with your Excellency and President Saddam Hussein of Iraq and what you agreed upon . . ."). This strongly suggests that the meeting was in fact conceived as a working session for ironing out the details of an already confirmed deal. In addition, the invitation seems almost to plead with the Kuwaiti prime minister to fulfill his previously negotiated obligation ("I have full confidence in your judgment and wisdom in fulfilling all that we are looking for and your Arab brothers are looking for . . ."). It should be noted that it is impossible to know the exact terms of the agreement, but it is clear that Saddam Hussein's demands for cash were still negotiable along with the Rumaila oil field dispute and his need for access to the sea through control of the coastal islands of Warba and Bubiyan.

If the Saudis were in truth confident that the al-Sabahs would do the proper thing at Jidda, they would soon be sorely disappointed. Scrawled across the top of the invitation is a handwritten note from the emir of Kuwait to the crown prince, Sheikh Saad, who would actually be representing the Kuwaitis at the meeting. In the note, the emir tells Sheikh Saad not to listen to requests for Arab solidarity from the Saudis or the

Iraqis; the Iraqis, the emir writes, are extortionists, while the Saudis wanted to deal Kuwait out of its share of the fabulously rich oil discovery made several years ago in the diamond-shaped neutral zone just west of the emir's southern border. The oil in this area, called the Wafra field, is shared by the Kuwait Oil Co. and Texaco. The latter has a profit-sharing agreement with the Saudis.

What's more, the note says that ignoring Iraq's demands and its consequent threat to invade was the advice of "our friends in Washington, London, and Egypt."

The emir closes portentously: "We are stronger than they think." The crown prince knew that, rather than cede claim to the disputed zone or pay billions to buy off the Iraqi army, at Jidda he would only offer $500 million dollars.

Translation of the emir's handwritten note to his prime minister:

> We will attend the meeting according to the conditions we agreed upon. What is important to us is our national interest. Do not listen to anything you hear from the Saudis and Iraqis on brotherhood and Arab solidarity. Each of them has their own interest.
>
> The Saudis want to weaken us and exploit our concessions to the Iraqis, so that we will concede to them (the Saudis) in the future the divided (neutral) zone. The Iraqis want to compensate their war expenditures from our accounts. Neither this nor that should happen. This is also the opinion of our friends in Egypt, Washington and London.
>
> Be unwavering in your discussions. We are stronger than they think. Wishing you success.

After the Iraqi invasion, King Fahd would tell King Hussein, "It's all the Kuwaitis' fault." A source close to the negotiations said that King Fahd was furious with the Kuwaitis for backing out of their prearranged deal, and that anger was expressed in a general way to King Hussein. When I showed this document to King Hussein—who has denounced both the invasion and the official annexation of Kuwait—he said he had made inquiries about its origin, and now believes it is authentic.

One reason everyone in the Arab world was so surprised by Saddam Hussein's bold seizure of Kuwait was that Egypt's Hosni Mubarak had met the Iraqi leader in the week before the invasion, and he had been assured that the troops on the border were merely there to pressure the al-Sabahs into settling their disputes with Iraq. Though Saddam Hussein had tried to swear Mubarak to secrecy about his "bluff," Mubarak had quickly told Arab and Western governments that he believed Saddam Hussein was only feigning an attack (which may or may not be the reason CIA chief Webster told President Bush on July 31 that he believed there might be an invasion, but it would stop at the disputed border). Once the invasion had taken place, Mubarak was quoted in the press as saying Saddam Hussein had lied to him.

But King Hussein tells the story differently. He insists that Saddam Hussein had indeed told Mubarak in late July that Iraqi troops were on the Kuwaiti border only to pressure the emir into settling their border and monetary disputes. The Iraqi leader had explained his ploy in strictest confidence, eager to reassure Mubarak about his intentions but anxious lest the Kuwaitis learn he was bluffing and refuse to pay him as much as Saddam Hussein believed they had, in principle, agreed to. The Iraqis later said Saddam Hussein had told Mubarak that he would not invade if the Jidda meeting gave an indication that negotiations would continue and he would be taken seriously.

Instead, the King said, "Mubarak violated a confidence." By his own admission, the Egyptian President quickly told the Saudis, the Kuwaitis, several reporters, and George Bush that Iraq would not invade.

Needless to say, that went a long way toward stiffening Kuwaiti resolve at the July 31 summit in Jidda. After all, not only did the Kuwaitis have Mubarak's assurances that Saddam Hussein's saber-rattling on their northern border was little more than a negotiating tactic, but for good measure they knew they had U.S., British, and Egyptian support for stiffing the Iraqis. As the emir's note put it, "We are stronger than they think."

SABOTAGE AT JIDDA, PART II

At about 5 a.m. on Thursday, August 2, King Hussein was awakened by a call from King Fahd of Saudi Arabia. There was a great sense of urgency in the voice of the Protector of Mecca: Saddam Hussein's troops arc racing across Kuwait. Please tell him to stop where he is.

King Hussein immediately placed a call to Baghdad. He finally reached Saddam Hussein at around 10 a.m.

King Hussein asked, "What did you do?!"

"Well, as you heard," Saddam Hussein replied.

"Please, tell me, don't stay there!"

"Well, I will withdraw, it is a matter of days, perhaps weeks."

"No, don't talk about weeks, only a matter of days."

"Yes, but I have learned that the ministers are meeting in Cairo and they want to condemn us . . . if they do I am afraid that will not help." Saddam Hussein was referring to the conference of Arab League foreign ministers, which was being held that day in Mubarak's capital.

As rivals to the mantle of Arab leadership handed down from Egypt's Gamal Abdel Nasser, there is little love lost between Saddam Hussein and Mubarak. But both Saddam Hussein and King Hussein realized that the chance for peace was now in Mubarak's hands. If the Egyptian leader chose to, he could lead the foreign ministers into a strong condemnation of Saddam Hussein's action, opening the way for Arab sanction of Western intervention in the gulf.

Saddam Hussein added, "Let them look into it seriously and then . . . not take it that way, because if they do we will not take it lightly and they will not like our reaction!"

King Hussein summoned his aides and told them, "Knowing the man, knowing his personality, if they try to humiliate him he will act adversely. We have to go to Cairo right away."

The Jordanians flew to Alexandria and met with President Mubarak about 4 p.m., the same day as the invasion. After witnessing Saddam Hussein's nearly apoplectic rage the day before the July 31 Jidda conference—and hearing the Iraqi leader's suspicions about secret cabals to cripple his nation—King Hussein knew all hope of a deal would evaporate if Mubarak denounced Iraq.

When King Hussein met him on that sultry August afternoon, Mubarak agreed on the need for discretion; he promised to be silent until the Jordanian monarch had a chance to go to Baghdad and talk Saddam Hussein into withdrawing. The king could carry with him an invitation to a mini-summit that would be hosted by the Saudis in Jidda on Sunday, August 5, as one last-ditch attempt at achieving an Arab solution.

As evidence of his sincerity, Mubarak gave the Jordanian foreign minister use of his helicopter to fly from the airport to the foreign ministers' meeting in Cairo to forestall any condemnation by the League. In the meantime, Mubarak said he would telephone the Egyptian foreign minister, who was chairing the sessions.

That's when President Bush called Mubarak, who left the king to take the call privately. It is not known if Mubarak informed Bush of the diplomatic maneuvers already underway; but when he returned, Mubarak invited King Hussein to the phone, saying Bush wanted to talk.

Jordanian diplomats say Bush raised two points: (1) he was worried about Americans in Kuwait, and (2) he wanted the Iraqis to withdraw. But he said nothing about any intention to send troops to the Gulf. The king told Bush that he was going to fly to Baghdad to attempt to find an Arab solution to the conflict, saying this could best be effected by an Arab summit in Jidda on August 5.

King Hussein then tried to call King Fahd to get approval of the mini-summit, but he couldn't get through. Mubarak finally reached the palace, spoke with Fahd and asked him to talk to King Hussein. But King Fahd demurred, saying he would return the call. He never did.

The confused Jordanians waited three hours at the Alexandria airport. Finally they gave up and flew back to Amman about 9:30 p.m., finishing a whirlwind day on a disappointing note.

The next morning, Friday, August 3, King Hussein—refreshed and confident after sleeping on his new plan for peace—flew to Baghdad, assuming that the Egyptians and hopefully the Saudis supported his efforts. As he left his palace in Amman, the Arab ministers' loud and angry debate over the condemnation issue wore on. There was no time to waste.

In the Iraqi capital, Saddam Hussein was receptive to the king's initiative and agreed to two points: (1) Iraqi troops would begin to withdraw as the meeting got down to business on Sunday, August 5, and (2) Saddam Hussein or a representative would personally attend the mini-summit. Saddam Hussein apparently knew that he had stepped too far by seizing the entire country—but he also felt confident he would hold a strong hand at the August 5 negotiations.

A pleased King Hussein tried to phone Mubarak at about 1 p.m. on the afternoon of Friday, August 3 with the news. He was told the president was at the mosque. Hussein waited, but like King Fahd the day before, Mubarak did not return the call. The king then phoned an aide in Amman, asking him to call a CNN crew to the airport for his arrival.

Returning to Amman from Baghdad at about 6 p.m., the king messaged a trusted adviser from his plane, asking him to notify the Arab foreign ministers meeting in Cairo that Saddam Hussein was willing to withdraw if the Kuwaitis and Saudis would live up to their initial agreement.

King Hussein thought he had made a historic breakthrough—there was a chance for an "Arab solution to an Arab problem," despite the failure of the July 31 Jidda summit.

But his spirits were dashed a few minutes later by a phone call from his foreign minister at the Cairo conference. Mubarak had sabotaged the peace plan by breaking the pledge made only hours before not to publicly condemn Saddam Hussein.

"Oh, my God, now the conspiracy is complete," the King said.

The frustrated Jordanians say that Mubarak acted after receiving a second telephone call from President Bush, but it is impossible to verify specific telephone calls. In any case, the Arab League denunciation of Saddam Hussein had become a foregone conclusion, and Arab participation in the American-led coalition was assured. Later, King Hussein said, he learned that Mubarak had been pressured to get the foreign ministers to pass the anti–Saddam Hussein resolution by 5 p.m. on August 3, in order to coincide with the presentation of the U.S.-drafted Security Council resolution calling for an economic boycott of Iraq.

Diplomats from several countries attending the Cairo meetings have confirmed that the Egyptians led the charge to condemn Saddam Hussein, aided by the Syrians and the Saudis. "There was a desire to get this on the record without delay," said one observer, who saw the foreign ministers' condemnation in writing three hours before it was approved.

These participants, with many years of experience in Middle East intrigue, agree that there was a heavy atmosphere of intense outside pressure and dread at the sessions.

"There was a general knowledge that the Americans and British were behind the Egyptian actions," one observer said. "This was discussed behind the scenes, but there were only a few reporters there, mainly from Arab countries where the press is heavily restricted, so the reality of the moment didn't get out," he said.

WOULD IRAQ HAVE INVADED SAUDI ARABIA?

In the wake of the invasion, the Arab world was thrown into a flurry of lamentation and diplomacy. There was wide speculation in the West that Saddam Hussein intended to press on to Riyadh, intent on seizing not only the richest oil fields in the world but the holiest sites in Islam.

Did Saddam Hussein intend to invade Saudi Arabia? "No way!" an agitated King Hussein insists. The King recalls how on August 7, after receiving an American cable warning that Saddam Hussein might gobble up the Saudi regime, he offered a visiting Saudi official "half of the (Jordanian) Army" if a genuine threat existed. But the Saudi said that help was not needed, that he had been with King Fahd that very day and the king had seemed confident and secure. Certainly no urgent need for Jordanian military help was mentioned.

But within 30 minutes of the Saudi official's departure, King Hussein received news that the first U.S. troops had arrived. President Bush cited the threat to Saudi Arabia in his decision to send the Rapid Deployment Force to form the first skirmish line of Desert Shield.

According to King Hussein, "The (Saudis) pressed the panic button" when they saw the CIA photographs of Iraqi troop movements brought by Secretary of Defense Dick Cheney to Riyadh. The CIA also sent King Hussein photos of tanks moving along roads near the Kuwaiti-Saudi border. The king argued that if Saddam Hussein had wanted to invade the Saudis, he would have moved immediately, when the only thing between him and the Saudi capital was a tiny and untested—if expensively equipped—Saudi army.

But Saddam Hussein's intentions were actually less critical at this juncture than Western intentions. In another conversation King Hussein had at around this time, with then British Prime Minister Margaret Thatcher, the Iron Lady, let it slip that "troops were halfway to their destination before the request came for them to come." (See "Exclusive Interview with King Hussein," below.) The television-paced war had already begun.

"PREPARATION FROM THE WORD 'GO' FOR WAR"

It now seemed impossible for Saddam Hussein to escape from what those who wanted to punish him began to see as a well-formed trap.

And in retrospect, there was no further chance for peace after those first few days of August—the first American-Arab war became a reality when "linkage" with the Palestinian issue emerged as a stumbling block in a series of last-minute negotiation attempts.

Greatly angered to see the hope for an Arab solution torn from his grasp, King Hussein confronted Mubarak over the phone. "I told him, 'It's your fault,'" the King said. Nettled, Mubarak complained that he had been under pressure from King Fahd of Saudi Arabia and from media people who were challenging his earlier assurances that Saddam Hussein had no intention of invading. When Mubarak said, "I'm so tired, I can't think," a fuming King Hussein shot back, "When you can think again, call me back!" It is difficult to know precisely when U.S. pressure was placed on Mubarak, but the record shows that billions of dollars of Egyptian debt were forgiven in return for Mubarak's faithfulness as a coalition partner.

From an Arab point of view, the war with Iraq could not have happened at a worse time. The Palestinian movement had been making steady progress toward recognition by the international community, and the fading Intifada had recently found a new surge of life after the brutal Israeli massacre at the Haram al-Sharif (Temple Mount) in October. The next major Arab move would have been to use its growing influence to force the Israeli-Palestinian issue to the fore, with Iraq, Egypt, and Syria vying for leadership of an international Middle East peace conference, the Saudis playing their usual behind-the-scenes power game and Jordan acting as a broker for compromise.

Instead, the Arab world fell apart. And the events leading to war in the desert seemed to have more to do with dodging peace than preserving it.

"Unfortunately, I've been convinced for a while that there was no effort to dialogue, no effort to reach a diplomatic solution," King Hussein said. "And that there was preparation from the word go for war."

EXCLUSIVE INTERVIEW WITH KING HUSSEIN

It is a war that we did not seek but it also is a war we will not lose.

—Secretary of State James Baker
February 20, 1990

Oh, my God, now the conspiracy is complete.

—King Hussein of Jordan
August 3, 1990

AMMAN, JORDAN—The official car arrived at the Intercontinental Hotel late Tuesday afternoon, February 19, to carry me to the palace for my interview with King Hussein. The car passed through a heavily barricaded gate onto the grounds of the Royal Palace, which looks more like a college administration complex than any American idea of a royal setting. The only sign of any official state purpose is the small group of soldiers whose barracks are there, but, like campus security guards, they work and casually talk in the cool autumn sunshine. Once inside the palace working area, there is a long, wide corridor and a series of high-ceilinged rooms that are the offices for the king's advisers, including the Minister of the Royal Court. One of the king's Bedouin palace guards served drinks to waiting guests from a gold-plated container slung over his shoulder.

It was six in the evening, and the king had already had a busy day. The news from Moscow and Washington was not encouraging, but there was still hope that President Bush would accept the Soviet peace plan—if so, there would be no ground war. King Hussein met me in a large sitting room filled with couches and arm chairs, but he took a straight chair next to a small end table that held the tape recorder. For more than two hours, the king patiently answered questions that concentrated on an alleged pattern of deceit that had led to war in the Gulf. He quietly described how he had discovered the plans of "some intelligence agencies" to discredit Iraqi President Saddam Hussein beginning in August 1988, after Iraq emerged as the strongest Gulf power in the wake of the Iran-Iraq War.

Americans have seen the king portrayed as a weak man, a onetime ally caught between his own Palestinian population and extraordinary pressures from Washington, London, and Israel, whose speech in support of Iraq on February 7 amounted almost to a betrayal. Actually, my impression was that the king is extremely comfortable with his decision to hold firm against what he sees as Western bullying. He is adamant about the need for holding to historical ties, culture, and tradition. He is equally proud of being a good friend—he made frequent references to his old friendship with George Bush—but it is clear that, for his part, the king feels violated by his old friends as well.

"I'm not angry with (the American people)," the king said. "I'm maybe angry for them, really, because I believe the United States—with all of the changes that have occurred in the world, many which came as a total surprise to us—had a great opportunity to help the world, (as) the strongest power on the globe, to see us move in a manner even toward helping us identify with the American people . . . (I mean), in terms of upholding lofty ideals and principles and treating problems equally wherever they are in the world, and to use its power sparingly and constructively. . . .

"I believe that every attempt that I made, that any of us made in this region to eliminate this bloodbath, this destruction, was unfortunately blocked. . . . I found a new situation that developed over the last few years. And that is an attitude which I don't believe is becoming of the United States.

. . . It is something along the lines of: You are either for us or you are against us."

During this interview the king was shown copies of documents purportedly taken from Kuwait City by the Iraqis. Up to this point, the king had avoided public speculation about the motives of Western and Arab leaders who, in his words, had "caused this war to happen." He was in the middle of a sentence explaining his reluctance to claim anything that could not be independently verified, when the door swung open and an aide softly announced bad news. CNN was reporting that President Bush had rejected Moscow's "program" for the Iraqi withdrawal from Kuwait, although the Soviets said it was in keeping with the intent of United Nations Resolution 660.

The king slumped back in his chair and murmured to himself in Arabic for a second before quietly responding. "I think a ground war will take place soon . . . I believe it is imminent . . . Obviously, it goes way past the liberation of Kuwait."

The thrust of his feelings then emerged, that the United States and Britain had together decided to paralyze Iraq after the end of the Iran-Iraq War and impose an American-designed regional security system—one that would ensure U.S. control of the region well into the twenty-first century.

PRIME MINISTER THATCHER'S ROLE

Much of his anger was actually directed at the British, the former colonial power in the Gulf, whom King Hussein suspects of encouraging the United States to make war on Iraq. The king chuckled while recalling what he described as "a loud argument" in London with British Prime Minister Margaret Thatcher after the allied troop buildup in the Gulf was already underway.

"It was one of the rowdiest discussions that I ever had with anybody. She was very strong on her side and so was I . . . very strong language . . . " the king said, registering a measure of the shock felt by practicing Muslims for a cursing woman. "But one thing came out. She said troops were halfway to their destination before the request came for them to come."

Thatcher later tried to back away from her comments, according to King Hussein, when they met again briefly at a conference in Geneva on November 20. But he didn't accept her explanation. "(Her original statement) was very clear," he said.

The king's communications with the then British prime minister tend to support the widely held Arab view that Thatcher, citing her experience in the Falklands War, had pushed President Bush toward the commitment of overwhelming military force in the Gulf. Thatcher told the king on August 7, after Jordan had refused to go along with the majority of Arab states in condemning Saddam Hussein, "I know (Bush), too, feels hurt about Jordan's action, especially as he has done so much to support your Majesty over the years." She went on to discuss what she saw as Jordan's hubris in siding with Saddam Hussein—in no uncertain terms.

"(She was) speaking of the President's disappointment . . . with the kind of language I wasn't used to from anybody," the king said. Thatcher was in the United States at the time, pushing for a concerted international campaign against Iraq—which became Desert Shield.

Bush himself later turned up the heat even more. "It's vital for Jordan's essential interests," Bush said, "that it not be neutral in the struggle between Iraq and the great majority of the Arab states."

JORDAN'S KING HUSSEIN GIVES HIS VIEW

Despite his disappointment over Bush's determination to ignore the effort to achieve a solution within the Arab world and his frustration over Thatcher's old-style, strong-arm tactics, the king reserved his greatest anger for those Arab leaders who continually left him out of the decision-making process—ultimately ceding control of events to the West.

The king was adamant on five major points:

1. Saddam Hussein did not lie to Egyptian President Hosni Mubarak about not wanting to invade Kuwait in late July, shortly before the August 2 invasion.
2. Iraq was provoked into its invasion of Kuwait by the intransigence of the al-Sabahs.
3. Iraqi troops never intended to enter Saudi Arabia.
4. Iraq did not and does not have a nuclear weapons capability.
5. In supporting Saddam Hussein, Jordan was not going out of its way to hurt legitimate U.S. interests, but was instead sticking to basic principles. And it is now being punished for sticking to those principles.

King Hussein said he had been deeply hurt by the Western perception that he had thrown in his lot with Saddam Hussein, shirking his obligations as head of a neutral country with ties to the United States.

His voice barely audible, King Hussein said, "It is fairly obvious the infrastructure of the whole country (Iraq) has been destroyed, or is in the final process of being destroyed. I've been convinced for a while that there was no effort to dialogue, there was no effort to reach for a diplomatic solution, and there was preparation from the word go for war. Unfortunately, it has come about, whatever the motives and reasons behind it."

In an effort to summarize many details of the origins of this war, the king was asked if he thought the Arab understanding was that Saddam Hussein had been provoked into his invasion—thereby stepping into a noose the allies had prepared for him. "I believe it is," the king firmly replied. The Kuwaitis, according to this view, had been assured of American support in the event of an Iraqi invasion, and therefore declined to join in an agreement to pay $10 billion in "war reparations" to Saddam Hussein. When the Kuwaiti prime minister instead offered a mere $500 million to Iraq at the Arab summit in Jidda on July 31, an angry Saddam Hussein launched his assault. "I believe it is most unfortunate that this has happened and I believe it will leave a very bitter taste that is going to be there for a long time . . . People of great responsibility in the Arab world have allowed this to happen . . ."

Coloring the entire interview was the king's evident disappointment in the West's lack of appreciation for the culture, values, and traditions of the Arab world. Scion of a family that has long played a prominent role in Arab history—a history that includes several galling humiliations—he, at times, bristled with pride in his own heritage.

Perhaps Arab pride explains the dismay here at the failure in communication. Throughout the war, the Western press had depicted the fighting as a one-sided video game, virtually cheering on the allies' long-distance pounding of an Arab country as if they were hometown scorekeepers at an electronic football game.

The Arabs are invisible people to Westerners, even in death.

EDWARD W. SAID

PEACE IN THE MIDDLE EAST

Ever since he addressed the Congress on March 6, 1991, President Bush has seemed set on convening a Middle East peace conference. There is now a tentative, if not completely clear willingness on the part of concerned Arab and Israeli governments to participate in the conference, which is scheduled to begin sometime in October/November 1991. During its meeting in Algiers at the end of September the Palestine National Council voted decisively in favor of entering the peace process, although it should be said at once that despite the fact that the Palestinian people are the principal aggrieved party to the conflict between the Arabs and Israel, and although this nation of people now suffers under the twin burden of exiled dispossession and military occupation, it alone has been prevented from supplying the conference with its own freely chosen representatives. Still, as I said, all the parties—including the Palestinians who will participate in a non-PLO grouping within the Jordanian delegation—all the parties will be present under the aegis of the United States and the Soviet Union for two days of politically insignificant ceremonial inauguration to be followed by two weeks of bilateral discussions. My subject here is not so much the conference itself, but to what crisis the conference is meant to be a solution, what sort of human problem and political conflict it seeks to address, and what we can and cannot expect. Most of all I want to talk about some of the large cultural and moral issues that seem important to me and do not get enough attention in this age of 15-second sound bites, a superficial and manipulative media, and a poorly informed mass audience.

One more thing. No one needs to be reminded that, when it comes to the subject of Israel and the Palestinians, public discourse in the

United States lags considerably behind that in Israel itself or in Europe. In both Israel and Europe today it is possible to speak and write and represent critical views of Israel and to speak and write about the Palestinian people with affection and support. This is very difficult to do here for reasons that are familiar to everyone. I have never allowed myself to be deterred by these hobbles on free discussion and thought, and in these comments I shall be as frank as possible. But that is not the point. I want to say quite simply that anyone who believes that there can be peace between Israel and the Arabs generally, the Palestinians in particular, without serious acknowledgment of the moral and existential case of the Palestinian people, now at an extremely low point in their fortunes, is seriously misleading him- or herself. My premise is that neither the Palestinians nor the Israelis have a military option against each other. Both peoples must learn to live in peace, and in mutual acknowledgment of each other's history and actuality. Yet we must also admit as a simple fact that today only one people, Israeli Jews, has sovereignty, has achieved self-determination, even as the other people, the Palestinian Arabs, live in a state of subordination and oppression. That the Palestinians struggle against and resist this state of affairs is a function of how injustice and suffering do not defeat a people, nor compel them into submission, but rather drive those people to resist more, and to struggle further for political justice and rights. Today, therefore, there is no parity, no symmetry between these two peoples who are destined to exist with each other. It is because the Palestinians' side of the conflict is most urgently in need of attention and help that I want to accentuate their tragedy and travail, and I want to do so in such a way as befits Palestinian history, the continued resistance of the people of Palestine, and their political perspectives. There are issues of principle and morality that I want to highlight, and if they are difficult and embarrassing and even unsettling I feel that they must neither be avoided nor rendered more digestible by being turned into platitudes and euphemisms.

So I shall start with the immediate background of the present and move from there to some of the other issues and concerns that must be addressed if we are seriously to assess the prospects for peace in the Middle East. Let us look first then at what has generally engaged and affected Americans most recently, the war with Iraq which, given the parking lot shenanigans of the last week of September as well as the threats of future military action against Baghdad, still continues today.

The world is full of cultural, religious, and political conflicts, most of them of short duration, some of them very long. Arabs and Americans are parties to the opposing sides of what appears to be one of the longest, the deepest and most complex conflicts of the modern world, that between the Arab-Islamic world on the one hand, and on the other, the Western, and more particularly the North Atlantic world. Some of us have lived anxiously and agonizingly through a particularly violent episode of that conflict, our feelings engaged with both sides, sometimes angrily and despairingly, sometimes sorrowfully and bitterly. Neither side, it seems to me, did itself much credit. The behavior of the Iraqi regime has been disgraceful; repressive at home, mischievously adventurous and violent abroad most recently in its illegal occupation and annexation of Kuwait, it brought destruction upon its own people, first through American bombing and mass devastation, then through a merciless persecution of its own population, especially the Kurds, grievously sinned against, persecuted, betrayed, and in danger yet again of being abandoned. Certainly Iraq's government did important things domestically to build a secular society, to take major steps in development, education, health, agriculture, oil, and housing. But along with almost all the other Arab governments it did very little—quite the contrary—for human rights. Democracy does not really exist as a result, and the shocking rampage against the sovereign state of Kuwait indulged in by the Iraqi army cannot at all be characterized as having anything to do with the best things about Arabism, Arab civilization, or the Arab people. Neither for that matter has the restored government of Kuwait done itself credit, as the abuse of innocent expatriates continues, the mindless corruption and despotism remain unruffled and the likelihood of further stagnation, inaction, and political hopelessness increase each day. So far as the United States is concerned, this was another imperial intervention, activated by oil, not principles, mainly to consolidate a faltering empire, distract attention from the troubles at home, gather in some triumphalism and military aura at the expense of a tailor-made villain whom, interestingly enough, the United States in a certain sense supported and apparently still wants to live with as a useful foreign devil. It is perfectly obvious, however, that along the way, getting Iraq out of Kuwait has accomplished next to nothing; the mess continues and once again, the United States and its allies show themselves to be largely devoid of ideas, values, and any appreciable sort of moral or statesmanlike courage, except bellicose declarations and saber rattling.

As I said a moment ago, this war must really be seen as an episode in a much longer and deeper contest. Recall that after its European wars, for instance, the United States quickly came to terms with Europe; the same was true of its conflict with Japan and with Indochina which even after both were devastated seem to have settled into a sustained mode of doing business with the United States. With its other antagonists we do not therefore feel that the conflict lingers on after the guns fall silent. Only with the Arab-Islamic world does one feel that after this particularly violent chapter the problems remain pretty much unsolved, pretty much simmering beneath the surface. There are wounds, betrayals, misunderstandings and antipathies that seem to be reproduced generation after generation, each of them quite different but each of them sharing with all the others the sense that an over-all contest between the West and Islam is still in place and still unresolved. To this level of tension President Bush has never addressed himself—and more's the pity.

But let me be paradoxical for a moment and allow me to contradict myself. Yes, there is a contest, but no, it is not as real and as enduring as one would think. What I am trying to say is that because of history and tradition many people in the West and in the Islamic world like to think that they are part of a contest that has world-historical significance. The fact is, I believe, that both the Arab-Islamic world and the West are constructions which human beings and institutions have made, and which they use for political ends. In speaking about the West we are not really speaking about anything so concrete and so fully inclusive as to be monolithic. There are many Wests: there is a Catholic West and a Protestant West, there is a Judeo-Christian West and a secular liberal West, there is the West as represented by Europe and the West represented by the United States, there is the West that colonized Ireland, Africa, Asia, Australia, and Latin America, and the West that fought for abolition, for decolonization, for justice and freedom. Much the same points can be made about the Arabs and Islam: there is the Arab world of Abbasid and Andalusian culture and that of militant fundamentalism, the Arab world of the intifada and the Arab world of the Gulf emirs, of writers like Abdel Rahman el Munif, Kanafani, Jabra, and of the official regime-sponsored journalism of al-Ahram—one could go on and on. The point I am trying to make is that one way of dealing with what we have too long thought of as this very enduring conflict between our worlds either as Arabs or as Westerners is to realize that the worlds themselves are not stable and watertight but shifting and unstable because they have been made, so to speak, by human beings who for all sorts of understandable reasons want to hold on to them. Perhaps it is useful therefore to say that the officially designated Arab world and the officially designated West are in conflict because in a strange way their official establishments require each other as enemies. Certainly it was true of George Bush and Saddam Hussein that each saw in the other an embodiment, in one case of Western imperialism, in the other of a foreign devil, each of whom had to be defeated not just militarily, but morally and culturally as well. This was why in the Arab world people supported Saddam Hussein, and certainly not because he was a real champion of Palestinian or human rights, and why also in the United States so many people supported George Bush as the personification of Western civilization reversing aggression. For those Arabs who were also of the West it was a peculiar misfortune to fall into both of these rhetorical and almost exclusively negative traps, yet there was little space or opportunity afforded anyone to dispute either the notion that Saddam Hussein was equivalent to the Arabs and Islam, or the equally false notion that George Bush represented America and the West.

Now it would be complete folly for me to deny that there was something of the Arabs in Saddam Hussein and something of the West in George Bush. That is so obvious as not to be very discussable. Given the present situation in the Arab world and in the United States, however, I feel that there is much more to be gained by critically discussing and disengaging from the large collective passions; this allows one to be more aware of what is contradictory or unsatisfactory about them. As we look around in the aftermath of Desert Storm I think we must conclude that on the level of the general and collective, such ideas as make it into public rhetoric, claims, and statements have almost all been either false or unsatisfying. No one can be convinced that today the collective Arabs any more than the collective Americans who speak the language of justice and rights are doing anything different than what they did before Desert Storm; and that what they do now has anything very much to do with improving the concrete human rights of Palestinians, say, or women, or disadvantaged minorities in the Arab world, or enabling free expression, or freedom of press, opinion, assembly, and the rest. The language of generality and collective identities is in fact a false language, not because it is not true in some of what it says, for instance, about the existence of an Arab people—there certainly is one—but because it has been highjacked by the state, and by the voices of official nationalism. And these, both in the United States and in the Arab world, have been locked in a frozen mold that has been completely overtaken by events and realities on the ground.

Let me give you one simple example. Every Arab state today proclaims the self-determination of the Palestinian people as one of its chief aims in life. All of the Arab states visited several times by Secretary Baker refused to take any steps toward a bilateral peace with Israel because, the leaders of these states said, there had to be movement on the Palestinian question first. Of course something has happened: steps toward a peace conference have been taken because the United States, as the major power, has taken them. In the meantime the intifada is well into its fourth year. Now what is interesting about the intifada, among other things, is that it actually is a galvanizing Palestinian process for self-determination; in other words it actually is the very thing that collective Arab rhetoric has been speaking about for so long. The intifada is Palestinian self-determination, and is not a figure of speech. As part of the intifada Palestinian men and women have taken their difficult lives under Israeli military occupation in their own hands, they have tried to construct a system of self-help and relative independence from the occupation, and they have thus roused themselves and the other Arabs into actualizing, almost for the first time in recent Arab history, a model for communal life that is not based upon the exclusive authority of one party, one sultan, one repressive state apparatus.

To this the Arab states well before the Gulf crisis have responded really very, very little. It is, I think, true to say that if you compare all the reams of paper published, all the tons of words spoken in support of Palestine since the intifada began by information agencies, foreign ministries, princes, kings, and presidents in the Arab world, you will see that none of it amounts to what the intifada was really in need of, namely, real (as opposed to token) financial and political support. Sadly we must conclude that the general Arab rhetoric abandoned the intifada on the ground and then took off into the higher realms of fantasy and self-congratulation. And Palestinian children, women and men were left to suffer and fight on the ground, more or less alone, well before the Gulf crisis began, well before the PLO displeased the Arab allies of the United States. Roughly the same argument can be made about the United States' official rhetoric of support for freedom and the rights of people everywhere. While the president sent off over 650,000 troops to resist aggression, his government continued to block votes in the United Nations that supported agreed upon rights for the Palestinian people. Over the years there have been 64 U.N. resolutions on the books, an additional 29 of them vetoed unilaterally by the United States, some of them even supported by it, enjoining Israel to stop its dreadful abuse of the Palestinian people, and its annexation and settlement of Arab territory. None of them practically speaking was ever as enthusiastically supported as was the liberation of Kuwait by the United States. So here too the general rhetoric is arraigned, indeed can be positively convicted by the specific and concrete.

In the late twentieth century it is the case, I believe, that the language and the rhetoric of large scale national and cultural identity is now seriously in disrepair. If we look at the contest such as it is between the West and the Islamic world, we will have to acknowledge that the resolution of such contests cannot be accomplished simply by buying into a fully deployed language of indiscriminate antagonism. In any case the conflict is too vast and too unreal in many ways either to be won or lost conclusively. Even more important, I think, is the fact that there are too many rascals, too many exploiters of the situation who have wrapped themselves in the virtuous rhetoric either of the West or of the Arabs to do much more than keep themselves going.

That is why I said it is important now, with the Arab world sunk in a dispiriting torpor, with the absence of collective vision and leadership mostly the case in the West and in the Arab world, for us to stand back critically and look at the situation before us, on the eve of a likely peace conference, with slightly fresher eyes, with a greater degree of discrimination, with a broader awareness of history, cultural possibility, and human responsibility, with a heightened sense of moral purpose, than the usual clichés about the Arab world, Islam, and the West afford us.

In the relationship between Europe and the Islamic-Arab world there is a very different history of problems, profits, and encounters than that between the United States and that world. Europe first encounters Islam as an Arab religion, when it emerged from the Arabian peninsula in the seventh century and swiftly swept across Western Asia, North Africa, and southern Europe. Throughout the Middle Ages and the Renaissance, the Arabs and Western Europe were linked in all sorts of ways, ways military as the history of the Crusades attests, ways cultural as the transmittal of knowledge from the Arabic scientific and philosophic tradition to European culture shows, ways theological as the whole history of Christian polemics and religious disputation against Islam beginning with John of Damascus testifies so eloquently and, alas, in so hostile a manner. Norman Daniel, Hisham Djait, Maxime Rodinson, and Albert Hourani have correctly stressed the presence in this extended encounter of a great many contradictions. True the anti-Muslim polemics of Pascal and later of Renan characterize much that has remained as a prevailing attitude to Islam within European culture, but what has also remained is what Rodinson has called a fascination with Islam. The first non-Arabic version of the Koran was produced in eleventh-century Cluny by Peter the Venerable, a labor of interest and attention emulated by many later scholars, poets, travelers, and religious figures: Goethe, Hugo, Burton, Massignon. The list of Europeans with a deep and abiding interest in the Arabs and Islam is a long and honorable one.

Yet I would argue that since the late eighteenth century the relationship between the Arab world and Europe has been shaped by a largely political contest that has taken many forms. Beginning with Napoleon and continuing with the British expeditionary force to the eastern Mediterranean, the French occupation of Algeria in 1830, the British occupation of Egypt in 1882, European powers have viewed the Arab world as a place to exercise their colonial energies. And this in turn has provoked a series of resistances to European colonialism that climax not only in various insurrections and nationalist agitations between World War I and II but also in such variously misconceived attempts as the partition of the Fertile Crescent, the promise of Palestine by the British government to the Zionist executive as a national home for the Jews, and—after 1870—the annexation of Algeria as a department of France. After a particularly bloody war, however, Algeria did achieve independence from France in 1962, and many of the countries of the eastern Mediterranean also gained independence and liberation from Britain or France, except Palestine.

Along with the struggle for political domination has gone a long-standing cultural and technological contest between Europe and the Arab-Islamic world. This too has been well studied and documented by a whole range of scholars and intellectuals. All of them agree in the main on three points. First, is that European advances in industrialization, technology, and economic power rendered the Arab world especially vulnerable to domination. In this the Arabs were hardly more unfortunate than say the Indians, the Irish, or the Africans, as the global reach of European navies, missionaries, merchants, and scientists impressed upon the entire globe the fact of what the historian Michael Adas has called "machines as the measure of man." In short, non-European men and women were found wanting, inferior, less developed, a fate which condemned many of them not only to subservience but also to slavery, poverty, and ignorance.

Second, Europe, referred to by David Landes as the unbound Prometheus, instigated in the Arab world and across a wide front a great wave of nationalist sentiment. This ran the gamut from religious fundamentalism (still present in different forms today), to modernization of the sort that stimulated mass education, translation, local industrialization, and reformism, to a very various assortment of local as well as pan-Arab nationalism. Much of this has been well studied both by Arab and European scholars, although the tendency has been to see things according to a simple model of the West acting, the Arabs reacting. For surely there were aspects of Arab cultural activity, for instance, that answered to an internal logic within Arab society that was neither available nor permeable to Western influence. But there is little doubt that much of the animosity felt by Arabs toward the West today bears within it the history of defensive responses to encroachments from Britain, France, Italy and so forth, all of them, in my opinion, shaped by such less than noble attitudes as the search for cheap resources, for ready markets, for strategic dominance, and the like. Rarely was the encounter an equal one, and even more rarely did it result, from the Arab standpoint, in a humane exchange.

Third and most interesting, there developed a certain intimacy between Europe and the Arabs that in another context Germaine Tillion has referred to as complementary enmity, that is a sort of hostility that also included a knowing affection, long years of mutually engrossing experience, and grudging acknowledgment of each other's actuality. This never precluded the most savage repression visited by one on the other, nor in the case of European colonial attitudes toward the Arabs, did it prevent attitudes of the most rabid racism, many of which still persist today. But—and this is the point—it was about knowledge and experience of a kind that has literally never existed between the Arab world and the United States, which in effect has succeeded Europe as the great outside power exercising hegemony over the Arab world, from the Atlantic to the Gulf. In 1936 the leading Egyptian intellectual, scholar, and public figure Taha Hussein published a tract titled "The Future of Culture in Egypt," in which as a man deeply involved in university education as professor (later to become rector of Cairo University) and as senior administrator (he was to become minister of culture) he outlined the topic from a perspective that was taken by many to be an official one. He spoke at length about Egypt's Islamic and Arab legacies and mission; but when he came to the country's future cultural orientation he spoke exclusively about Europe. For Taha Hussein, Egypt's role as the principal Arab country meant its recognition of its debt to the Greeks, the European Enlightenment and above all to European industrial and scientific modernity. For indeed Hussein accurately articulated the Eurocentrism of an Egypt that ever since Mohammed Ali's reign [Pasha of Egypt, 1805–48] had locked itself into the European orbit, consciously and happily, despite the travail of colonial rule and imperial exploitation. Hussein makes no mention at all of Egypt's cultural links with Africa and Asia, both of which in the revolutionary era that succeeded his, Abdel Nasser's, were to be of central importance. [Interestingly enough, in the recent scholarship of Martin Bernal and Basil Davidson these links are also of the first magnitude.] For Taha Hussein the mainly Arab-Islamic character of Egyptian culture would be oriented toward Europe, and not the United States.

Most Americans have little idea of the world beyond the United States' borders, and most seem convinced that the United States is the world's policeman, entitled to intervene at will more or less everywhere and, what is more depressing, having intervened and (as was the case with Panama, Vietnam, and Grenada) having savaged whatever the place, it thereafter left that place behind, forgotten, consigned to oblivion. I felt this in particular about the tremendous media campaign against Iraq. No matter what one feels about Saddam Hussein, and his government, it is also true that the United States did nothing serious to avoid war or to help Iraq in its search for freedom and democracy. One had the impression that Iraq was a tremendous desert with a mad Hitler-like figure sitting on top, and that it was not only alright but an excellent thing for the United States to pour a huge amount of firepower onto the place and virtually destroy it as a functioning country.

In fine, Iraq was reduced to a noncivilization, a noncountry, and its people were simply ignored, although it was, of course, they far more than Saddam and his supporters who bore the terrible brunt of the United States attack. Now during the whole of the war, as well as the period before and after it, no one who had access to mainstream public discourse (in the media or the government) suggested that in spite of the current U.S. war with Saddam, Iraq was after all the inheritor of a great culture, its people were remarkably gifted and had done perhaps more than any other Arab people in the twentieth century to further artistic, literary, and architectural production in the Middle East. This, I think, might have been a small deterrent to the fury of the military attack on Iraq—but that deterrent was not there in the United States precisely because relationships between the Arabs and the United States are so humanly, culturally, and historically attenuated, so abstract, so dehumanized and in so many significant ways nonexistent. In the United States the Arab world has no cultural status at all; the few images of the Arabs are essentially negative and frightening, images such as those of terrorism, fundamentalism, and so on. This need not be so at all, since it is also true that given an opportunity the people of the United States can be singularly generous and open when it comes to other cultures and societies.

So far then I have been arguing that far from there being a monolithic West and an equally undifferentiated Arab world, there are important distinctions to be made, of which one of the most important so far as the West is concerned is the one today between the United States and Europe. When we turn to the question of Palestine—surely the longest lasting matter at issue between the modern Arab world as a whole and the West—it first engaged modern Europe in conflict with the Arabs, before it engaged the United States in a continuation of the same conflict, not just with one Arab people, the people of Palestine, but with the whole Arab world. The present struggle between the Palestinian people and the state of Israel very much belongs to the historical relationship created over time between the Arabs and the West. So far as any Palestinian is concerned, the destruction of our society in 1948, the expulsion and dispossession of our people since then, as well as the military occupation of the West Bank and Gaza since 1967 are seen as extending and deepening the ravages in our midst of what began originally when Napoleon invaded Egypt in 1798, West European colonialism. In its earliest stages Zionism was of European provenance; its earliest institutions referred to and identified themselves as colonizing undertakings in the manner of the European colonization of Africa and Asia; its whole rhetoric and ideological language borrowed heavily not only from Jewish theology but also from the rhetoric and language of the British in Africa and India, or the French in Algeria. Central to the enterprise was the qualitative distinction between incoming Jews from Europe, and those natives who were variously depicted as absent altogether or, in the words of Ben-Gurion [Israel's first prime minister], like red Indians, that is a negligible quantity entirely.

As I suggested, the complexity and richness of Palestine, however, have involved Europe well before the onset of modern Zionism in the late nineteenth century. One could say of this small, largely unprepossessing bit of land between the Jordan River and the Mediterranean that more than any other on earth it is literally drenched in religious and cultural significance, not only for Judaism and Christianity but also for Islam, in whose tradition it has always had a unique sanctity. Until the Renaissance, Jerusalem—the city of my birth—was placed at the center of the earth on most European maps of the world. Crusades were fought over Palestine, and although the actual physical territory was unknown to most of the people who referred to it, it was the center of imagination, of culture, of world history for generations of Europeans, from Shakespeare and Dante to the humblest village dwellers in France and Ireland. Without actually ever being seen, Palestine informed the iconography of Western art; it underlay Rome and the Roman Church and, ironically, it also undergirded the entirety of the Protestant Reformation. It is perhaps a comic, perhaps even a pathetic fact that when West European and American missionaries came to Palestine in the nineteenth century they ended up by converting no Jews and no Muslims; they succeeded only in making converts of the local Eastern Christian sects who, for reasons having to do with a free education and other emoluments of this world, joined the Anglican community (like my paternal grandfather in Jerusalem) or the Baptist church (like my maternal grandfather in Nazareth). The point is that Europe in particular, and the West in general had designs on Palestine that go back to the beginning of the Christian era, designs that entailed the overriding of native communities in Palestine, designs that entailed a huge amount of conflict with the native cultures of the place.

Yet when it came to the politics of an actual Palestine and the wishes of its actual inhabitants, one always senses in the Western consciousness an agenda of far greater consequence is at stake than that imagined by some essentially insignificant Palestinian individuals. Consider the following sentences from a memorandum written by Arthur Balfour [then British Foreign Secretary] in 1919:

> The contradiction between the letter of the Covenant [the Anglo-French Declaration of 1918 promising the Arabs of former Ottoman colonies that as a reward for supporting the Allies they would have their independence] is even more flagrant in the case of the independent nation of Palestine than in that of the independent nation of Syria. For in Palestine we do not propose even to go through the form of consulting the wishes of the present inhabitants of the country, though the American Commission has been going through the forms of asking what they are. The four great powers are committed to Zionism and Zionism, be it right or wrong, good or bad, is rooted in age-long tradition, in present needs, in future hopes, of far profounder import than the desires and prejudices of the 700,000 Arabs who now inhabit that ancient land. In my opinion that is right.

Not merely the expression of an opinion, this remark and many others like it made possible the availability of Palestine for literally millions of Jewish immigrants, in the past as well as in the present and they in turn took over the land, dispossessed and exiled the natives, and today sit in military occupation over approximately two million Palestinians on the West Bank and Gaza. In 1948, my entire family was turned into a scattering of refugees, none of whose older members ever recovered from the trauma. Since the occupation began in 1967, the Palestinian people have had no political rights at all; since the intifada began in late 1987 until the end of June 1991, 983 have been killed by the Israeli military (this is three times the number of blacks killed by South African troops under apartheid for the same length of time) and over 120,000 wounded and beaten. Israel has forbidden Palestinians to conduct themselves as if they belonged to a national community. On the West Bank and Gaza the word "Palestine" is forbidden by military law. It's against the law to pronounce the word "Palestine." It is even against the law to use the colors of the Palestinian flag or to show the Palestinian flag. You've seen pictures during the intifada of young kids waving the flag around. This is a capital offense in Israel. The colors of the Palestinian flag, for example, once used on a birthday cake in Gaza, earned the user of those colors a term in jail. An artist, also in Gaza, using the colors of the Palestinian flag—black, white, red and green—in a painting was sent to jail for six months. So there is, in addition to the absence of political rights, also a programmatic war against the very concept of Palestine, as if what Israel has in mind is the extermination of Palestinian national identity.

Palestinians in the West Bank and Gaza under Israeli military occupation are subject to the closure of schools and universities. I speak now of the period in particular after the beginning of the intifada, from December 1987 until the present. What is astonishing to me is that beginning in February 1988 Israel closed all seven universities on the West Bank and Gaza and for many, many months at a time. They also closed the primary schools, high schools, and vocational schools, all as punitive measures using the excuse that they were doing this to prevent terrorism. We're not talking about one school. We're not talking about one university. We're talking about all the schools and universities, with the result that Israel has, in fact, denied an entire generation of Palestinian children their education. So that today seven, eight and nine year old children are illiterate. They haven't been able to attend school. And Israel has made it even more difficult to preserve education by making alternative education illegal, so that if you educate your children in little groups, that too is against the law. There is a code against these attempts by Palestinians to lead their own lives, a code of military laws now numbering over a thousand. They're done by edict, and so there's no appeal against them. To this day (Fall 1991), Bir Zeit, the leading university on the West Bank and Gaza, is still closed. It is a scandal that Israel, which is the state of the Jewish people, the people of The Book, the people who are above all others committed to learning, to humane values, to moral values inscribed in the Old Testament, should be in the position of persecuting another people on matters to do with education. There are over a thousand books banned on the West Bank and Gaza today. I supported the movement to prevent Salman Rushdie from being censored by the Iranian government or possibly being killed. I believe absolutely in the right to freedom of speech and opinion. The moral hypocrisy is that at the same time that we were demonstrating for Salman Rushdie's rights, The Merchant of Venice, Plato's Republic, and Hamlet were forbidden on the West Bank by the Israeli government. To this day (October 14, 1991) the leading university is still closed. Where is there in all of the expressions about the need for freedom of opinion and democracy that we hear from the president and every elected official in this country about opening the universities in Palestine? It is a colossal, outrageous breach of moral law that entire institutions of learning should be closed by the Israeli government on the grounds that they are incitements to terrorism.

In addition to preventing education, Israel has another policy which is particularly effective, which is not only to confiscate land but to uproot trees. These are punitive measures conducted against Palestinians by the Israeli occupation army that were never done in South Africa. Since the beginning of the intifada, they have uprooted 112,000 trees. For example, if an unarmed kid is caught throwing a stone at a jeep or an Israeli tank, this can earn the kid's village the loss not only of some more land, but it can also result in the uprooting of fruits and vegetables which require a permit from the military government to be replanted. You cannot plant anything on the West Bank and Gaza, nor build anything, without a permit. There was an article some years ago by an Israeli lawyer named Avigdor Feldman called "The Israeli Government versus the Eggplant." He was talking about a particular law, in which the Israeli military governor declared that no fruit tree or vegetable can be planted on the West Bank or Gaza, without express permission of the government. If something was planted it would be destroyed and the person who did it would be put in jail for six months.

Another unique contribution of Israel to the annals of persecution is the punitive demolition of houses. This means that if you are suspected of or have, in fact, committed an offense against the Israeli military, whether it be a child or an adult, you are marched back to your house by the soldiers, given a few hours to pack your belongings, and the entire house is blown up. There have been over 2,000 houses blown up in the last four years.

Finally we come to two very grave measures which have to do with political prisoners and deaths. Since the intifada began, there have been over 100,000, some say close to 200,000 prisoners put in Israeli jails. By put in jails I don't mean as a result of a trial. The Israeli military occupation is entitled to bring in anyone that it wishes without charge, without trial, without lawyer and incarcerate that person for six months and then renew the incarceration for another six months. There are approximately 15,000 prisoners in Israeli jails on those grounds, and the only grounds usually given are security offenses. If you want to compare this with South Africa, you would have to say that during the 30 years of the state of emergency in South Africa this would have meant that 234,000 prisoners would have been incarcerated. This is three times more than actually were. Israel has established a record, and it is, in fact, the highest number of prisoners per thousand population of any place on earth.

Then we come to the deaths. Since the intifada began there have been over 1,000 Palestinians killed by Israeli bullets. I'm not talking about accidents, I'm talking about the practice of the Israeli army of killing Palestinian men, women and children who demonstrate, who try to circumvent the strictures of the occupation. And add to that the various days, months, weeks of curfew. During the first three weeks of the Gulf war, for example, the entire West Bank and Gaza, two million people, were kept under twenty-four-hour curfew. For 40 days they were not allowed to leave their houses 24 hours a day. The number of people who died as a result of that was more than twice the number of Israelis who were killed during the Scud attacks, three times the number.

I'm sorry to have to recount all these figures to you, but I come to the most important figure of all: The United States, we, the taxpayers, have been paying for this. On September 24, 1991, for the first time in a clear and consistent way, there was an article in the *New York Times* which was giving background on the discussion of the loan guarantees which Israel is requiring from the United States. The amount of money since 1967 that the United States has given to Israel is $77 billion. In 1990 alone the United States gave Israel $4 billion, and you'll recall recently in a speech the president said this amounts to a thousand dollars per Israeli man, woman, and child. We're talking about the largest single handout in the history of U.S. aid, relative to the population and in absolute terms. The question I'm asking is, how is it that we have done this, in light of the colossal number of violations of human rights to Palestinians that have occurred during that period? It is an irony that I find so scandalous as to be unable to understand it that the United States every year for the last five or six years, in its own State Department annual survey of human rights, has condemned Israel for all the abuses I've been referring to and then some; and at the same time continues to pour money into Israel, without regard for the rights of the Palestinians.

Despite Israel's unqualified hostility to the Palestinian people, and as one Israeli government after another has moved further to the right, become more and more intransigent and rejectionist, Palestinians have become more moderate, more reasonable. The Palestinian political program as set forth in 1988 by the Palestine National Council (PNC) has been unambiguously clear. Although official Israel has refused to accept any of the provisions of the Palestinian political program that program remains as is, despite the Gulf War. Passed in late 1988 the Palestinian program calls for two states on a partitioned Palestine, it recognizes Israel, it accepts the validity of U.N. Resolutions 242 and 338, and it envisions an end to the armed conflict between Israelis and the Palestinian people through political negotiation. Israel's response has been unambiguously clear and unambiguously negative: no withdrawal, no Palestinian state, no end to settlement, no end to confiscation, no dealings with the PLO.

Now, of course, the political positions of the Israeli government are well known and, as I shall be showing, have played far too great a role in determining the U.S. position in the upcoming peace conference. What I want to stress now is the fact that what Israel does to Palestinians it does against a background, not only of the long-standing Western tutelage over Palestine and the Arabs that I discussed earlier, but also against a background of an equally long-standing and equally unflattering anti-Semitism that in this century produced the Holocaust of the European Jews. We cannot fail to connect the horrific history of anti-Semitic massacres to the establishment of Israel, and nor can we fail to understand the depths, the extent and the overpowering legacy of suffering and despair that informed the postwar Zionist movement. It would be inhuman and deeply wrong not to. But it is no less appropriate for Europeans and Americans today, who support Israel because of the wrongs committed against the Jews, to realize and acknowledge that support for Israel has, alas, included, and still includes, support for the sufferings, the exile and dispossession of the Palestinian people. I would put it as bluntly as this: the Palestinians today and since 1948 are the victims of the victims, and are kept in this unforgiving position to a great extent by Europe and the United States, both of whom look away and excuse Israeli behavior because Israel is seen as a state of survivors, and must be excused. Moreover, as a state whose economic and political well-being depend to an enormous degree on generally Western, and specifically American support—almost 25 percent of Israel's GNP today takes the form of American aid which since 1967 has totaled the staggering figure of $77 billion—we are entitled to draw the conclusion that Israel's occupation policies on the West Bank and Gaza are in fact subsidized by the West.

Nor must we overlook the sad fate of Israel's Palestinian citizens, 780,000 of them who today constitute 18 percent of Israel's population. They are underrepresented in the Knesset, that is, at about 1 percent of the entire membership. Their juridical status in the state of Israel, which unlike every other state in the world today is not the state of its citizens but the state of the entire Jewish people, their status is confined to that of "non-Jews"; they receive less than one percent of the education budget, and their life expectancy and rate of infant mortality are dramatically worse than that of Jewish citizens of Israel. But it is when it comes to land holding that the worst discrimination is enacted against them. Since 90 percent of the land in the state of Israel is held in trust for the Jewish people, non-Jews are allowed neither to buy nor to lease land, privileges reserved totally for Jewish citizens. As recently as September 16, residents of the town of Ramyah—close to the development town of Carmiel—have had their land expropriated for use by incoming Russian Jewish immigrants. Thus it is clear that far from being a threat only to the well-being and landholding of Palestinians in the Occupied Territories (where Israel has expropriated 90,000 acres, more than 50 percent of the land), the massive waves of Russian and Ethiopian immigrants to Israel, whatever the obvious humanitarian reasons for their arrival, are also a threat; their arrival means that Palestinians will be dramatically, catastrophically less well-off as a consequence. To make matters worse, the ordinary democratic freedoms of expression and opinion allowed Jewish citizens of Israel are curtailed for non-Jews. Thus a well-known Palestinian-Israeli writer, Shafik Habib, a distinguished poet who is also a non-Jewish citizen of the state of Israel, has been on trial and convicted of terrorism because a book of his poetry has been found "dangerous" to the state. Were it not for groups such as PEN, abuses against Palestinian writers and artists would go unreported and unprotested by Western liberals who on the other hand, and quite justifiably, supported Salman Rushdie's right to publish freely.

But it would be too simplistic to say that the West, especially Europe, no longer owed the Jewish people restitution for what is a terrible history of anti-Semitism. In the United States, for example, a long history of enslavement and racial discrimination against black people has subsequently produced what I think is a fair practice of affirmative action, that is, minorities are actively helped to achieve what historically they have been deprived of. And whereas it is scant reparation for what white American society did to the African-American people, it is something. So, one could argue, this is what Israel represents, reparation for what the West did to the Jews, up to and including the dreadful massacre of European Jews. There has therefore been little time for and scant inclination to listen to the pathetic bleats emitted by Palestinians, whose society was destroyed in 1948 and who in the main have had no political rights since then, most of the time living under the subjugation of, in fact, the state of the Jewish people. But in reality the situation has been changing, as more and more Palestinians have forced themselves upon the Western consciousness, as more and more of them actively resist the colonial measures administered against them in their ancestral land by Israeli soldiers and colonial officials.

At a time when most of the tyrannies of Eastern Europe, Latin America, and the Soviet Union have collapsed, three places remain—Ireland, South Africa, and Palestine/Israel—where hostility between communities has prevailed for decades. In each of them, a minority is surrounded by an unreconciled majority; it has appeared important therefore for the embattled minority, like the Israelis or the white South Africans, to maintain a state of siege against the majority, the Muslim and Arab majority in one instance, the black majority in the other. The problem with this model, as any visitor to Ireland, South Africa, or Palestine can readily see, is that it is flawed in at least two ways. First, it suggests that the minority just because it is a minority is to be forgiven, despite any or all of its provocations and sins against the majority; second, the model ignores the fact that important change can take place and has taken place in at least two places, South Africa and Ireland. Far from the situation being frozen into an unending siege, an immensely significant transformation has occured to require a change in perspective. A scant eighteen months ago the ANC was considered a terrorist organization, banned from the country, most of its leaders either in exile or in jail; today, you can visit ANC headquarters, as I did recently when I went to Johannesburg, in the downtown Shell House, and its leaders, Nelson Mandela, Oliver Tambo, Walter Sisulu, and Joe Slovo are major political figures in the country. There are negotiations, and, of course, there are still huge problems. The point, however, is that the situation is now transformed so that both the majority and the minority are involved in discussions about the future of the country, about power-sharing and about enfranchisement.

The Irish situation is also vastly different today than it was a decade ago. There is an Irish state, there is an Anglo-Irish agreement, even though there is partition and British forces are still in Northern Ireland. People speak about unification, and they also speak about the past, and about the British occupation with frankness and passion. Change is occurring, not soon enough, not quickly enough, but unmistakably. In both Ireland and South Africa, of course, violence is still a major ingredient of the current political situation.

Only in Palestine, that other partitioned and internally divided land, is the political situation frozen and the tragic plight of the Palestinian people largely unacknowledged, except for a few individuals and groups. How different from South Africa! For at least ten years it has been internationally impossible to say a good word about South Africa, because South Africa has been irrecusably attached in the public mind of the West with apartheid. Not only was South Africa banned from international artistic and sports events, but a widely sustained policy of economic sanctions and a cultural boycott have remained in effect for a considerable period of time. In the United States a successful campaign against investment in South Africa was waged on the campus, with results in divestment policies and a raised political consciousness that have been dramatic. To a large degree change has come about due to the ANC's international success in connecting South Africa's identity as a nation directly to its racial policy.

No such connection has been made with regard to Israel and its treatment of the Palestinians, half of whose number now resides outside Palestine as refugees, stateless persons, and persecuted exiles. Today people can oppose apartheid in South Africa and say not one word about Israel's practice of apartheid on the West Bank and Gaza. Writers and intellectuals can quite easily refuse—as many do—to visit South Africa in observance of the cultural boycott, whereas they can go and give lectures in Israel, completely ignoring what Israel has done to Gaza, which is a great deal worse than Soweto. If today a film or theatrical producer wishes to put on a Palestinian play or film the dangers of commercial suicide are too great; think of what happened to Vanessa Redgrave. Books and articles are prevented from being published and they are opposed so forcefully when they are published, not because they don't tell the truth, but because they do. A new tactic has been to impugn the person and completely ignore what he or she says if that happens to be accurate and sheds an unflattering light on Israel.

In both the American and the Israeli cases I have discussed instances of courage, of speaking out, of intellectual responsibility, but these cases have been overridden by the fear and self-censorship of the majority concerned. People follow dogmas quietly on their own since these have been internalized as constituting unquestioned norms for what should or should not be said. Yet I want to underline my conviction that only a revitalized conception of the intellectual vocation itself can remedy the situation. Almost seventy years ago Julien Benda accused intellectuals of failing in their mission when they compromised with the truth and succumbed instead to what he called the organization of collective passions. We live in a more difficult world today. Intellectuals have become vastly specialized into various fields of knowledge and expertise; they do not cross over from one field into another, nor in general do they challenge the prevailing consensus, which in the West is like a lucrative Kuhnian research paradigm that guarantees consultancies, jobs, promotion, and the like. In the second place, the manipulation of public opinion and what has been called the manufacture of consent creates large monolithic blocks of patriotic sentiment; these then congeal into ideological abstractions that quickly and unthinkingly mobilize people around slogans like "the West," or "America," or "Israel," or "Islam"; with that has gone a remarkable resurgence of ethnic particularity and a new kind of indiscriminate patriotism.

To return to the Palestinian-Israeli case and the challenge it offers to the intellectual conscience: I do not want to be interpreted as saying that Palestinians are innocent, or that as a people they have been passively tolerant of their fate. Such words as innocent have no place in discussions of this sort. We are discussing attributions of responsibility based on an intellectually discriminating and accurate representation of the collective historical reality. It is therefore imperative for us to insist that Israelis are not white Afrikaaners; nor are they like French settlers in Algeria. They have a history of suffering and of persecution that has made the state of Israel a compellingly attractive resolution for that history, with its amazing longevity and duration, despite genocidal attempts, exile, and dispersion.

Yet none of this, in my opinion, can lessen the truth of what all this has meant for the Palestinians, a truth that needs, indeed cries out for expression. The intellectual task for Jews and Palestinians alike is to connect and to face up to these two histories with something more creative and audacious than reiterated appeals to a divisive nationalism. For Palestinians there is now a major threat to their culture and national existence, a threat which is neither theoretical nor just a vague possibility. Most of all, however, since the Palestinian-Israeli conflict has always had so important an international cultural component there must also be scrupulous attention to making the kinds of connections between history and modernity that too many people have shied away from. This of course is a moral as well as a political and intellectual task that goes to the very heart of the matter, since it is not Israelis who are threatened by Palestinians but quite the other way around. The question to be asked therefore is how long can the history of anti-Semitism and the Holocaust in particular be used as a fence to exempt Israel from arguments and sanctions against it for its behavior toward the Palestinians, arguments and sanctions that were used against other repressive governments such as that of South Africa. How long are we going to deny that the cries of the people of Gaza—a recent visitor told me that she could not open her hotel window for three days, so great was the stench—are directly connected to the policies of the Israeli government and not to the cries of the victims of Nazism?

A generation ago political and intellectual change in the Third World was often spurred by one of the two super powers. It's certainly true, for instance, that the successful liberation movements of Africa, Latin America, and Asia were helped by the Soviet Union, as were a number of subsequent dictatorships. [The U.S. record in this context is hardly an admirable one.] Yet today the international context has changed completely: the United States now has a startling ascendancy which places new responsibility on independent citizens such as are gathered here. None of us should want to live in a new world order governed exclusively by the market, by lobbies, or by governmental experts and technocrats.

At the very threshold of a Middle East peace conference we should understand concretely that what is truly at stake is neither a $10 billion loan guarantee to Israel, nor a patched-together arrangement between unpopular Arab rulers and Israel. The real issue is Palestine. The Palestinian people have accepted an extraordinary set of compromises, required of no other participant. As a result, only we will not be represented by our political representatives the PLO; no one from East Jerusalem will be allowed to attend; no one from outside the West Bank and Gaza will be allowed to participate even though the Palestinians are one people, half of whose number live in forced exile outside Palestine.

So not only will Palestinian participants be a subordinate part of the Jordanian delegation, they will have to face an Israel armed with what might be unconditional U.S. support and a series of inflexible positions that commit it to no withdrawal, no end to settlements, no negotiation on Jerusalem, no compromise on Palestinian self-determination. As Michael Lerner put it in his lead editorial for the September/October *Tikkun*:

> The conference is set up in such a way as to make substantive progress extremely unlikely. Israel will get its way on matters of procedure. After a largely ceremonial opening session, separate negotiations between Israel and the surrounding states will take place. But Shamir has reassured his constituency over and over again that there will be no compromise on the Golan Heights—and no compromise that would grant sovereignty or national self-determination to the Palestinian people . . . [They would get "limited autonomy" which] would allow Palestinians control over municipal functions such as fire and police services, garbage collection and street repair. Shamir's plan would not allow Palestinians' control over land and water resources, would not protect them from the increasing expropriations of land on behalf of Israeli settlers.

In spite of all this, Palestinians have accepted what even Abba Eban has said is something unprecedented in the history of conflict, that one side, Israel, can pick both the team for the other side and the agenda. The United States has in effect gone along with this, although President Bush's position on the loan guarantees is the first instance of his administration even suggesting that not everything about the Middle East should be dictated by Israel and the Israeli lobby.

We have no choice but to support the president's position of course, but we must also speak out and say that the realities on the ground are too tragic, too horrific and violent for the Palestinian people to permit only a cosmetic peace to occur. One cannot in good conscience condone the endless enslavement of a people and the exile of many of its number and also expect silence and compliance. But that, I am sorry to say, is what the peace conference might portend if Israel and its supporters work their way further on the United States, which has already incorporated too many Israeli designs into the structure of the agenda of the conference. These designs—I must say categorically—

are scandalously unjust, unworthy of the Jewish people in whose name Mr. Shamir and his colleagues purport to speak. To the current Israeli government Palestinians are at most aliens on Jewish land; according to Mr. Shamir and his colleagues, they cannot have a status that in any way diminishes exclusive Jewish control over the entire land of historic Palestine. Even to Israel's staunchest supporters such a vision of the future must clearly appear to be a formula for virtually unending conflict. No one can suppose that having resisted decades of unjust Israeli rule, the Palestinian people are about to give up and play dead. We have no strategic ally, the Arab environment is deeply hostile, Israel has an almost complete monopoly on the means of violence and coercion. But we do have hope; we are a resourceful and unendingly courageous people who will never submit to brute force; and above all we have a more just and, I think, a truer picture than our enemies of a future built on reconciliation and peace. The answer is not exclusivism and unending hostility. It is rather reconciliation, sharing, community. We're talking about two people in a small land connected to that land urgently and in many, many ways. The question is how many people we can persuade of this before there is another holocaust, and it's a Palestinian holocaust that I'm talking about now. What is left to Palestinians today is the moral force of the argument that says (a) there is no military option, and (b) you have to live with us, we have to live together as Israelis and as Palestinians, and we have to discover modes of sharing. Palestinians have agreed to participate in the peace conference; we have submitted a list of acceptable candidates; we have cooperated with the conveners, and have done so imaginatively and intelligently. What we worry about is indifference and silence, especially in the United States, where it has too long been the case that because people are afraid of the Israeli lobby they simply turn away from the truth. This must no longer be the case. The issues are clear, the dangers too obvious to be gainsaid. Peace is for everyone, not just for one people who happen to be in the ascendant. As Americans we have an urgent role to play as witnesses and referees to what might be the last chance in a generation for an opening toward peace in the Holy Land. Yet no one must shy away from the responsibility to speak out, to call injustice, and to appeal not to present fears of the past but to future actualities and to the abiding truth about justice and peace.

Postscript, August 1992:

The Madrid peace conference was held under the conditions described above. Bilateral and unilateral talks did begin with no significant change in the situation. The Israeli elections on June 23, 1992 returned the Labor party and Yitzhak Rabin, who promptly signaled a change in the policy of increased settlement, and shortly thereafter appeared in the United States to claim the $10 billion loan guarantees. He got them on the spot from President Bush who seemed desperate to enhance his fading election prospects. The talks will perhaps resume with an autonomy agreement as their purpose: this will give the Palestinians control over municipal affairs (something they had in 1975), and none over security, defense, foreign affairs, land or water. Rights of return, compensation or repatriation will be denied the more than three million Palestinian exiles (who make up over 50 percent of the Palestinian people). Since both Israel and the United States categorically oppose Palestinian self-determination, it therefore seems likely that a tiny Palestinian enclave on less than 20 percent of historic Palestine will in effect be a Bantustan, if the autonomy agreement goes through as planned. But this will not settle the question of Palestine.

PART II

SILENCE = DEATH

The Body As Battleground

MARLENE FRIED AND LORETTA ROSS

REPRODUCTIVE FREEDOM

Our Right to Decide

INTRODUCTION

We women have always fought to control our fertility. We have always wanted to have sex and children on our own terms and we have resisted efforts—whether by individual men, governments, judges, or anti-abortionists—to prevent us from having that control.

The persistence of this struggle reveals its importance. At stake is nothing less than the power to shape our own lives. It is not rhetoric but reality to say that if we cannot control whether, when, and under what conditions we will have sex and children, there is little else in our lives that we can control.

During the 1960s and 1970s, the women's movement and other progressive/liberation movements in the United States made real gains. Even though what we won was so much less than what we wanted, or needed, those gains were a threat to the systems of power that control our lives. We challenged traditional hierarchies and rejected fundamental forms of social control.

The civil rights movement and the women's movement indelibly changed our society, and by the 1980s, these movements presented a formidable front against ongoing assaults. We saw this coalition during presidential campaigns and in fights against conservative Supreme Court nominees.

Defenders of the status quo have responded to these sweeping social changes with a consistent effort to reverse the gains that our movements fought so hard to win. This effort includes campaigns of repression—legal, illegal, and increasingly violent.

This is the context of the current battles over abortion in the United States. Not only are we fighting to win back funding and abortion rights for teenage women, today we must also resist the effort to overturn *Roe v. Wade. Roe* had a profound impact on the daily lives of women. Without legal abortion, thousands of women died in back alleys, thousands more suffered serious medical complications, and all women's health was threatened. After *Roe*, for those women who had access to legal abortion, a dangerous and desperate experience was transformed into a safe and legitimate health care option.

Together with legalizing contraception, abortion legitimized the separation between biology and procreation. This is a necessary step in the struggle for sexual freedom—heterosexual women could choose to have sex and choose not to be pregnant. And by breaking the link between sexuality and reproduction, it opened the door to sexual self-determination for lesbians and gay men.[1]

Now after almost 20 years, we are on the brink of losing legal abortion in the United States. In its most recent decision (1992, *Planned Parenthood v. Casey*), the Supreme Court upheld *Roe* by a narrow, 5 to 4 majority (with four justices ready to overturn *Roe*). At the same time, the Court dealt severe blows to abortion rights by allowing states to place restrictions such as mandatory waiting periods, biased "informed consent" requirements, parental consent regulations, and by weakening the standard against which further constraints will be judged. As with all of the previous erosions of abortion rights, these restrictions hit hardest at the most vulnerable women in our society—low-income women among whom women of color are disproportionately represented, young women, any women who depend on the state for their health care.

As we plan our strategies for resistance, we find that the popular focus on the judicial arena obscures our own history of struggle. Legal abortion wasn't a gift from the Supreme Court, but a victory of a women's movement that was fighting on many fronts for a range of rights and freedoms. And this is what it will take again to protect legal abortion and to win other reproductive freedoms.

We write as activists and participants in this struggle, hoping to contribute to the dialogue. We are angered by the state of siege under which we must live. We are pained by the militaristic terms we must use to describe this assault. But when women are singled out to die, especially poor women, it feels like a war, complete with bombs and terrorists.

We are not going to allow Supreme Court justices, legislators, or antiabortion terrorists to make fundamental decisions about our reproductive lives. We are going to do whatever is necessary to help women get safe abortions and to save women's lives.

FROM ABORTION TO REPRODUCTIVE FREEDOM

The attack on abortion rights is symptomatic of a sweeping assault on women's reproductive health and lives:

- The federal government has waived its Medicaid regulations to allow Wisconsin to implement legislation which penalizes low-income women for having more children. The state will not pay increased benefits to women who have more children while they are on AFDC. The Bush administration has encouraged other states to adopt these regulations.
- Prenatal care for women of color is inadequate: nearly one-third of African American, Native American, Puerto Rican, and Mexican American women receive no care in the first three months of pregnancy.
- Norplant, the first new birth control device to be marketed in the United States in twenty-five years is already being used coercively against poor women.
- Sterilization remains the most prevalent form of birth control in the world.
- In the Third World, reproductive health problems cause the death of at least one million women each year; another one hundred million are maimed. Complications from childbirth and pregnancy and illegal abortion are the leading killers of women of childbearing age—about half a million women die annually from illegal abortions.[2]
- The single greatest cause of injury to women in the United States is domestic violence. More women are seen in emergency rooms for injuries caused by battering than from muggings, rape, and car accidents combined. The F.B.I. estimates that a woman is beaten every fifteen seconds by her partner.

- There are renewed attacks on the rights of lesbians and gay men to be parents, including challenges to retaining custody of their own children; regulations against adoption or being foster parents; and the lack of "family insurance" coverage that extends to lovers and children. All of this comes in a context of escalating hate crimes against lesbians and gay men.
- In the United States, women are the fastest growing group of people with AIDS; 80 percent are black and Latina. Although women with AIDS generally die faster, they have been excluded from the vast majority of experimental AIDS drug trials, and have fewer services available to them.

These are just a few examples; unfortunately, we could describe many more. Services to women and children around the world are decreasing, while efforts to punish and control them are on the rise. Pregnancy, birth control, abortion, and childbearing continue to threaten our health and our lives. Our bodies, our sexuality, and our reproduction are manipulated by others. Our struggle to control these areas is a struggle for survival.

We need to act out of a wider vision which acknowledges the breadth of this struggle. In that vision abortion rights are the cornerstone of the fight against racism, poverty, sterilization abuse, infant mortality, and medical malpractice. We must demand a higher quality of medical care—one that leaves us, not doctors or courts, in charge of decisions that affect our bodies. We must demand sexual freedom, lesbian and gay liberation, decent jobs, housing and education.

The abortion rights movement cannot win the struggle for reproductive freedom without incorporating these issues and formulating strategies that touch all women throughout their lives. There is a transformation in progress, from a movement narrowly focused on abortion to one concerned with all aspects of reproductive health and freedom. Although the course is not smooth, this is a positive process. It brings together the pro-choice movement, which has been primarily white, with its sister movement for reproductive health rights which has been primarily women of color. That movement has linked abortion rights to economic and social conditions, seeing it as one of many issues in a continuum of race and class discrimination.

While these two have been divided by differences in analyses, strategies, and tactics, the strengths of each can bring about a new movement—one that is based on the understanding that sexism, racism, classism, and heterosexism are all inseparable challenges to reproductive freedom. In this process we can learn from our weaknesses. Both movements have had leaders without strongly developed constituencies and even though the majority of American women favor abortion, they don't actively support our movements. This means we have not yet effectively translated our vision into strategies that activate, rejuvenate, and sustain people.

Creating this alliance requires each of these movements to transcend itself in order to build an effective coalition against its common adversary and win its goals. Doing so requires us to reevaluate our strategies and analyses. For example, when the pro-choice movement uncritically adopts a civil libertarian perspective on abortion, the same approach which leads to a defense of the First Amendment rights of the Ku Klux Klan, it loses credibility among men and women of color. Similarly, when civil rights organizations accepted antiabortion amendments to the 1988 Civil Rights Restoration Act, it undermined pro-choice allies.

Often the abortion rights movement has isolated itself from other progressive struggles because of its narrow focus and the racism and elitism inherent in that perspective. The "abortion only" image and agenda has weakened the reproductive rights struggle.

And sometimes alliances have been undermined by other progressive groups. In the civil rights, human rights, peace, and environmental movements we encounter not only a reluctance to defend abortion rights, but an effort to carve out a "left" antiabortion position in which opposition to abortion is seen as consistent with an overall peace and social justice agenda. We need to struggle against these views. Women's lives cannot be compromised by any movement claiming to be progressive.

The current attacks on reproductive control provide us with many opportunities for understanding our common ground and for building coalitions that enable us to pursue our wider vision of reproductive freedom.

In this pamphlet we are putting the current abortion crisis in a broader perspective. We will talk first about reproductive control and then look specifically at the battle for abortion rights. Finally, we will use our analysis to think about political agendas, strategies, and organizing.

WOMEN'S CONTROL NOT POPULATION CONTROL

We see the fight for abortion rights as part of defending the rights of all women to make their own decisions about reproduction. Unfortunately, historically and today, not all advocates of abortion rights share this understanding. Too often arguments supporting legal abortion and contraception have appealed to racist and genocidal notions about "overpopulation" by Third World people. Now there is an effort by mainstream population control groups and environmental groups to claim that fertility rates in the Third World are the source of global environmental degradation.

Rejecting population control perspectives means that along with our resistance to attempts to prevent women from having abortions, we also oppose efforts to coerce women not to have children. Women have a right not to have children, and they have a right to have them. It means respecting every woman's reproductive decisions and fighting for the conditions that enable women to have the children they want to have. It means rejecting the population control assumptions about poverty and population. Social and political inequalities, especially the worldwide subjugation of women are the cause of poverty which in turn leads to high population rates.

Overpopulation arguments are used to justify coercive, top-down population control programs that treat women's control over their reproduction as a threat to global survival. Women of color in the United States and throughout the world have been the primary targets of the population control policies of the U.S. government and the population establishment. Women have been used to test contraceptive technologies without their consent and without being given the facts needed to make informed decisions. The history of sterilization abuse provides one of the clearest examples of reproductive coercion.

STERILIZATION ABUSE[3]

Female sterilization is the most prevalent form of contraception in the United States and worldwide. It is also the most permanent form of contraception. While it is technically possible to reverse the operation, doing so is very expensive, the operation is hard to obtain, and the success rates are very low. Hence, reversibility remains a virtual impossibility.

The U.S. government has historically promoted sterilization programs among those groups which the majority of society has seen as undesirable. This has included the poor, people of color, the mentally disabled, and those labeled "genetically defective." Such programs have resulted in estimated sterilization rates (based on reported statistics and anecdotal evidence) for Puerto Rican women (45 percent) and Native American women (50 percent) that are among the highest in the world.

Widespread sterilization abuse by the government was revealed in the 1970s. This included sterilizing without the woman's consent; obtaining consent by giving false or misleading information (e.g. saying that the operation was reversible); giving information in a language or complex terminology the woman did not understand. Low-income women were told they could not get jobs, health services, or welfare benefits without agreeing to be sterilized.

Women have also been subjected to less direct forms of coercion. As abortion has become less accessible, sterilization has been all too available for women of color. The federal government stopped funding abortions in 1977 but has continued to pay for sterilization. Subsequently, there has been a dramatic rise in sterilizations.

Many feminists fear that Norplant, the contraceptive implant, will be used in the same coercive ways. Although it has been in use here for less than a year, there is already evidence to substantiate these fears. In California, a judge ordered a woman to have Norplant inserted as a condition of her parole. Not only did the judge violate her basic human rights, he did not know that his sentence was medically dangerous for this woman. He is after all a judge, not a doctor.

As a Louisiana state legislator, David Duke advocated making Norplant use a condition of receiving welfare benefits. Others have proposed reintroducing government-sponsored eugenics programs to reduce the "welfare burden." This extremism is not limited to extremists. The Kansas legislature is considering a proposal to pay cash benefits to women having the implant. These are all efforts which will turn a technology that could empower women into a means of controlling us.

Legal abortion and contraception will continue to be used coercively as tools for limiting Third World populations and for reducing the numbers of "undesirables" as defined by the politically powerful. Currently, pregnant women who are HIV infected, overwhelmingly women of color, experience pressure to have an abortion. There is also concern that these women will become targets of forced sterilization.

When we put together this racist history and the continuing virulence of racism in the United States, there is little question as to why people of color link abortion to genocide.

This does not mean that women of color do or should oppose abortion and birth control. Access to both are essential for all women, but so is women's control over their use. These examples of coercion and abuse underscore the risks when judges and legislators (mostly male and white) make decisions about women's reproduction.

CONTROLLING PREGNANT WOMEN[4]

Efforts to criminalize abortion have not yet succeeded, but other attempts to control women's reproductive behavior have been more successful. Pregnancy has become an excuse for legislators, doctors, and judges to exercise greater control over women. Increasingly, pregnant women are seen as threats to their fetuses. Attention is on the fetus, while the needs and rights of the pregnant woman are ignored. And punishment rather than treatment and education is the vehicle of social control.

Prosecutions for drug and alcohol use and failure to follow doctor's orders are on the rise. From the first prosecution in 1987 to 1992, ninety women in twenty-three states have been prosecuted. Women have been fined, jailed, and subjected to harsh probationary conditions. They have had their babies removed from them at birth. As with population control, low-income women of color are the primary targets. All of the prosecutions to date have been of low-income women and more than 70 percent have been black women. Drug and alcohol use are spread across race and class, but efforts to detect that use in pregnant women are overwhelmingly concentrated among low-income women of color.

The punitive approach ignores the fact that there are few available services. Virtually all drug treatment programs exclude pregnant women and many treatment programs exclude women on Medicaid. Most drug treatment programs are designed for men and ignore the important realities of women's lives such as whether they are survivors of rape or incest, or whether they are in battering relationships. Very few programs provide child care. And the lack of access to either contraception or abortion increases the chance of pregnancy among women who do not want to be pregnant precisely because of their addiction problems.

Prosecuting pregnant women is dangerous to their health. It drives women away from the health care system, making it even less likely that they will receive prenatal care. And while drug and alcohol use during pregnancy are receiving widespread attention, there is little focus on much more pervasive threats to the health of children and women—inadequate prenatal care, lack of health care, battering, poor nutrition, and poverty. These are the real problems that proposed solutions must address.

THE ANTIABORTION MOVEMENT

Faced with the social changes underway in the 1960s and early 1970s, the far right movement in the United States attempted to change itself from a defeated, marginalized movement into a significant political force. A constellation of organizations came together including religious groups and white supremacist groups, all outside of the political and social mainstream.

Simultaneously, a new right movement emerged in the 1970s which saw abortion as a vehicle for shaping a political agenda that would let them work within the political system to recapture the presidency and regain control of institutions like the Supreme Court. They organized themselves around a series of social issues under the banner of support for "traditional" family values.

Opposition to abortion was made the centerpiece of this social and political agenda. Abortion was linked to a litany of "social evils" ranging from the destruction of the traditional family to infanticide.

Abortion became the symbol of women's rights, sexual freedom and all that had undermined these values. Combining this with an anti-social welfare economic agenda, a powerful political alliance was forged. Abortion was used as a tool to gain legitimacy and power. It served as a bridge between extremists and conservatives.

This "pro-family" coalition swept Reagan into office, ushering in a backlash era in which the rights of women, poor people, and people of color were all under attack. As they experienced a boost to their legitimacy and power, their initiatives multiplied in legislatures, in the courts, and in the streets.

The coalition has also had frightening ideological successes. Terrorism to stop abortion is acceptable because one is on a "mission from God." Poor people are seen as burdens on society, responsible for their own poverty. Most frightening, however, is the fact that some of the victims believe the myth, too—the sponsor of a New Jersey bill which penalizes poor women for having children is an African American.

The antiabortion movement exploits the deep ambivalence in our society about whether women ought to have control over their reproduction and their lives. Their political successes show the depth of the threat to established systems of order that women's reproductive freedom poses.

ERODING ABORTION RIGHTS/ATTACKING THE MOST VULNERABLE WOMEN

The goal of the antiabortion movement is to outlaw all abortions—not to stop abortions or save lives as they self-righteously claim. They want to punish women who have abortions. If abortion is recriminalized, they will succeed. Women will continue to have abortions as they did before *Roe.* Abortions will not be stopped; they will once again be made dangerous, life-threatening operations. And once again, women trying to control their *own* lives will be criminals.

The antiabortionists are pursuing their long range goal of criminalization by working on several fronts to make abortion increasingly less accessible for increasing numbers of women. They attack public funding of abortions, try to close down clinics and attempt to pass as many restrictive laws as possible. They have also tried to control the imagery surrounding abortion, shrouding it in messages of guilt and shame. In all of these areas, the attacks have come first against the most vulnerable women—poor women, young women, women of color.

The most dramatic erosion came soon after *Roe v. Wade.* In 1977 Congress passed the Hyde Amendment prohibiting the use of federal Medicaid funding for abortion. For low-income women, Hyde effectively undermined *Roe*—if you cannot access abortion, it might as well be illegal. Because a disproportionate number of low-income women are women of color, curtailing access to abortion hits this group the hardest. Rosie Jiménez has become the symbol of this discrimination. She was the first woman known to have died from an illegal abortion after the Hyde Amendment was passed. She was, of course, not the last.

State funding has also been attacked. Only thirteen states and the District of Columbia continue to fund abortions. These restrictions affect all women who depend on the federal government for health care. This includes women on Medicaid, Native American women on reservations, women in the military, and federal employees. The Supreme Court has upheld these funding restrictions.

Access to abortion has also been undermined for young women. Thirty-four states have parental consent or notification laws. The Supreme Court has upheld their constitutionality.

The antiabortion movement's legislative strategy is to try and pass as many restrictive laws as possible. In the first year after Webster, 400 such laws were passed, 300 in the following year. Although most of these efforts failed, those that did pass have provided the courts with opportunities to weaken and perhaps even overturn the constitutional protection.

Their judicial strategy has involved gaining the appointment of large numbers of judges and Supreme Court justices who oppose abortion. As of 1992, over 70 percent of the sitting federal judges and a majority of Supreme Court justices were appointed during the Reagan/Bush era in which opposition to abortion was used as a litmus test qualification for appointment.

This has resulted in eroding the constitutional right piecemeal through court cases that chip away at it. And these decisions invite further antiabortion legislation like the Pennsylvania law recently upheld by the Court. There are several other cases already in the pipeline, any of which could be used to overturn *Roe v. Wade* or at the very least, to continue to weaken it.[5]

Negotiating so much of the abortion battle in the courts tends to hide the real impact that these decisions have had. Courts and judges are far removed from the world they control. In that world millions of women have already been harmed by these decisions and laws. For example, before Hyde, one-third of all abortions were Medicaid funded. Without federal and state funding, low-income women with unwanted pregnancies are forced to have babies, be sterilized, or have abortions using money really needed for food, rent, and other necessities. The illegal and extralegal attacks on abortion clinics are an especially outrageous part of the antiabortionists' strategy.

Over 80 percent of all abortion and family planning clinics have experienced some form of harassment—anything from picketing and bomb threats, to kidnapping doctors and death threats against doctors, other clinic personnel, and Supreme Court justices. Fanatical groups like Operation Rescue and the Lambs of Christ have kept up a steady assault on clinics, clinic personnel, and women seeking abortions.

In addition to these highly visible attacks on abortion, there has been an ideological offensive. The antiabortion movement has been successful in making fetuses prominent in the moral, legal, and political debates surrounding abortion. In fact, fetuses have more legitimacy and reality than pregnant women. Fetuses are projected as independent beings, deserving of full human rights and endangered by "selfish" women seeking abortion on demand. In the antiabortion moral calculus, fetuses, not women, deserve empathy, legal protection and societal resources. The church and the state project the voices of fetuses, while suppressing those of women. Fetuses after all are innocent; sexually active women are not. The National Council of Catholic Bishops is currently spending $3–4 million in a propaganda campaign aimed at "persuading" women of the immorality of abortion. This doesn't count other monies spent in their antiabortion work.

This array of strategies placed the pro-choice movement on the defensive. The movement was forced to protect gains already won rather than advancing women's reproductive freedoms.

THE PRO-CHOICE MOVEMENT RESPONDS

A strong, multi-issue women's liberation movement fought for abortion rights as part of a broader agenda for women's freedom. The feminist movement fought for women to be able to control their own reproductive lives. Legal abortion was a necessary step toward this goal, but only the first step.

By comparison with this vision, *Roe v. Wade* was a compromise. It did give us legal abortion. But abortion that was controlled by doctors and the state, and protected by the right to privacy.

After *Roe,* the abortion rights movement virtually disappeared. Although a broad spectrum of groups fought against the Hyde Amendment, this attack on poor women did not galvanize large numbers of pro-choice people, nor did it cause public outcry. It wasn't until the threat of a constitutional amendment that would ban all abortions was posed in 1981 that a visible mainstream abortion rights movement re-emerged.

The mid-1980s saw the rebirth of marches and demonstrations for abortion rights and increased organizing by women of color. But there was no mass mobilization until two events translated the steady erosion of abortion rights into a crisis for middle-income women. In 1987 Becky Bell, a white teenager from a stereotypical middle-American family, died from an illegal abortion. And in the 1989 Webster decision, the Supreme Court seriously weakened the constitutional protections for abortion rights by allowing broader restrictions on abortion than it had since 1973. And, some members of the court signaled their willingness and commitment to overturn *Roe.*

The pro-choice movement that emerged in the 1980s was reacting to the intensive antiabortion backlash we described earlier. As the ideological and political landscape shifted to the right, the pro-choice movement responded by trying to make itself and its demands seem less radical, hoping to make them more acceptable to those in power. The language of the movement was sanitized—talk of individual choice and privacy replaced calls for women's equality. In fact, women were almost entirely forgotten in the public debate over abortion. The effort to make us less threatening also made us almost invisible.

Sex was also lost in this process. Privacy and choice language, seemingly safer than talk of sex and sexual equality, missed the obvious—that in large part the fight over abortion rights is about women's ability to have sex with whom you want, when you want. The antiabortion movement opposes sexual freedom—they attack gay and lesbian liberation, birth control, and sex education. From pulpit proclamations that gay men deserve to die of AIDS for their "immorality," to pressure for increased federal censorship of lesbian-oriented art and safer sex AIDS information, the antiabortion right continues to aggressively promote the view that the only acceptable sex is married and heterosexual. This view was affirmed by the Supreme Court in 1986 when it rejected a challenge to Georgia's sodomy laws, ruling that homosexual sex was not protected under the right to privacy. [6]

BEYOND INDIVIDUAL PRIVACY AND CHOICE

The successes of the antiabortion offensives have forced a reassessment of the ideology and strategies of the pro-choice movement. We think the privacy and choice framework has become increasingly problematic. It is inadequate both to defend abortion rights and to encompass a broad vision of reproductive freedom.

The dangers of the individual choice and privacy framework were clarified when it dovetailed with policies of cutting social welfare and other government supports for basic survival. In the case of abortion, this happened soon after legalization. The idea that private decisions do not have any claim on public resources enabled the Supreme Court to uphold the Hyde Amendment, making it painfully clear that privacy rights do not protect poor women's reproductive decisions. Thinking about abortion decisions as exercises of privacy and personal freedom masks the experience of millions of women for whom abortion, like all health care, is an economically determined necessity. Individual freedom of choice is a privilege not enjoyed by those whose reproductive lives are shaped primarily by poverty and discrimination.

The dangers inherent in this framework pervade all of the issues we have addressed. There are common threads in public policies that restrict abortion, coerce birth control, advance population control and criminalize pregnant women. In each area the government uses the ideology of individual choice to escape responsibility for the conditions of people's lives. It locates the cause of and the blame for poverty in women's individual choices—women are poor because they have too many children. This mentality also legitimizes state control when individual decisions are not to the liking of those in power. Hence the rights of pregnant women can be so easily ignored in the name of fetal protection.

Privacy and individual choice are weak responses to the antiabortion charge that abortion is immoral. Countering their attack challenges us to articulate our values. Our response should be that legal abortion is crucial to women's lives and health, that women's lives have value. We believe in the moral authority of women to make their own abortion decisions, ". . . not because they are victims who are suffering, but because doing so is integral to being able to chart one's own destiny."[7] We think that all women should be able to control their reproduction and thus we are fighting for a vision of social justice that transcends any reality we have ever known.

STRATEGIES FOR THE FUTURE

Our analysis of the abortion struggle leads us to the need for transforming the agenda, the strategies, the membership, and the leadership of the pro-choice movement. The current crisis is full of possibilities for accomplishing these changes. There is a need for many forms of political activism and for activists working in different arenas to find ways to support each other's activities. After all, it is the ability to translate our collective rage, vision, and hope into collective action that is our power.

New leadership is emerging among women of color and young women. This leadership is creating a far reaching agenda for reproductive freedom, providing a chance to include women who have not traditionally been in the forefront of this struggle. The abortion rights movement should look for ways to directly support these efforts. We can bring this agenda into all of the organizations and arenas in which we work.

Acknowledging that the judicial system will no longer be an avenue of relief for the foreseeable future requires political action on every front. We must continue to resist efforts to criminalize abortion even as we prepare ourselves for that eventuality. And we must emphasize access to abortion and fight to restore funding, even as the legal right itself is in question. As we fight for specific goals we will also be working toward our larger vision.

Many activists are involved in the legislative and electoral arena. Those doing this work face difficult challenges as they try to carry the fight into an arena to which women have insufficient access. We believe the central challenge is to avoid single-issue politics which result in narrowing the agenda of the abortion rights movement. Failure to meet this challenge has narrowed the movement's base of support and alienated potential allies. At the same time the right, clearly understanding the power of making connections and alliances, has broadened its agenda and its political base.

While we respect those working in this arena, we also think that it has eclipsed other important tactics and spheres of struggle.

RESHAPING THE DEBATE

In 1977, the Third World Women's Committee of the Abortion Action Coalition in Boston talked about the need to reframe the debate to make clear that the right to abortion can be a woman's right to life. In 1989 Alice Walker echoed this: "Abortion for many women, is more than an experience of suffering beyond anything most men will ever know; it is an act of mercy, and an act of self-defense."[8]

These sisters remind us of the need to project a vision of abortion that is true to women's lives. This involves rejecting abstractions of fetuses in favor of the many voices of women who want and need the right to abortion. Speak-outs in which women talk about their abortion experiences are especially effective ways of affirming women's realities.

All women's experiences must be included—women who really have a choice, and those who are having abortions out of necessity. We must deplore the social conditions that prevent some women from being able to bear the children they want just as strongly as we condemn the policies that force women to have children they do not want. In both we are emphasizing the need to struggle for access to services and rights.

We can all participate in the process of transforming the debate by adding our own voices and experiences. The battle over abortion and reproductive freedom is about women, it is about us.

DIRECT ACTION

Since the Webster decision there has been a revival of interest in the "in the street" and underground movement. In the upsurge of activism that followed that decision, thousands of women publicly stated their intention to commit civil disobedience by having abortions, counseling other women about abortion, and providing abortions, no matter what the legal status. Women are certainly not going back. New formations like WAC (Women's Action Coalition) and WHAM (Women's Health Action and Mobilization) represent some of the fastest growing and most vital tendencies in the abortion rights movement.

And the widespread anger and outrage is affecting mainstream groups as well. National NOW has called for "OPERATION FIGHT-BACK! An Unprecedented Campaign of Political Action and Nonviolent Civil Disobedience." Even though this represents only part of

NOW's strategy, it is a significant indicator of the appeal of direct action tactics within the abortion rights movement.

FIGHTING THE RIGHT

We must continue to strengthen our opposition to the antiabortion terrorists. While we have been preoccupied with defending legal access to abortion, antiabortion opponents have built massive networks in churches and a wave of legal and extralegal organizations.

To adequately respond, the pro-choice movement must establish a national research and monitoring project to study and identify anti-choice opponents at both the local and national level. Currently no major women's organization maintains a data base on the opponents of abortion. We need to develop appropriate intelligence techniques that allow us to study them as intently as they have studied us so we have the capacity to predict their next moves, so that we become pro-active.

CLINIC DEFENSE

Continuing to defend the clinics is another important strategy.

The antiabortion attacks on the clinics has been the most visible and one of the most direct challenges to abortion. Large numbers of abortion rights supporters have been drawn to clinic defense and counterdemonstrations.

This strategy, too, has its challenges. Sometimes clinic directors do not want us at the clinics, preferring to rely on court injunctions and the police. They argue that the safety and privacy of their patients and their ongoing ability to operate is compromised by direct confrontations with antiabortionists.

The prominence of the police, while inevitable, is also problematic for us. Our goals of wanting to keep the clinics open and making sure that the police uphold women's constitutional rights involve some amount of cooperation with the police. The challenge is to do this without taking political direction from them.

PROVIDING ABORTIONS

Those who work on the front lines are in a crucial arena—providing abortions, and teaching birth control methods, and safer sex education and methods. Even though abortion remains legal, service providers have been functioning under the increasing hardships of harassment by the antiabortion clinic invaders, and by the IRS. The attacks on clinics and clinic personnel has made clear the political nature of this service. If *Roe* is reversed, the ranks of these women will provide one avenue for safe, illegal abortions.

Many activists are currently focusing their energies on bringing RU 486 to the United States and increasing its access worldwide.[9] This new drug is an effective method of early abortion. Its use in the United States, even for research, has been opposed by the antiabortion movement. At the same time, feminist health activists have raised concerns about health risks and side effects, especially for women who do not have access to good quality health services.[10] Another area of concern is its effects on women from different racial, ethnic, cultural, and socioeconomic backgrounds. Clearly more research is needed. Acknowledging this, the National Women's Health Network supports the availability of RU 486 in the United States.

We do not, however, see RU 486 or any other technology as the solution to the abortion battle. Even if it were widely available, surgical abortion services must be preserved for women who want them or need them and for cases of later abortion. And since the opponents of abortion are really after women's ability to control fertility, they will shift the battlefront. We must defeat them politically in order to secure that control.

EXPANDING TRAINING AND ABORTION SERVICES

The political attacks on abortion rights have taken their toll in terms of shrinking services. There are 600 fewer hospitals providing abortions today than there were a decade ago. Only 13 percent of OB-GYN residency programs require training in first trimester abortions and only 7 percent require training in second trimester abortions. As a result of this and of ongoing political pressure, fewer doctors provide abortions.

There are many possibilities for grassroots organizing which would address these issues: Campaigns to pressure medical schools to offer training; targeting hospitals who don't provide abortions and pressuring them to do so, especially public hospitals; advocating for new training facilities outside of medical schools; challenging the ethic that allows doctors and medical facilities to retain their legitimacy while refusing to provide abortion services.

We can advocate for expanding the category of providers to include other trained medical professionals such as midwives and physician assistants and trained lay people as well.

SELF-HELP AND EMPOWERMENT

The National Black Women's Health Project has developed a self-help model that adds another dimension to the importance of women telling our stories—the need to bring women together to share those stories. Byllye Avery, founder of the Project, describes this as a necessary step in the process of self-validation and empowerment. Advocating wellness, a wholistic notion of women's health, the Project locates abortion rights along with other health concerns as part of a total women's survival agenda.[11]

Another tendency identifying itself within the self-help tradition is that focused on menstrual extraction. Here too women's empowerment is the issue. Menstrual extraction is not just a reponse to fears about impending criminalization, but also a rejection of the medicalization of abortion, a process which disempowers women. Those practicing menstrual extraction in self-help groups see this as a way for women to take control over their own bodies.

Before *Roe*, some feminists and lay midwives provided abortions despite the law. The JANE collective (an underground feminist abortion service which existed in Chicago from 1969–73) and self-help groups are inspiring many activists today who see the need to create alternative institutions. "Jane" too was about women taking power. "We wanted to give women some ammunition in their lives, and, by acting directly, show them that it was possible to take action in their own behalf and in behalf of other women . . . If there's something that needs to be done . . . We can go ahead and do it ourselves."[12] This same spirit has led contemporary activists to revisit the history of our movement and to discover that direct actions to solve the immediate problem of the inaccessibility of abortion were a significant part of that history.

In whatever sphere of activism we choose—education, agitation, inspiration, legislation—whether we are building organizations or creating alternative structures and communities of resistance, we must trust in our ability to find answers from our own lives. "We are the ones we have been waiting for."[13]

We want to acknowledge and appreciate the many women with whom we have worked politically over the years. Our political commitments and understandings have been developed through activism and struggle.

[1] "From Privacy to Autonomy: The Conditions for Sexual and Reproductive Freedom," Rhonda Copelon, in *From Abortion to Reproductive Freedom: Transforming a Movement,* ed. Marlene Gerber Fried, ed., South End Press, 1990, p. 34.

[2] From "Women's Reproductive Health: The Silent Emergency," The Worldwatch Institute, 1991.

[3] Information for this section comes from: *Women Under Attack,* Committee for Abortion Rights and Against Sterilization Abuse, edited by Susan Davis.

[4] Sources for this section: "Perspective of a Reproductive Rights Attorney," Lynn Paltrow. "The Future of Children," Spring 1991. "Drug Addicted Mothers," Dawn Johnson, *Harvard Law Review,* vol. 104, 1991.

[5] The Pennsylvania law imposes a series of restrictions including husband notification, antiabortion lectures, and physician-only counseling; a mandatory twenty-four-hour waiting period; and parental consent. Other laws (Louisiana, Utah, and Guam) make virtually all abortions illegal. In its decision in *Planned Parenthood v. Casey,* 1992, the Supreme Court upheld all but the spousal notification provision.

[6] Hardwick, 478 U.S. 186 (1986).

[7] "From Privacy to Autonomy: The Conditions for Sexual and Reproductive Freedom," Rhonda Copelon, in *From Abortion to Reproductive Freedom: Transforming a Movement,* Marlene Gerber Fried, ed., South End Press, 1990, p. 37.

[8] "Right to Life: What Can the White Man Say to the Black Woman?," Alice Walker, originally printed in *The Nation,* May 22, 1989.

[9] For more information write the National Women's Health Network, listed at the end of this book.

[10] See *RU 486: Misconceptions, Myths and Morals,* Janice Raymond, Renate Klein, and Lynette J. Dumble, Institute on Women and Technology, 1991.

[11] "A Question of Survival/ A Conspiracy of Silence: Abortion and Black Women's Health," Byllye Avery, in *From Abortion to Reproductive Freedom: Transforming a Movement.*

[12] *Abortion Without Apology: a Radical History for the 1990s,* Ninia Baehr, South End Press, 1990, p. 29.

[13] "Poem for South African Women," in *Passion: New Poems, 1977–1980,* June Jordan, Beacon Press, 1980, p. 42.

ROSALYN BAXANDALL

WOMEN AND ABORTION

The Body As Battleground

SEXUAL ACTIVISM, THE BODY AS BATTLEGROUND

A score and four years ago fifteen radical feminists invaded a hearing on abortion at New York City Hall. Reproductive policy was then decided by fourteen well-to-do white men and a nun. Many of the invaders had abortions, and all feared they were pregnant at some time or another. This isn't unusual as demographers calculate that from a third to half of all women of reproductive age undergo at least one induced abortion in their lifetime. (Tomas Frejka, "Induced Abortion and Fertility," *International Family Planning Perspectives*, December 1985; quoted in Jodi Jacobson, "The Global Politics of Abortion," *World Watch Paper 97*, July 1990.) Of course, they were expelled from the hearing with the help of New York's finest. The *Daily News* headlines read, "Gals Squeal for Repeal."

However, we didn't let being bounced out stop us. We, a group called New York Radical Women, had for two years been doing consciousness-raising and actions, guerrilla theatre, zap-attacks, large demonstrations, the first Miss America demonstration, and holding marches and rallies. In those days of many social movements and excellent press coverage for radicals, we felt we could change the world and people would listen. We had learned a lot from black people in the civil rights movement and we believed in the philosophy of "tell it like it is" and "speak bitterness to recall pain." If we dared to struggle, we could win. We didn't let ourselves get pushed around. We fought back ourselves because we had stopped relying on others to defend us. As one anonymous woman put it, "I think the times were extraordinary and it gave us the right to be more extraordinary in our action and activism. The timing was right. The times called for extraordinary strength out of all of us and changed us all. But we weren't by any means superwomen.

We were lucky because we got a chance to put our politics into practice. The late 1960s and early 1970s was a river of action." ("Jane" quoted in Diane Elze, "An Ordinary Group of Women," *Our Paper,* Winter 1987, pp. 12–13; quoted in Ninia Baehr, *Abortion Without Apology, A Radical History for the 1990s,* South End Press, 1990, pp. 29–30.)

Abortion had become a significant issue in the late 1960s due to a falling birth rate, delayed childbearing and marriage among middle-class women, higher college attendance and labor force participation among women, an increased number of female-headed households, continued low wages for women and an active civil rights and antiwar movement that showed the potential ordinary people had to change their world. Since the early 1960s, there were civil libertarians asking the legislators for abortion reform and talking about abortion as a public health issue, a doctor's rights or a population control issue. But radical feminists made people see that it is essentially a women's rights issue. We wanted repeal. We wanted it removed from the law entirely. If abortion is merely legalized, the state remains in control. We wanted women, not doctors, or legislators to decide how and when we could reproduce. (Cisler, Lucinda, "Abortion Law Repeal (Sort Of): A Warning to Women," in *Radical Feminism,* Anne Koedt, Ellen Levine, Anita Rapone, eds., Quadrangle, 1970. Cindy Cisler, who started New Yorkers for Abortion Law Repeal with Jim Clapp, was the architect of this idea.)

Women all over the United States were challenging the antiquated abortion laws at this time. Many of their stories remain untold as they didn't have the time or energy to write about their achievements. It is documented that in the early 1960s in San Francisco, Pat Maginnis, Rowena Gurner, and Lana Clarke Phelan comprised an army of three to repeal all abortion laws. These three working-class females, all who'd personally experienced illegal abortion, conducted street surveys, gave classes on abortion (including how to induce abortion yourself), kept lists of Mexican abortionists and relevant abortion information, wrote letters to legislators in favor of total repeal, and courted arrest. (Ninia Baehr, *Abortion Without Apology: A Radical History for the 1990s,* South End Press, 1990.)

In Los Angeles, Carol Downer (a mother of six) and Lorraine Rothman began a self-help movement, first educating women about their bodies and then giving women abortions themselves. They perfected a new safe method of abortion using a suction device made from a mason jar, a cork with two holes in it, two lengths of fish tank tubing and a syringe. Like most of the early radical feminists, their view of abortion was militant but not narrow. Abortion was the key issue to women's self-determination. As Carol Downer put it, "I think what we really need to have, first of all, is the recognition that a woman has the right to her own body. That means she has the right to do self-examination if she wants, to have children, if she wants not to have children, to have sex if she wants, not to have sex, to be able to use condoms in her heterosexual relationship to get the man to use a condom. If she has children, (she has the right) to expect this society to take responsibility to make sure the child has good schools to go to, to support her in all the ways that anybody deserves support for their children to grow up healthy and happy . . . Our rights for this are not just to go down to the abortion clinic and get an abortion. It's much deeper. This is absolutely not a single issue. It really goes to the heart of our right to have our own sexuality. It's so fundamental." (Ninia Baehr p. 23–24.)

In Chicago there was JANE, a women's liberation abortion service that performed over 11,000 safe, affordable abortions between 1969 and 1973. At the time, abortionists usually charged between $300 to $2,000 per operation. JANE charged $100 and actually only received on the average $40 for each abortion. No woman was turned away for lack of funds. First they referred women, and later when they realized that the abortionists they were referring women to weren't doctors, they taught themselves the technique. They performed the abortions themselves in friends' houses, usually twenty to thirty a day. Many of these militant activists were working in low-paying jobs, participating in the social upheaval of the 1960s, and gaining confidence and experience in organizing.

Women knew we were the experts, people who had thought about and experienced illegal abortion, and we wanted to share our insights with the public and hear others' reactions. Defining our problems ourselves through consciousness-raising and taking actions to change them was empowering. In deciding sexual policy, it is necessary to include a jury of one's peers. This is true for policies of sexual harassment on campus as well as federal abortion regulations.

To continue the narrative, the NY Radical Women tried to educate the policymakers then meeting to decide on abortion legislation. After being ousted from City Hall, we rented Washington Square Methodist Church (whose ministers had been doing illegal abortion referral for years), sent out a press release, and held the first abortion speakout. We stood up before an overflowing crowd and remembered the details of our illegal abortions and made what had been private and personal, political and public. Keeping sexual secrets imprisons and isolates women; sharing confidences empowers. We talked about abortion as a lived experience. Some told horror stories of back alley, sleazy procedures, others of wanting a child, but not being able to afford one mentally or economically. Judith Gabree testified about trying to get a legal abortion, which meant presenting her case to a board of white male psychiatrists, who then decided that she was mentally distraught enough to deserve a legal abortion. The operation took place in the hospital and the physicians took every possible occasion to humiliate her. She spent the night in the maternity ward, and the proud mothers kept asking her whether she had a boy or girl. Barbara Kaminsky, a working-class woman who testified, lived in Brooklyn and never found an abortionist. So she was sent away to have her child and give it up for adoption. Irene Pesilikis, who was then nineteen years old and living in Queens, had to go to an unknown doctor in Ohio. She pointed out that her abortion left a mark on her for life. It was her first realization that women were not equal. She had felt independent having sex, but it illustrated to her that female freedom was limited.

I was first to stand up and speak and I was scared. Remember, at this time abortion was illegal—you could lose your job, your reputation and whatever social amenities you might have, which might be negligible, but you risked losing them. My abortion took place in Milwaukee. I was at college in Madison, Wisconsin. My boyfriend's dad arranged it. The abortionist practiced in an opulent office building and I don't believe he was a doctor; he seemed more like a get-rich-quick businessman. The procedure cost *one thousand dollars*, which was staggering in 1961. We borrowed money from everybody we knew, which meant that the word got round that I was pregnant. The operation was painful, as there was no anesthesia. I moaned and groaned and the abortionist said, "There's no reason to scream. You're no nigger." The abortionist was a slick operator. I remember that he took more care in counting the money than in comforting me. He also told me that if I had any problems not to call him. I was in pain and went to the bathroom to sob. He ordered my boyfriend to go in and get me as he would be liable if I "lay about."

I had a hard time concentrating in my classes. Every time I'd feel a cramp or bleeding I'd imagine my insides spilling out on the lecture hall floor, or being carted to jail. I worried that word would get out that I was a bad girl and I'd get an even worse reputation than I already had. This fear was real, as years later I'd meet people from the University of Wisconsin and they'd say, "Hmm, aren't you the girl that got an abortion?" My panic subsided though as women in the audience stood up to talk about their abortions. Women were telling the truth for the first time and the air was electric and liberating. "It was like the sun rising after a night of secret and horrible nightmares. The shame, the guilt, the horror quickly began to vanish as the truth came tumbling out of women's mouths sometimes amidst the tears of painful memories. Truth is a powerful weapon in the struggle for justice." (Carol Hanisch, "The Case for a Positive Abortion Law," in *Meeting Ground,* no. 11, November 1989, P.O. Box 1287, Port Ewen, NY 12466.)

The next day I was terrified when my grandmother called me to tell me she had seen me in the *New York Times.* She said, "Dearie, you only had one abortion, let me tell you, I had thirteen." She then proceeded to tell me about the Russian and Italian midwives of Manhattan's Lower East Side and how skilled they were. They not only did abortions, but visited you afterward to make sure all was well, brought you some soup, and let you pay in installments. Well, my consciousness was raised! I realized that we, the generation who thought of ourselves as leading a cultural revolution, were far from unique. What has changed is our openness to discuss sexuality rather than the acts themselves. Abortion is indeed a universal phenomenon.

The transformation is not the practice of birth control, but the moral and legal regulation. Even the Catholic Church did not explicitly or publicly condemn abortion until 1895. Until 1873, when the Comstock Law made it illegal to mail or advertise birth control, abortion was neither a crime nor a sin. History indicates that prohibitions have merely forced women underground in search of reproductive control. The most recent example is Romania, where Ceausescu's fourteen years of legislating against abortion and contraception was a failure and nightmare. A secret pregnancy police oversaw monthly checkups of female workers, pregnant women were monitored, and married women who didn't conceive were kept under surveillance. A special tax was levied on unmarried people over twenty-five and childless couples without medical reasons for infertility, and no Romanian woman under forty-five with fewer than five children could obtain a legal abortion. In spite of these severe laws and controls, women continued to control their fertility. Both abortion and abortion-related mortality rose precipitously in Romania at this time. One survey found that Bucharest Municipal Hospital alone dealt with 3,000 failed abortions in 1989. (Michael Dobbs, "Dictator's Dream Took Harsh Toll," *Washington Post,* January 5, 1990, quoted by Jodie Jacobson.) After abortion was made legal in the United States in 1973, abortion-related mortality among women in North America fell from thirty per 100,000 live births to 5. (From abortion-related mortality rates in the United States, W. Cates et al., "Legalized Abortion: Effect on National Trends of Maternal and Abortion-Related Mortality," *American Journal of Obstetricians and Gynecologists,* vol. 132, 1978, in *The Global Politics of Abortion.*)

The universality of birth control practices illustrates that women's reproductive freedom is not simply a matter of developing more sophisticated techniques. With the movement away from home-concocted potions—orange halves and stones to vacuum aspiration—RU486 and Norplant represent a gain for women. But reproductive freedom remains a political agenda, not a technological one, which feminists need to pursue over and over again—twice in my own lifetime. The major advances in reproductive rights have occurred at the same time as the advances in women's freedom and equality. Progress in reproductive rights coincides with the gains made in periods of social activism, essentially in the 1870s, the 1910s, the late 1960s and early 1970s. (Linda Gordon, *Woman's Body, Woman's Right, Birth Control in America,* rev., Penguin, 1990.) Collective struggle, marches, rallies, petitioning legislators, disruptions, theatrical skits, and guerrilla actions made it possible to widen the latitude of socially permissible activity for women and to discard the lies and silences about women's psychological and physiological sexuality.

It was a strong women's liberation movement—not physicians or scientists—that demanded repeal of the abortion laws in the early 1970s and pressured the government and courts to change the laws. Today's women's liberation movement is challenging the laws as well as traditional sexuality. The technology is here and it is up to women collectively to make it cheap, available and safe. For example, RU486, sometimes called the French abortion pill, is now available in France. It was to be available here but the FDA's (Food and Drug Administration) banning of it was directly due to pressure from antiabortion legislators: Senator Jesse Helms, Representative Henry Hyde, Robert Dornan, Bill Dannemeyer, and others. There was not even an attempt on the part of the FDA to document the supposed risks posed by the drug. England, Scandinavia, and the Netherlands will distribute RU486 this year; and Spain, Russia, and Sweden are expected to follow. The World Health Organization is conducting tests on it in China, India, Hong Kong, and Cuba. But American drug companies were threatened by the right-to-lifers and decided under pressure to not even pursue testing.

PHILOSOPHICAL UNDERPINNINGS

Two essential ideas underlie a feminist view of reproductive freedom. The first is derived from the biological connection between women's bodies, sexuality, and reproduction. It is an extension of the general principle of "bodily integrity," or "bodily self determination." The slogan, "women should control their bodies," that is, their procreative capacities, derives from this materialist view. The argument emphasizes the individual dimension of rights—self-determination. This philosophical framework, one of natural rights, assumes a fixed biological person.

The second philosophical idea is based on the historical, changing, social position of women. This position states that in so far as women, under the existing division of labor between the sexes, are the ones most affected by pregnancy and most responsible for child-rearing, it must therefore be women who decide about conception, abortion and child-rearing. This argument implies a social arrangement that may be changed. It emphasizes the principle of socially determined needs, rather than natural rights. Both these concepts are necessary for a feminist reproductive platform. (Rosalind Petchesky, *Abortion and Woman's Choice, the State, Sexuality, and Reproductive Freedom*, Longman, 1984.)

In the ground-breaking 1973 Supreme Court decision *Roe v. Wade*, the justices based their decision on the Fourth Amendment which guarantees the right of people to be secure in their persons and houses. It is based on the right to privacy and personal liberty. This position has two contradictory principles. Privacy was compatible with a legal tradition of noninterference in marriage; a tradition which denies women legal relief from economic and physical abuse of their husbands, a tradition which also enforces male dominance in the home. Privacy buttresses the conservative idea that the personal is separate from the larger social structure and that structure has no impact on private individual choice or action. Women should be in control of decisions over abortion, but noninterference by the state should reinforce rather than undermine women's autonomy—which is a clearer concept than privacy. Actually, there are two notions of privacy: the liberal idea of privacy as the negative and qualified right to be left alone; and the more radical idea of privacy as the positive liberty of self-determination and equal personage. So the privacy doctrine is practically and theoretically double-edged, having the tendency to constrain as well as expand reproductive rights. Privacy in the liberal sense makes it impossible to challenge traditional gendered reproductive and sexual norms. Privacy can also imply secrecy and shame. The negative right of privacy carries no corresponding obligation on the state to facilitate reproductive rights and obscures the public responsibility for reproductive freedom. To avoid the narrow interpretation of privacy the social aspects need to be emphasized here as well. (Rhonda Copeland, "From Privacy to Autonomy: The Conditions for Sexual and Reproductive Rights," in *From Abortion to Reproductive Freedom: Transforming a Movement*, Marlene Fried, ed., Boston, South End Press, 1990, pp. 27–43.)

The nature of a radical reproductive position is therefore both individual and social and operates at the core of social life as well as within and upon women's individual bodies. The nature of these arguments is complex and confusing and can seem contradictory in comparison to the simplistic right-to-life, biology-is-destiny position. While radical feminists believe it is a woman's fundamental right to control her own sexuality and reproduction, we also ask men and society to take more responsibility for children and conception.

Reproduction is a shared female experience that transcends class division and permeates work, politics, community involvement, sexuality, creativity, and dreams. Yet sexuality takes place in a particular society at a particular historical period. The sexual experience is therefore socially constructed and experienced differently by different classes, races and in different historical times. The acknowledgment of biological reality can't be mistaken for biological determinism. Biology is a capacity as well as a limit. Biology can be a source of female power as well as of female confinement. We want the right to control our bodies, but we don't want to be defined or circumscribed by our capacity to reproduce.

THE RIGHT TO CHOOSE VS. THE RIGHT TO FREE SAFE ABORTION

Women's reproductive situation is never the result of biology alone, but of biology mediated by social and cultural organizations. Birth control methods are limited by technological developments, access to them, class divisions, and the distribution and financing of health care, nutrition, employment, the state of the economy, women's social networks, family friends, providers, employers, doctors, and the church. For example, in 1930 the diaphragm was the most effective form of birth control, but it was virtually inaccessible to working class and poor women due to lack of access to private clinics and medical instruction, and lack of privacy and running water. The fact that female sterilization, an irreversible procedure, is the most widely used, economically reimbursable by welfare (which abortion isn't now in most states) raises questions about the reproductive choices available to most women, even now.

The right to choose is both problematic and politically compelling. It ignores the fact that peoples' desires are often contradictory. A woman may want to be a mother, but not want to be a mother-like-her-mother. A poor woman may desire a child and a personal life outside of poverty which a child would prevent. The principle of free choice evades the moral questions about when, under what conditions, and for what purposes reproductive decisions should be made. A woman may get an abortion on grounds that she prefers one gender over another, which amniocentesis can now determine. Such a decision would be sexist in a society where the majority of people asked say they prefer to have male children. Another potential danger in the assertion of women's reproductive rights as absolute or exclusive is that it excludes men from decision-making in the reproductive process.

The right to choose means little when women are politically powerless. In cultures where illegitimacy is stigmatized and female infants are devalued, where is the real alternative for women? Why should the choice be a job or a child? The American Cyanamid plant in West Virginia gave women an option between sterilization or losing their jobs. Is that a real choice? The reproductive rights movement could focus less on choice and more on how to transform the social conditions of choosing, working, and reproducing. Corporate and state interests in the management of reproduction have defined the choices of all women in a way that is biased according to class and race. Poor and third-world women are more likely to be used as experimental subjects in international population control programs for testing or dumping contraceptive chemicals or implants whose safety may be questioned by the FDA.

In spite of this lack of options, it would be wrong to picture women of any class as passive victims of medical, commercial, and state policies of reproductive control. Women of all classes have successfully challenged and changed laws on birth control, summoned drug companies and doctors regarding the severe health hazards of the pill, coil, deprovera, and other synthetic hormones. Groups of Mexican-American, Native-American and African-American women have fought together with women's health groups against involuntary sterilization.

The phrase *right to choose* was actually a step backward, a compromise with the growing right wing who used the better sounding slogan *right to life.* The right to choose ignores the essential feminist truth that in a male supremacist society no choice a woman makes is entirely free or entirely in her interest. Many women have had abortions they didn't want or wouldn't have wanted if they had plausible means of caring for a child. Countless others would not have gotten pregnant in the first place were it not for inadequate contraception, sexual confusion and guilt, male pressure and other stigmata of female powerlessness. Women who have abortions are also victims of ordinary miscalculation, technological failure, or vagaries of passion—all bound to exist in any society. (*Meeting Ground*, December 1979, July/August, 1980, November 1989.)

In the women's liberation movement of the 1970s we asked for total repeal of all antiabortion laws and free abortion on demand.

During this period, we referred to forced pregnancy as slavery. Feminist lawyers argued that criminal abortion laws imposed a formal servitude that violated the Thirteenth Amendment, which ended slavery. Reproductive control is a necessary condition for equal participation in the economic and social life of the nation. This was a stronger, less ambivalent argument than the right to privacy. It was clear that abortion was a women's rights issue and a necessary condition for women's autonomy. In the late 1980s and early 1990s, abortion began to be referred to as a human rights issue and the life referred to was abstract. Without this emphasis on female rights, we leave the door open for a discussion of fetal rights and parental consent. It's almost as if in the 1990s people are afraid either to use the word abortion, or to state that abortion is a female issue. Abortion and feminism have become dirty, shameful words. So we use the word choice and speak of parental and human rights. This is a sign that we have become defensive and are losing ground to the neo-conservatives.

Our radical history is being forgotten or purposely suppressed. As Kathie Sarachild pointed out, "it was the public actions of the radicals, the consciousness-raising section of the movement, that put the women's liberation movement on the map. Consciousness-raising actions, like [the protest of] the Miss America contest, develop techniques for mass organizing and producing journals, newspapers and books which are widely disseminated."

Radical theory and strategy was not only the source of widespread mobilization—what sparked the interest of the masses of women—it was also what produced the most concrete results and changes in women's lives. The greatest achievements of the women's liberation movement have been increased freedom in the area of birth control and abortion, freedom from oppressive dress codes, and the growth of feminist theory and consciousness. These were the changes that the radicals first demonstrated for and organized around.

At that time, radical feminist activity was strongest and most advanced in New York. It was there that the first concrete breakthroughs of the women's liberation movement in the United States were achieved. The abortion law of New York turned that state into "the abortion mill of the nation." A few years later, the United States modeled its guidelines on abortion after New York. It was the radical strategies of (1) opposition to reform and demand for repeal led by Lucinda Cisler, (2) mass consciousness-raising on abortion with women testifying to their "criminal" acts in public and in court, (3) the development of feminist self-help clinic ideas and their promotion of simpler, new abortion techniques that led to the national reform in five years time.

In 1975, Kathie Amatniek predicted a right-wing counterattack. She comments, "It has been only six years since the women's liberation movement mushroomed, and already the radical women who initiated the movement's theory, organizing ideas, and slogans have been buried from public consciousness, and the liberals have taken over claiming credit for the radicals' achievements. If this goes on much longer feminism will go under once again and we will lose almost all of what was gained in the last years—both the radical consciousness and the practical reforms. It won't be long until the liberals will be gone, too." (Kathie Sarachild, ed., "The Power of History," *Redstockings of Women's Liberation, Feminist Revolution,* New York, Random House, 1975, pp. 20, 13. Available now from the Archives Distribution Project, P.O. Box 2625, Gainesville, FL 32602.)

RECENT DEVELOPMENTS, OR FURTHER INVASIONS OF THE BODY SNATCHERS

The recent Supreme Court decision, *Planned Parenthood v. Casey,* announced June 1992, is a continuation of the chipping away of women's right to abortion.[1] The current ruling further accentuates the erosion of abortion rights and the perils of the liberal reproductive rights agenda. Poor women, rural women, and teenage girls will now have an even harder time obtaining an abortion. In Pennsylvania, they will have to wait twenty-four hours and be humiliated by doctors who are required to hand out antiabortion material published by the government, even if the women are totally convinced of their decision. Due to the normal bureaucratic nature of institutions, these delays will most likely be more than twenty-four hours, and increase the aggravation, anxiety and expense. Women will need to stay over in hotels, take more time from work and arrange for child care. The Court made it clear that the purpose of the counselling prescribed by the state is not neutral, but "rather to persuade the woman to choose childbirth over abortion." As Blackmun, one of the few real liberals left on the Court stated, "this type of compelled information is the antithesis of informed consent and goes far beyond merely describing the subject matter relevant to the woman's decision. That the Commonwealth does not and surely would not compel similiar disclosure for every possible surgery or of a simple vaccination, reveals the antiabortion character of the statute and its real purpose . . . A visual preview of an operation to remove the appendix plays no part in a physician's securing informed consent to an appendectomy."[2]

Forced parental consent, another feature of the Pennsylvania decision, is a straitjacket for a teenage girl, who may fear her parent's wrath or want to assert her autonomy and certainly doesn't want to jump through hoops and act contrite for a judge who may be antiabortion and autocratic. Parental consent is of course not required for sexual intercourse or childbirth.

In some way, the Supreme Court decision is a victory for women's rights, and there are so few victories for feminism these days that we can cheer. After all, it wasn't the worst outcome, and in that way it was a standoff and defeat for the antiabortionists. The Guam, Louisiana, and Utah laws, which would have made abortion a criminal offense will no longer stand under the current ruling. Spousal consent was also struck down. The decision appeared reasonable.

While affirming abortion as a "liberty," *Casey* allowed major incursions into the right to choose. It left some people complacent and relieved, others confused, and many more militant. *Casey v. Planned Parenthood* didn't sign a death certificate to women's abortion rights. The majority decision makes clear that the reason *Roe* wasn't thrown out entirely had to do with *stare decisis*, respect for the Supreme Court and its precedents, not concern for the mother or potential child. Justices Kennedy, O' Connor and Souter state, "the immediate question is not the soundness of *Roe*'s resolution of the issue, but the force that must be accorded its holding." The new decision does not recognize a woman's right to decide to terminate her pregnancy. Women are treated as minors, impaired and uninformed. The woman's right to choose has become subordinate to the state's interest in promoting fetal life. "Her choice exists in theory, but not in fact"[3]

Roe originally said that states would be under "strict scrutiny" if they intervened against abortion. The *Casey* ruling allows a new level of state intervention. Restrictions on abortion are now constitutional, unless they place a "substantial undue burden, an obstacle in the path of a women seeking an abortion," as interpreted by antiabortionists. The door is opened for further state curtailments, years of costly legal expenses, and time wasted battling state by state. Like the period before the Civil War, there will be free-abortion states and those that support reproductive slavery. Abortion states will become magnets as in the years prior to *Roe*, attracting financially able women from other states seeking abortions, an undue burden on the free states.

The majority of women will no longer have access to safe legal abortion. The law provides a medical emergency exception to "prevent death or substantial irreversible impairment of major bodily function," but women will be at the mercy of the decision-making power of doctors and state authorities. Many women will figure that illegal abortions are cheaper, closer to home and less of a hassle; the scuzzy profiteers will again begin to practice. Feminist underground abortion networks might also appear.

In this context politicians are opportunistic about abortion, which makes them unreliable, but also subject to pressure. When Reagan was governor of California, he signed that state's abortion law. Before Bush became president, Barbara Bush was on the board of Planned Parenthood and Bush was not antichoice. Yet when they assumed the presidency, both took an antiabortion stand on supposedly staunch moral grounds, supported Operation Rescue, and hosted their demonstrations. Of course, if Vice President Quayle's daughter and Bush's grandchildren wanted abortions, both men would have publicly stated their support for choice. There has been and will be choice for an elite. On the other side, both Clinton and Gore are on record as supporting state antiabortion laws. Clinton declared that fetuses were "unborn children" in 1986, opposed state funding of abortion for poor women, and supported parental notification. But due to mass feminist pressure and desire to win, Clinton and Gore are now the candidates of choice. Their switch indicates a resurgence in the pro-abortion forces, or as Justice Scalia says, "maybe today's decision not to overrule *Roe* will be seen as buckling to pressure from that direction."

Unfortunately, most of the large pro-choice national groups like NARAL (National Abortion Rights Action League), NOW (National

Organization of Women), and Planned Parenthood are politely opposing the Pennsylvania decision as victims on narrow turf, talking about choice rather than abortion and not connecting abortion to sexual freedom, class and race inequality, health care, jobs, day care, and housing. However, a growing wave of radical feminist groups like WAC (Women's Action Coalition), WHAM (Women's Health Action and Mobilization), and No More Nice Girls, which has been in existence since 1977 have recently emerged into the national spotlight. These zap-action theatrical groups are confronting Operation Rescue courageously and successfully with wild and wooly, hit-and-run tactics. In the process, these organizations are pushing the liberals to take public action and winning battles in Buffalo and New York City. Operation Rescue is now divided and discredited and trying to retreat to respectability. Perhaps the tide is pulling conservatism out to sea.

PLEASURES AND DANGERS

> *Eroticism is a realm stalked by ghosts. It is a place beyond the pale, both cursed and enchanted.*
>
> —Camille Paglia

We have to dare to say that to oppose abortion is to oppose women's sexual power and autonomy relative to men. Abortion is essential to gender equality and women's capacity to participate equally in society as full persons. Opposing abortion means embracing a conservative sexual morality, one that subordinates pleasure to reproduction. Much of the opposition to abortion is opposition to sex, and women's freedom. Sex is only tolerated if it leads to something else, never in and for itself. Sexual passion and love are important human needs. However, in a male-dominated society female sexuality is a more complex matter than men's. For women sex spells potential danger as well as pleasure. (Carole Vance, "Pleasure and Danger: Toward a Politics of Sexuality," *Pleasure and Danger: Exploring Female Sexuality,* Carole Vance, ed., Routledge and Kegan Paul, 1984, pp. 1–27.) A feminist politics about sex, if it is to be credible as well as hopeful, must seek to protect women from sexual danger as well as to encourage their pursuit of sexual ecstasy. The feminist preachers of sexual prudery, like Andrea Dworkin and Catherine MacKinnon make no distinction between rape and intercourse, marriage and prostitution, or fantasy and reality. MacKinnon even sees abortion reform as removing women's last protection from men's pressure for sex.

Focusing only on the dangers of sexuality (violence, rape, incest) ignores explorations of the body, curiosity, intimacy, sensuality, excitement, and human connection. Sex is delightful and scary because it touches on the nonrational and infantile. Sexuality activates a host of intrapsychic anxieties: fear of merging with another, the blurring of bodily boundaries, dependency, the wish to be dominated or to dominate, the loss of control, our own aggression, our wishes to incorporate body parts, even entire persons. Freud observed that pleasure threatens civilization. But what if there is no end to desire?

Sexuality also raises the fear of competition, as we recognize our own wishes to compete for attention and for love objects. Whether women are lesbian or heterosexual, the competitors are other women—an unsisterly prospect. For women, experiencing desire can signal the giving up of vigilance and control—the responsibility of a "proper woman." Desire causes profound unease about violating the boundaries of traditional femininity. Transgressing gender roles raises the specter of separation from other women—both the mother and the literal and metaphorical sisters—leaving one isolated and vulnerable to attack. These subterranean pulls on women are no less powerful by remaining unnamed. Our unspoken fears are added to the sum of sexual terror. Without a better language to delineate these other sources of danger, everything is attributed to men, thereby inflating male power and impoverishing ourselves. We have to try to comprehend our own fears so we don't project them. Otherwise we leave the irrationality and volatility of sex open to manipulation by others, as in right-wing campaigns against sexual deviance, degeneration, and pollution.

The hallmark of sexuality is its complexity; its multiple meanings, sensations and connections. It is all too easy to cast sexual experiences as either wholly pleasurable or dangerous. Our society encourages *yes/no* and *either/or* thinking. Actual sexual experience is complicated, difficult to grasp and often unsettling. As the male world has overemphasized women's enjoyment of rape, the feminist community in opposition has emphasized the ubiquity of humiliation and danger. Initially useful as an ideological counterpart to even the odds, this critique now shares the same one-dimensional and simplistic focus as its opposition. There is an interplay between power and desire, attraction and repulsion, acceptance and denial.

In my experience I have often said *no* when I was really ambivalent, my mind and body in contradiction. However, in a male-dominated society no should be read as "NO." This is difficult because so much of sex and courting involves unspoken body language and marvelous expectation and mystery. However, without learning to communicate verbally, men and women who are socialized differently around sex will speak different body languages.

In order to understand the rich brew of our sexuality, we also have to be tolerant of difference. Women and men have a wide diversity of sexual experiences; what is pleasurable to one, might be pain to another. We must dare to discuss the details of our experiences, desires and fantasies, otherwise we fall back on myth and texts that are prescriptive and too generalized. Sexuality is a particularly fluid and ever-changing arena, evolving through adult life in response to internal and external vicissitudes. This is why it will always be a problematic domain for regulation. There can and should be political movements around issues of sexuality, but we cannot have rigid standards of politically correct behavior. We also need to understand that there are privileged forms of sexuality. Heterosexuality, marriage, and procreation are protected and awarded by the state and subsidized through social and economic incentives. Those engaging in privileged acts, or pretending to, enjoy a good name and good fortune. Marriage is a priviledged form, which is not to say it's not difficult and doesn't involve struggle. Less privileged forms of sexuality are regulated and forbidden by the state, religion, medicine, and public opinion. Those practicing the less favored forms of sexuality suffer from stigma and invisibility, although they also resist.

Sex is neither shameful nor trivial. It is very much part of our political landscape. Some people feel that sexuality is a topic, important only to the affluent. The right wing has been more vocal about its conservative sexual political desires, which can be summarized as *Just Say NO*, or *The 3 W's: Worship, War, and Work.* Defining our sexual ideology prevents our being constantly caught off guard and merely reacting to the right and stepping backward to win favor from the ubiquitous middle. Ignoring sexuality means letting the powerful in our culture speak and leaving individual families in control, rather than forcing the state to take social responsibility and assure equality of sexual treatment. We have to question the dichotomy between public and private in matters of sexuality. Private means that often women decide alone and men and public institutions aren't responsible. In the United States, we have a private, for-profit, competitive health care system that makes the best available only to the rich. The direction of research is decided by dollar amounts, not prevention; research is not shared, but kept secret for commercial reasons. Secrecy prevents public scrutiny and informed choice. Science and technology in the United States are largely in the hands of drug corporations, physicians, and male researchers, who are motivated by profit, not social need. We must demand to know who funds the so-called neutral research.

Historically, women have been perceived as either good girls and madonnas or bad girls and whores. Aborting women are stigmatized as bad, selfish, and immoral creatures while mothers and women with many children are seen as good, self-sacrificing martyrs. Women are taught by the mass media to be the objects of men's desire, rather than the subjects of our own desire. As sex objects we have been violated and used to sell products. Part of our project is to reclaim our sexuality and see ourselves as desiring subjects in the full sense of the word; not just as victims of men's sexuality, but as active seekers of our own pleasure.

THE PRESENT

Our era is characterized by trials of violence and sexuality: the Willie Smith (Kennedy nephew) rape trial, the Central Park jogger rape trial, the Mike Tyson rape conviction and all the hullaballoo about it, including the protest of the Baptist Church, rather than cases of political momentum like the Rosenberg, Hiss or the Scopes trials. Our potential presidents are judged not by their programs, but by their sexual infidelities and whether or not they smoke or inhale marijuana. In an era of total corruption and lack of political imagination or vision Gary Hart and Bill Clinton are raked over the coals for marital infidelities. Sexual correctness has become a real diversion from real political abilities and leadership.

It's interesting that we are exposed to sexual words, symbols, languages, nuances, and titillation in our supermarket's magazine rack, on our TV, and movie screens; yet when it comes to talking publicly about the reality of how women experience sex in our real lives there is still such shame, guilt, and fear to be reckoned with. Pregnancy and abortion are the result of sex. As one sign at the spring NOW (National Organization of Women) march in Washington (1989) put it, "If abortion is a crime, fucking is a felony." (Carol Hanisch,"The Case for A Positive Abortion Law," *Meeting Ground,* November 1989.)

Our current society is sexually contradictory. On the one hand there is plenty of noncontractual sex around, telephone sex, 900 numbers, sex cable stations, mail order porn, home-made sex porn videos, and on and on. At the same time, though, temperance, marriage, and chastity are in. There is even a National Chastity Association, which includes a dating service and whose beliefs include premarital sexual abstinence. It's almost like the Victorian age where sex was so hush-hush and forbidden that people saw sex everywhere; back then even chair legs had to be covered for fear of arousal.

Americans are similarly sex obsessed. All around us are ads where the camel's face is clearly a penis and balls. Almost naked asses stare at us from the backside of buses. Sex, skin, and shock are used to sell us products. Yet we are a society of prudes banning nude bathing and public breast feeding. Sex negativism, which prescribes repression and puritanism as an antidote for AIDS and teenage pregnancy is part of illness, not the cure. All this caution and fear and sexual talk in the newspapers have not made Americans more knowledgeable about sex. In what is billed as the "first representative survey of what people know about sex" conducted by the Kinsey Institute and Roper Organization, Americans couldn't answer ten out of eighteen questions correctly. (*New York Times*, September 6, 1990.) The questions were about basic physiology, like whether women can get pregnant during menstruation. We can.

These current attitudes are not only caused by the fear of AIDS; we live in a scary, volatile, violent time. One can't be sure one has a job, bank savings, retirement or home, or that one can't be shot randomly or killed by carelessness in a plane or car or in high school. Safety standards have been lifted and everyday existence is deregulated. Is the body the last bastion of freedom against an ever invasive, precarious society? Somehow people have the idea that if only they can control their physical selves through such things as exercise and eating the right foods life will be secure. Not to eat meat, smoke, drink alcohol, now means that you are a moral, together human being. In fact, the United States is in the midst of a major new Temperance movement, the third in its history. (*New York Times*, January 1, 1990.)

The physical body has become the site of something we can harness, in a world barely held in check and coming apart at the seams. This is true in East Europe, where abortion is being reconsidered, i.e. made more difficult, as well as in the United States. Restraining sexuality often goes with rising nationalism. For the patriot, a woman's place is to populate the fatherland. Sexuality which is less controllable is therefore seen as a danger rather than a pleasure. The body has become the site of the new world order, or is this the order of the new world?

[1] The ruling rejected the trimester approach used in *Roe.* That doctrine, in which the state could limit the right of abortion depending on the development of the fetus, was used to evaluate the permissibility of any given abortion regulation. Under *Roe,* states could issue almost no regulations concerning abortion during the first trimester. In place of this trimester approach, the Court said it would evaluate the permissibility of abortion rules based on whether they "unduly burden" a woman's ability to obtain an abortion. The Court ruled that parental consent and at least a twenty-four-hour waiting period were not an "undue burden," that is they were not an obstacle in the path of a woman seeking an abortion. Spousal consent was viewed as an "undue burden."

[2] Supreme Court of the United States, *Planned Parenthood of Southeastern Pennsylvania et al. petitioners v. Robert P Casey et al.* etc., June 29, 1992.

[3] Blackmun from *Casey v. Planned Parenthood.*

GEORGE CARTER

ACT UP, THE AIDS WAR, AND ACTIVISM

ACT UP

ACT UP, the AIDS Coalition to Unleash Power, is "a diverse, nonpartisan group of individuals united in anger and committed to direct action to end the AIDS Crisis. We meet with government and health officials; we research and distribute the latest medical information. We protest and demonstrate; we are not silent." The slogan SILENCE = DEATH refers to the complicity that permits events like the Holocaust of World War II to take place. ACT UP has over 100 independent chapters in North and South America, Europe, Australia, and South Africa.

With the inspirational abrasiveness and dedication of author and playwright Larry Kramer, ACT UP was formed in New York in March, 1987. A group of people—primarily gay men and lesbians—gathered in anger at the near total neglect of AIDS by politicians, doctors and researchers. The very first action was a march and civil disobedience on Wall Street to protest pharmaceutical giant Burroughs Wellcome's profiteering from AIDS. After the demonstration, the Food and Drug Administration (FDA) announced the shortening of the drug approval process by two years. Other demonstrations have targeted health care organizations and research centers such as the National Institutes of Health (NIH), as well as diverse organizations such as the Presidential Commission on AIDS (for its inadequacies early on), Northwest Orient Airlines (for refusing to carry people with AIDS), *Cosmopolitan* magazine (for stating that women were at low risk for contracting HIV), the New York Stock Exchange, as well as state and city governments nationwide. Presidents Reagan and Bush have been frequent targets due to their nearly absolute neglect of the burgeoning AIDS pandemic in their blind pursuit of a militaristic agenda that obstructs the country's urgent health care needs.

ACT UP has had remarkable success; treatments and therapies are closely monitored and information on them disseminated. New studies of alternative drugs have been initiated due to efforts by ACT UP. Government officials and media have been forced to recognize and at least begin to address specific AIDS issues. Pharmaceutical companies and the insurance industry have been brought into sharp relief as inefficient and wasteful organizations, designed to maximize profits with little or no concern for the effect on people's lives. Universal health care is at the forefront of today's political debates.

Nonetheless, the problems that remain are monstrous. The federal government still refuses to have open, clear discussions about the transmission of AIDS and sexuality. The research on how the immune system is destroyed in AIDS is nearly nonexistent. Treatments are few, toxic, and costly. Homophobia, sexism, and racism continue to dog the best efforts of activists. Unfortunately, the work of ACT UP must continue into the foreseeable or unforeseeable future; the dramatic and revolutionary changes necessary to end the AIDS crisis require widespread and concentrated efforts. The AIDS crisis has only just begun.

ACT UP is more than just an organization that holds uncompromising demonstrations. This pamphlet underscores the unseen side of ACT UP and highlights some of the subtler effects it has had. In addressing issues, an assessment is made of the problem and its impact. The problem is researched and studied—there is incredible expertise and experience in the ranks of ACT UP. Contact is made and, where possible, a resolution is achieved through talks. Frequently government, pharmaceutical or insurance companies maintain an air of arrogance or indifference. Often mass phone or letter "zaps" are used. When all else fails, we take to the streets.

According to Harvard's Global Policy Program, anywhere from 40 to 110 million adults will develop AIDS worldwide by 2000. Many more will be infected with HIV, widely considered the cause of AIDS. AIDS is found almost equally among men and women. AIDS is most often transmitted sexually, and globally, heterosexually. The virus continues to spread in the local populations where it is prevalent. One-hundred-and-fifty thousand Americans have died of AIDS over the past twelve years of the pandemic, primarily gay men and people of color.

People with AIDS (PWAs) continue to fight the perception, often spread by the media, of being AIDS "victims." This stems in part from the doctor-patient relationship which tacitly presumes that the patient is the helpless victim and the doctor is the savior. Compounded by the indifference, ignorance, homophobia, and racism associated with AIDS, PWAs and their advocates have been forced to respond with activism. PWAs more and more act as partners with their health care providers.

Unfortunately, the struggle simply to discuss lifesaving strategies such as safer sex education, women's sexual empowerment, and safer drug use takes place, all too often, in an atmosphere of fear and ignorance. The global response highlights class distinctions between poorer and richer countries, and the poor within wealthy countries. Folk without access to adequate general health care, treatments or condoms are most often the people with AIDS.

I became an AIDS activist in part because of the fear of infection. I am gay, formerly an intravenous drug user and have lived in San Francisco and New York—a high-risk profile, to put it mildly. More, I keep losing friends.

AIDS illuminates how our societies address crises. AIDS unveils our views on sexual behavior, gay men and lesbians, people of color, women and drug abuse, along with issues of housing, access to and availability of medical treatments and insurance, and the conduct of medical research. AIDS tests our ability to love. I write this to provide vital, potentially life-saving information. In part, my intention is to make you angry. With this anger and with love, I hope you will act.

THE BIOLOGY OF AIDS

Acquired Immune Deficiency Syndrome (AIDS) is a breakdown of the body's defenses against diseases, many of which are potentially present in our bodies but are held in check by a healthy immune system. Leading health authorities maintain that AIDS is probably a result of infection by a type of retrovirus called Human Immunodeficiency Virus (HIV). After infection, it takes on average six months before the body develops antibodies which will show up in a blood test. It can take from a few years to over a decade before symptoms appear that lead to a diagnosis of AIDS, although such symptoms do not always appear.

Breakdown of the immune system is connected with the destruction of important blood cells known as T-helper cells (made in the thymus). These white blood cells mediate immune functioning by assisting in the identification of foreign organisms (antigens). After an infected cell is identified, it is marked for destruction. Thus, the loss of T4 cells in AIDS destabilizes the immune system; exactly how this occurs remains unclear.

As AIDS develops, the body becomes increasingly susceptible to a variety of infections from bacteria, protozoa, other viruses, and fungi that it can normally fight off. These "opportunistic infections" (OIs) are often what kill people. OIs, including sexually transmitted diseases, often reside harmlessly in people with healthy immune systems. The OIs most commonly associated with AIDS are TB (primarily in Africa but increasingly so here in the United States), PCP—a fungal pneumonia, Kaposi's sarcoma, toxoplasmosis, candidiasis, cryptococcal meningitis, cytomegalovirus (CMV) and mycoavium intracellulare (MAI or MAC). When one develops an OI and has a positive test for HIV, then one is diagnosed with AIDS.

An HIV-positive test is not a death sentence. Not everyone who is positive goes on to develop AIDS. Not everyone who develops AIDS dies of the disease; a few have been living with AIDS for over ten years. Cofactors are probably required to initiate HIV's activity. Such cofactors include the presence of other viruses (such as Epstein-Barr) and bacteria or sexually transmitted diseases (particularly resident syphilis), poor nutrition, substance abuse, toxic medicines, stress and others.

The spectrum of theory regarding the causes of AIDS is broad. The prevailing model driving treatment research, increasingly under fire, is that HIV causes AIDS by infecting T-cells, replicating inside the T-cell and subsequently destroying it. Why only a tiny percentage of T-cells are found to be infected with HIV remains a core paradox which leaves the precise mechanism of HIV murky. Others believe HIV may be merely a "passenger virus" that is often found, but has little or nothing to do with AIDS. Another model posits that AIDS may be primarily an autoimmune disease. T-cells may in fact attack each other, as opposed to being destroyed by HIV infection. Unfortunately, minimal research has been conducted to develop a viable model from which treatments may be based. It is not scientific common sense to cook up drugs in a lab to treat a condition without concurrent and vigorous efforts to find out everything possible about how a particular condition arises. Each model suggests different therapeutic approaches—some radically different. After developing an accurate model, we then face the formidable task of redirecting research and developing therapies that must be available to all PWAs.

Two tests are traditionally used for determining HIV infection, the ELISA and Western Blot tests. These tests detect the presence of antibodies that develop as a result of HIV infection. The polymerase chain reaction test, which is more expensive, looks for HIV-DNA. A "p24" antigen test can be used before an antibody response.

Globally, two different viruses may result in AIDS: HIV-1 is prevalent in the United States and West Africa; HIV-2 was noted originally in East Africa and has recently been found in Maryland. It is here, and not detected by the same tests as HIV-1. So far, the incidence of infection is very low. Confidential and anonymous testing facilities for HIV-2, though costly, may be wise.

HIV is not easily acquired. The routes of transmission are through sharing needles, tainted blood products, and sex. Sharing needles isn't relegated simply to addicts: many Third World countries' health care workers routinely reuse syringes due to chronic shortages. Cleaning a needle with bleach helps arrest disease transfer, but none of the "works" (the spoon or cooker, cotton, and water) may be shared without infection risk. Blood products in the United States are screened closely, reducing the chance of infection. Hemophiliacs primarily have suffered infection through a tainted blood factor needed for their survival.

Those who choose to be sexually active must understand safer sex practices. Safer sex means men use condoms during vaginal, oral, or anal sex. Safer sex means that people use dental dams during vaginal, anal, or oral sex. Safer sex is for heterosexual, homosexual, and bisexual individuals. Safer sex means not sharing sex toys, such as dildos, and using condoms on them. Safer sex is for tops and bottoms (that is, the penetrator and the receptive person are susceptible to infection from each other). HIV is not spread through saliva or by mosquitoes.

THE CDC DEFINITION

The federal Centers for Disease Control (CDC) in Atlanta defines AIDS based on opportunistic infections (OIs) suffered primarily by gay white men. This definition has been almost universally adopted by international health-tracking agencies which monitor many diverse populations. However, gay white men, women, children and people of color, among other populations, progress to AIDS in different ways.

Since 1989, ACT UPs nationwide, led by their women's committees, have run a vigorous, multitactic campaign (petitions, lobbying, lawsuits, demonstrations, civil disobedience) to broaden the CDC's AIDS definition to include infections that kill women, intravenous drug users (IVUs) and other HIV+ people. ACT UP's position has been endorsed by hundreds of AIDS organizations and public health authorities, including the American Medical Association.

The definition is important for three reasons: It gives guidelines to doctors on AIDS-related conditions to monitor, test and treat; it is widely used to determine eligibility for financial benefits; and it is the basis for both fixed government funding formulas and political pressure to increase AIDS spending.

Currently, many women do not get diagnosed with AIDS until after death! Meanwhile, women with AIDS—over 80 percent of color—die much faster than men, due to poverty-related lack of primary care and definition-related denial of benefit payments. Worsening the problem is the ignorance by mostly male doctors of the need for HIV- and HIV-related-screening of women with common conditions such as abnormal PAP smears and atypical menstrual cycles. These problems are rooted in the medical system's institutional sexism which often ignores women-specific disease research and doctor education.

ACT UP's campaign demands that HIV+ women with illnesses such as pelvic inflammatory disease, cervical cancer, and chronic yeast infections be counted as having AIDS. Also urged for inclusion are common infections of HIV+ IVUs, such as endocarditis and kidney and liver disease.

The CDC has adamantly rejected the change, calling it "too cumbersome"—a stance placing bureaucratic convenience over the lives of PWAs. A change might open the door to vastly increased Medicaid and SSI (disability) payments, particularly to poor women of color. However, activists won a partial victory in 1991 when the Social Security Administration facing a lawsuit, agreed to broaden benefits eligibility for some PWA women beyond the narrow CDC definition, but imposing stringent eligibility criteria.

Under activist pressure, the CDC in the summer of 1991 proposed adding additional illnesses, including some specific to women, to criteria for early stages of HIV infection, but not full-blown AIDS. This change, while a small step to strengthen doctors' monitoring, falls far short of the need for full inclusion. Meanwhile, the agency proposed expanding the AIDS definition to include all HIV+ persons with a T-cell count under 200. While this category would boost the AIDS statistics, it would be arbitrary (since T-cells fluctuate) and unavailable to many lacking financial or geographic access to this blood count. Still unaddressed are the demands to add several infections to the definition. The CDC, despite a storm of public opposition, scuttled its plans to make any change in the definition, in an election year in which an accurate assessment of AIDS deaths is undesirable.

Another problem with CDC statistics on PWAs is their breakdown by "risk group" (gay men, IVDUs, hemophiliacs, etc.) rather than risk behavior. In 1985, Haitians in the United States successfully fought to have their unjustified listing removed. When PWAs are surveyed, the questions asked are "Are you gay or bisexual?" or "Have you had sex with other men?" They are not, for example, "Have you engaged in anal sex?" "Have you shared needles?" The questions concern whom you were with as opposed to what types of behaviors you engage in.

Behavior is crucial to understanding the epidemiology. Populations are not so isolated, and unsafe behaviors may result in an explosion in populations hitherto only peripherally affected—as in the gay community during the early 1980s and among African Americans, Latinos, Asians and Native Americans in the mid-1980s. Two fast-growing populations of HIV infection in this country are high school and college students and women, particularly people of color among both populations. The definition must address transmission modes: the exchange of blood, semen, vaginal fluid, infected needles, anal, vaginal or oral sex, or tainted blood products.

CORPORATE DRUGS FOR AIDS

Over a decade into the epidemic, the U.S. medical research establishment has authorized only three toxic, expensive drugs to fight HIV infection: AZT was approved in 1987, ddI in 1991, and ddC in 1992. All are produced by corporate giants: Burroughs Wellcome, Bristol-Myers-Squibb, and Hoffman LaRoche. These drugs, known as "nucleoside analogs," work by disrupting a specific mechanism of virus replication.

This effect is temporary in many due to resistance developing to the drug. All have serious side effects in a large minority of users. AZT can seriously suppress bone marrow and produce anemia, requiring blood transfusions, and other painful ailments. Animal tests and early analysis of long-term human trials strongly indicate it is cancer-causing. ddI can cause pancreatitis, a potentially fatal condition. All can produce peripheral neuropathy (severe pain in the extremities).

Meanwhile, AZT's strongest proponents, and even the most glowing studies, have only claimed life-extension of a few months and a temporary reduction of a handful of AIDS symptoms. Mounting evidence indicates that survival is unaffected with use of AZT. An initial highly publicized study claiming to show that AZT slowed down deterioration of HIV-positive people with few symptoms was later contradicted by more extensive studies. ddI and ddC have less of a track record; thus far it has only been shown to temporarily increase the number of T-cells.

Yet the nucleoside analog juggernaut grips the entire international medical community. From the moment one tests HIV-positive, AZT is almost automatically prescribed, with talk of side effects minimized or even omitted. Massive ad blitzes, multimedia conference presentations, and slick journal articles stoke the fires of adulation and dogma.

One ACT UP success has been to force the FDA, which approves drugs and sets prescribed doses, and Burroughs Wellcome to acknowledge (after a year's delay) studies showing that AZT at 600 mg/day was no less "effective" than 1200 mg/day. This profits-over-health mentality probably hastened many PWAs' deaths from side effects. The lowest effective dose is still not known.

The dose reduction, combined with militant ACT UP protests against the original $12,000 annual price tag, have cut the figure to $3200 today. This type of profiteering—on several AIDS-related drugs—has been a frequent theme of ACT UP pressure campaigns.

ACT UP's numerous actions, most prominently the national demonstration and civil disobedience at FDA headquarters in 1988, have substantially chopped approval times and eased import policies of drugs for all life-threatening illnesses, but long delays remain. ACT UP chapters have repeatedly succeeded in speeding the laid-back timetable of corporate and government clinical trials by a combination of research, meetings, and protests—particularly the 1000-strong, nationally publicized "Storm the NIH" demonstration in May, 1990. In addition, many ground rules about medical research have been forever altered by ACT UP's and other activists' successful advocacy of pro-patient provisions, patient participation in study designs and government research communities.

The most concrete result has been the speeded-up approval of several new drugs to aid in the treatment of prevention of some major OIs, but many other potent AIDS therapies remain bottled up in corporate and government pipelines. In addition, inadequate safeguards exist to monitor toxic reactions and side effects of already approved drugs, compounded by limited or no long-term patient follow up.

ALTERNATIVE TREATMENTS

At the street level, hundreds of clinics have growing, increasingly documented evidence of PWA life-extension, health improvements, sometimes dramatic rebounds with over one hundred drugs, vitamins, herbs and other approaches not recognized by the medical establishment. Beyond specific treatments, many PWAs in Western countries are benefitting from incorporating other healing systems—many long-established and scientific, such as Chinese medicine and acupuncture. Meanwhile, the World Health Organization estimates over 80 percent of PWAs, particularly in the Third World, have no access to Western medicine and rely on indigenous medicine such as herbs and diet, yet studies of these approaches are often excluded from scientific conferences. PWAs have built "buyers clubs" in several cities to sell experimental and sometimes quasi-legal treatments. Community research projects have been started by PWAs, their advocates and practitioners, to do quicker—but still scientific—versions of the clinical trials which the FDA requires for approval.

Yet, after over $1 billion in AIDS research spending (hard-won by activist battles since the early 1980s), the National Institutes of Health (NIH) has little to show. The pattern of AIDS research mimics that of other diseases, particularly cancer: vast sums spent on toxic, minimally effective drugs while numerous promising nontoxic treatments are ignored. Why? Without the sponsorship of a pharmaceutical giant, it is almost impossible to move through the complex, multimillion-dollar process of clinical trials and paperwork required to win market licensure by the FDA. But big companies will only invest in products with a large projected market, patentability, and a comfortable profit margin. Many vitamins and herbs already on the market, or drugs approved for other diseases, lack one or more of these attributes and so go nowhere. A major obstacle is that natural substances, even extracts, often cannot be patented. The crime is that many of these are well established as safe and prudent health measures. For example, megadoses of Vitamin C have been found by numerous doctors to decrease the incidence of OIs and speed recovery from those OIs that do occur.

The PWA community is often forced to rely on individual stories—important information, but grossly inadequate—to make life-and-death decisions. Where studies exist, that information is rarely made available by hospitals, conventional clinics, or the majority of doctors—due to ignorance or periodic "anti-quackery" campaigns by organized medicine and insurance interests which falsely paint alternative medicine as useless or fraudulent. And those who do take unapproved treatments can rarely get reimbursement from private or government insurance, thus further skewing survival rates by class and race. Access is further impaired by constant FDA harassment, sometimes including armed raids on nutritional supplement companies and practitioners of complementary medicine. ACT UP has joined other freedom-of-medical-choice groups to protest these abuses.

NIH's priorities in AIDS research have stayed consistent: over 80 percent of patients in AIDS Clinical Trial Group (ACTG) studies have been given AZT or ddI. NIH decision-making committees are stacked with scientists closely tied to big drug companies via consulting fees, investments or research grants—sometimes for the very drugs under consideration. Thus, treatments developed by small companies without the right connections won't get mega-corporate, government, or university sponsorship. The rare few companies whose products have enough research to apply for FDA approval face a reviewing process from staff members cozy with big companies and/or biased against natural medicines.

These systemic problems have proven the most resistant to ACT UP's numerous activist interventions—confrontational and quiet, public and private. Thus, the total reordering of research priorities and an end to corporate manipulation of NIH's agenda remains at least as important a demand as more AIDS research funds.

HOLISTIC APPROACHES TO HEALTH

Even the most promising individual treatments (for any immune deficiency disease) can only work in the context of long-term attention to basic principles of physical, mental and spiritual health maintenance. This means careful testing and full treatment for often hidden, contributing infections generally overlooked by doctors, such as candida (yeast) overgrowth, latent syphilis, and parasitic infections. It also means addressing such immune-suppressive factors as toxic chemicals, junk food, addictions (alcohol, drugs, nicotine, etc.), psychological stress, lack of self-esteem, social isolation, homophobia, racism and sexism, and many more. Increasing evidence proves that the mind is a powerful force over the body—for good or ill—and that nutritional deficiencies and imbalances play a crucial role in determining the course of AIDS. Yet this holistic approach to health is anathema to the sick-care establishment with its single-viral cause, "magic-bullet cure" approach. Thus, studies of such factors rarely get funded. First, because any evidence of immune-suppressive aspects of particular drugs would undermine sales and confidence in the medical establishment. Second, awareness of the full impact of "lifestyle" factors on health could challenge doctors' claimed monopoly on healing knowledge. Finally, educating the public about the need to change our view of corporate, high-tech modern life would not only save many lives, but might also set off revolutionary changes—first in buying habits, and then in political allegiances.

AIDS and other life-threatening illnesses also cannot be separated from broader environmental concerns. Toxic chemicals in the air, water, dumpsites and nuclear radiation emissions are just a few of the pollutants which exacerbate immune system disorders. Twenty-five percent of U.S. pharmaceuticals are derived from plants. The rapid corporate destruction of rain forests not only threatens genocide of its human inhabitants, but is forever destroying thousands of species, some of which may be the key to tomorrow's medicines.

INSURANCE AND ACCESS

No matter how many treatments are available for people with AIDS, or even if a cure is found today, the U.S. insurance industry is antithetical to guaranteeing that those most in need will receive available treatments. In the United States, alone with South Africa among industrialized countries, health care is a privilege of the wealthy and not an inalienable right. Approval of Foscarnet for the treatment of cytomegalovirus (CMV), a virus which often leads to blindness and death in PWAs, is typical: it is the most expensive drug—$30,000/year—for this OI. What good is it if one can't afford it?

Insurance costs have skyrocketed. Premiums went up 400 percent in the 1980s. The top executives of Blue Cross/Blue Shield, despite their being "not-for-profit" organizations, garner salaries that are obscene even by industry standards. Many other insurance carriers are openly for profit. It was only after a coalition of health-oriented consumer groups organized by ACT UP, using focused letter zaps and participation in public hearings, that a price hike by Blue Cross/Blue Shield in New York was averted. AIDS is inaccurately claimed to be the straw that broke the insurance industry's back, but AIDS costs are no greater than any other serious illness. Nonetheless, the insurance industry preferentially excludes people with HIV: even if one can afford it, it is unattainable. No insurer has gone under paying AIDS claims, and none are likely to. Many PWAs do not have health insurance! AIDS activism has simply highlighted a system that is in a disastrous state resulting in as many as forty million Americans being uninsured and another fifty million underinsured.

More people are discovering that decades of premiums do not translate into decent health care. Sixty-eight billion dollars a year is spent on administrative, clinical and systemic waste, and red tape—more than is spent in total on heart or cancer patient treatment. For every dollar spent on AIDS research, six dollars are spent on insurance overhead and billing.

For the uninsured millions, health care is dismal to nonexistent. Nationwide, public hospitals are in disastrous shape. In less populated areas, many procedures are performed unnecessarily, depending on who pays the bill. In overcrowded cities, patients are routinely placed on gurneys in hallways with a number marking their location; but often, unrecognized by hospital kitchens, they go hungry. Emergency room waits are gruesomely prolonged. This is due to understaffing and underfunding.

The demand has risen sharply for universal health care. The World Health Organization (WHO) states that "the highest attainable standard of health is one of the fundamental rights of every human being . . ." Certainly this is not the case in the United States. What kind of universal health care should the United States adopt? The models of Germany, Canada and Australia all highlight the cost effectiveness of such systems. Over 12 percent of the U.S. GNP is spent on health care, yet millions of Americans have no coverage. Germany, for example, spends only 8 to 9 percent of its GNP on health care which covers everyone. The German system is one of the most expensive health care plans in Europe! A compilation of universal health care options is clearly articulated in *Universal Health Care: We Demand a Cure for the AIDS Crisis*, published by the ACT UP Network.

HOUSING

Some three million people in the United States are homeless. At least thirty-five thousand Americans are homeless people with AIDS. While the homeless continue to swell in numbers, formerly middle class individuals becoming symptomatic are faced with insurance that dries up in short order, an inadequate public health care system, and the likelihood of joining the ranks of the homeless. About thirteen thousand homeless people in New York City have AIDS. It is a holocaust that is happening before our eyes—eyes jaded by the daily sight of starving, sick, and dying people.

Due to withholding vacant apartments from the market and to unpaid taxes resulting in city ownership, there are more empty housing units than there are homeless people. Yet the primary "solution" the city offers is police sweeps of places where homeless reside, offering them the abysmal alternatives of armories or shelters. The New York City administration shut many shelters and ended medical care in those remaining. More blatantly, rather than house the homeless, New York preferred to sweep people from Tompkins Square Park, fence in and lock up the park and spend millions in police overtime and costly renovations.

As a result, homeless people are left with three possibilities: shelters, prisons or, when ill, hospitals. Each of these places are hotspots for spreading tuberculosis. Due to failures at all levels of government and defunding of TB interdiction programs, an otherwise curable disease has become not only epidemic, but resistant to many of the first and second line drugs. This has helped to spawn what is called "multidrug resistant TB," or MDR-TB. Some drugs with low profit margins—simple, cheap ones like streptomycin—are simply not available in the United States! For people with compromised immune systems, MDR-TB is extremely dangerous and far more quickly fatal. Clear answers are available—such as providing adequate air flow, UV lighting (to kill TB bacteria), appropriate masks, and so on. Cheapness and indifference on the part of city, state, and federal governments compromise such efforts.

A clear alternative to homelessness is to provide permanent housing. Although this alternative is more humane and cheaper, it is ignored. In New York, a municipally appointed Commission of Homeless proposed saving $55.5 million from the city's original five-year plan by adding tiny amounts of additional permanent housing; yet that same commission report let the government off the hook by placing service provision on the backs of nonprofit community organizations.

It costs about $65/day for home care for a PWA—but $79/day to keep this person in a shelter. But people in shelters die faster, so it costs less! Out of $156 million that was authorized, only $50 million has been appropriated by Congress for the 1990 National Affordable Housing Act. Bush asked for nothing in his 1992 budget.

One of the most successful efforts for housing PWAs is the Housing Works program, the result of the growth of the Housing Committee of ACT UP. Clients include PWAs with drug abuse problems as well, whom Housing Works endeavors to enroll in available treatment programs. Despite facing huge challenges, Housing Works is forging ahead with building a residence for homeless PWAs with substance abuse problems that, if successful, will serve as a model for future programs.

OPPRESSION

Fighting a grindingly slow bureaucracy and a profiteering pharmaceutical and medical community is taxing in any struggle for fair and just health care treatment. Since the first cases of Gay Related Immune Diseases (GRID) were discovered in the United States ten years ago, the war against AIDS has also meant fighting institutional homophobia, sexism, racism, and classism. As numerous sources document, federal funding was insignificant despite the spread of the disease and its pandemic nature. As with sickle cell anemia and systemic lupus erythematosus, which primarily occur in people of color and, in the latter case, women, so far AIDS in the United States has primarily occurred in gay men, IVUs, people of color, and hemophiliacs: marginalized populations. It wasn't until 1985, a full four years after AIDS was recognized, that the United States developed its only feeble plan for AIDS.

Hostile and irrational societal attitudes toward lesbian and gay people pervade society at all levels. Sen. Jesse Helms (R-North Carolina) and Rep. William Dannemeyer (R-California) are exemplary of such hatred. Constantly vigilant against any expression of our existence, such people have lobbied extensively against our civil rights measures, NEA funding for lesbian and gay artists, and expansion of education curricula to include raising awareness and sensitivity. They obstruct the fight against AIDS through support of costly and ineffective strategies like mandatory testing and opposing universal health care. This is magnified by those homophobic researchers, doctors, and nurses who impede patients' access to quality treatment.

People of color—African Americans, Latina/Latinos, Native Americans, Asians, and Pacific Islanders—face systemic racism. Only the most feeble attempts to enroll people of color in clinical trials has been made, despite the prevalence of AIDS in these communities. Racism flourishes more virulently when inability to pay is added to the equation.

The Catholic Church, led in this country by Cardinal O'Connor of New York, routinely condemns gay people. O'Connor had members of the gay Catholic group Dignity arrested for simply standing in protest. I heard O'Connor say from the pulpit that "the separation of church and state is a misinterpretation of the U.S. Constitution." If this view were accurate, then it would follow that the Church ought to pay taxes!

Activists object not merely to the homophobic and misogynist tenor of Catholic doctrine, but specifically the way the Church influences public policy. For example, New York State asked for bids for AIDS hospices. Despite many lower bids, the State awarded the Church millions of dollars to build AIDS hospices. After five years the property reverts to the Church. A nontaxable gift of public lands! ACT UP's action at Saint Patrick's Cathedral in December 1989 denounced this violation of public funds. It was timed to occur during Cardinal

O'Connor's homily, which he has used not as an act of worship but exploited as his political rostrum.

Despite New York State law, the Church initially refused to provide safer sex information. They reluctantly agreed to provide a sealed envelope containing information merely on where to go for such information! In addition, they refused to give gynecological care or information about safe use of needles.

Women, particularly women of color and lesbians, have consistently been ignored in the AIDS crisis. Exclusions of women-specific OIs, lack of lesbian transmission studies and an almost complete exclusion from AIDS trials are examples of how the health care system's misogyny has been disastrous for women with AIDS. As a result, women in ACT UP have undertaken intensive research around women's medical issues, disseminated copious information, and spearheaded many actions to address these inequities.

AIDS fear and bigotry is most blatant in U.S. prisons. The condition of prisoners with AIDS is more than appalling; it is genocidal. Throughout the country, prisoners with AIDS have access to only the worst of medical treatment, which often amounts only to aspirin! They are frequently denied family visiting rights. They have been arrested and sentenced to multiyear prison terms charged with having spit at or bitten guards, even though HIV cannot be spread in this fashion. ACT UP chapters across the nation address these issues with letter zaps and demonstrations. One success includes the simple right to conjugal visits for prisoners with AIDS in New York State that elsewhere are routinely denied.

NEEDLE EXCHANGE

Drug abuse is worldwide and not just in large cities. The war on drugs, according to top correctional officers, policymakers and law enforcement officials in the United States, is a horrible, costly failure. Since the United States continues to address drug abuse as a legal instead of a medical problem, huge costs for arrests, judicial time and incarceration are incurred, and mindlessly repeated. No progress has been made in thirty years. Insufficient attention and funding is allotted for treatment, rehabilitation and job training. Profits are huge at every level: at street level, kids make the "choice" between working for minimum "slave" wages or the flash-cash, high-risk venture of selling narcotics. At the highest levels of corporate and governmental America, funding for covert operations and arms sales around the globe are facilitated by drug profits.

Despite such interests, ACT UP has been extraordinarily successful in causing cities across the nation to institute needle exchange programs. One strategy was involvement in a coalition of thirty-four AIDS and other service organizations calling upon the New York City Department of Health to demand a change in the law. The coalition recognized the imperative need for such measures given the woefully inadequate number of treatment slots for impoverished addicts and the lack of treatment on demand. Primarily, the effort was won with members of ACT UP and the AIDS brigade providing needle exchange in high drug use areas. In return for their dirty needles, addicts received a kit containing sterilized water, bleach, bilingual safe injection and safe sex information along with a condom. This program is so successful in stemming the tide of HIV infection that New York City has reversed its stance and authorized a needle exchange program. Even, the conservative *New York Times* ran an editorial calling for city-sanctioned needle exchange. Initially however, seven ACT UP members were arrested during the needle exchange program, and, with testimony from health and public officials on their side, were found not guilty. Their defense of medical necessity was upheld by the judge as preventing a greater harm than obeying that law. Activists in a similar case in New Jersey were also acquitted for the same reason.

Needle exchange is only the first step. The answer lies in treatment on demand, a cessation of huge drug dealing profits in part through recognizing substance abuse as a medical problem, not a judicial one, and a vigorous program to provide wide-ranging services for the abuser of any substances, including alcohol and tobacco.

MANDATORY TESTING AND DISCLOSURE

While Sen. Jesse Helms continues to be bankrolled by the tobacco industry (one of the biggest killers in the world), he has repeatedly raised the call for mandatory testing and disclosure of the HIV-status of health care workers and patients. Congress has considered—and at one point the Senate passed—such an irrational plan contrary to infection-control procedures and good medical judgment.

Despite CDC regulations seeking disclosure for invasive procedures, many institutions, catalyzed by surgeons, doctors, dentists and activists, have rejected the call for mandatory testing and disclosure. Among them are the New York State Department of Health, the California Medical Association, former Surgeon General Everett Koop, and others.

Media coverage of Arthur Ashe, an Aetna insurance spokesperson, and Kimberly Bergalis, who claimed she was infected by her dentist, accelerate AIDS-phobia by conferring upon them "innocent victim" status. Implicit in such attitudes is that others somehow deserved or desired AIDS. No one deserves AIDS. Having AIDS is not a crime. Calls for mandatory testing and disclosure of health care workers for HIV is nothing short of hysteria.

The irony of the Bergalis case is that she may not have contracted HIV directly from her dentist, Dr. Acer, who died of AIDS. It seems quite likely that she contracted it through infected equipment due to his not following procedures known as Universal Precautions. This means that a health care worker need not have HIV, but may have not properly sterilized the medical equipment. Thus knowing a health care workers' HIV status would not be any protection from this kind of infection.

The cost estimated by the Service Employees' International Union is $1.5 billion to test four million U.S. health care workers. Does this also mean that each worker would have to be tested after every procedure? Since the body's antibody response to HIV infection can take up to six months or more, would they have to wait this long or would even costlier tests be used? The stigmatization of HIV-positive health care workers would result in the loss of many trained personnel. As it stands, Ms. Bergalis and the other four patients who were allegedly infected by Dr. Acer or his equipment are the only known incidents of such infection.

Mandatory testing and disclosure is foolish for another simple reason: the chance of HIV infection by a health care worker are about one in twenty-three million. A survey of nine thousand patients of infected health care workers revealed no HIV-infected patients. Universal precautions will protect people from any kind of infectious disease if observed. They include the following:

- The proper use of sterilization and disinfectant equipment (such as an autoclave);

- The use of disposable needles and other equipment used once per patient; and
- The use of protective clothing, including disposable rubber gloves to prevent infection from patient to patient, doctor to patient, or patient to doctor for any kind of infection.

Finally, the Occupational Safety and Health Administration's (OSHA) adoption of the blood-borne disease standard is designed to protect workers and patients from hazardous work conditions by spelling out universal precautions, infection control procedures and sterilization techniques. Also included are employer requirements that equipment and protective clothing be provided; this involves private dental practices and medical offices as well as hospitals. This standard includes protection from diseases more virulent than HIV, such as Hepatitis B and TB.

THE FEDERAL GOVERNMENT'S RESPONSE TO AIDS

The Reagan and Bush administrations have only worsened the AIDS crisis. The federal government is the source of the U.S. trend in problem-solving through violence or indifference. Such methods retreat from addressing underlying causes and working upon obvious solutions.

The National Commission on AIDS, including several of George Bush's handpicked appointees, spent two years interviewing PWAs, doctors, nurses, and health care administrators. Their report blasted him for his criminal inaction in this crisis. They say, "the patchworked, ill-planned, and poorly implemented system of care that now exists should no longer be tolerated." Bush has remained silent, except to admit he hasn't done enough.

Bush actively supports mandatory testing and disclosure and the inclusion of HIV on the Immigration and Naturalization Service's (INS) list of infectious diseases. One hundred thousand letters were sent to have it removed. Despite the Department of Health and Human Services' recommendation that only infectious tuberculosis remain on the list, the Justice Dept., at Bush's urging, reinstated HIV on the INS list. Hepatitis B—one hundred times more infectious—is not included! As it is, immigrants who might have reason to believe they are infected will be driven underground. Due to this irrational policy, the International

Conference on AIDS rejected Boston as the site for the eighth Conference, switching to Amsterdam in protest.

While more money is needed, many noncost elements, policies, and strategies must be implemented. Among them are speaking out to challenge vicious public attitudes and misperceptions. However, Bush says he is "not ready" to accept the ordainment of lesbian and gay priests into his Episcopal faith. Far from initiating education of Americans with frank discussions of safer sex, he seeks to destroy public education *in toto* while espousing a narrow, oppressive definition of "family values."

Myriad issues inspired ACT UP to organize its first demonstration against Bush at his "ancestral family home" in Kennebunkport, Maine on September 1, 1991. Over two thousand activists marched through the streets and staged a massive die-in in front of police barricades blocking access to the house.

Included among a twenty-five-point national plan for AIDS developed by ACT UP and sent to Bush are the following:

- Issue an executive order defining the responsibility of all US citizens to end the AIDS crisis;
- Appoint a cabinet-level Director of HIV Disease to coordinate the efforts to stop this pandemic along with a national advisory board to streamline efforts and reduce bureaucracy, a board which includes people with HIV/AIDS;
- Support adequate funding—and appropriate the money;
- Expand the CDC definition and SSI benefits;
- Explicitly discuss the modes of transmission of HIV and safer sex in all relevant languages;
- Ensure funding is spent wisely and unspent funds reallocated;
- Oppose mandatory testing and disclosure;
- Reform eligibility criteria for Medicaid /Medicare and eliminate the twenty-four-month waiting period for Medicare;
- Begin trials of nontoxic and nonpharmaceutical treatments, as well as alternative and holistic therapies and modalities;
- Enforce broader coordination of research efforts in the NIH and encourage collaborative research and timely, effective modes of communication . . .

Bush has said ACT UP exercises an "excess of free speech." After ACT UP's action, he said he had more concern for the unemployed than for those with AIDS, endeavoring to create divisions between the unemployed and PWAs—as if many PWAs are not also unemployed! Yet, hypocritically, he vetoed a bill to extend unemployment benefits. He has never had a veto overturned, a testament to his near-totalitarian power over Congress.

MONEY FOR AIDS

AIDS is infectious and can kill faster than heart disease and cancers. At a conservative estimate, eight to ten million people worldwide are infected with HIV. The perception that money must be allocated to one disease over another is misleading—the war against AIDS should not be in competition with any other health care need!

Despite the government's misrepresentations, there are three areas where AIDS research and health care require additional funding. The first is the ACTG research budget. The clinical trial system held competitions that did not increase the minimal thirty-two sites, but instead reduced seven sites' funding until the end of the year.

Second, due to the huge increase in AIDS caseloads and the general increase in health care costs, Medicaid costs for AIDS have increased. Since many PWAs require Medicaid, payments for their care are made to hospitals by law. As more people require financial help, Medicaid payments associated with AIDS per force rise, making it appear as if more has been spent on AIDS care. The Bush Administration has falsely claimed to be spending over $4 billion on AIDS. This inflated figure was arrived at by including such payments—which is not done for any other disease. A standard review of the AIDS budget reveals that the latest increases have not kept pace with inflation, resulting in reductions in AIDS research funding. Even those amounts made available are sometimes lost—failure to make timely distributions results in mandatory forfeiture. The Ryan White bill seemed to address funding needs, but only about a quarter of the amount authorized in 1990 was appropriated.

Finally, AIDS education receives only the most minimal federal funding. The single pamphlet that the Surgeon General mailed to most Americans was a feeble measure. Sexually explicit information was almost nonexistent. ACT UP's YELL (Youth Education Life Line) has made great strides through distribution of condoms and safe sex literature to New York City high schools. The NYC Board of Education endorsed a condom distribution plan. An "opt-out" program that would have permitted parents to prohibit their children from receiving condoms was defeated, in large part due to activist pressure. To prohibit access to information and protection is exceedingly dangerous, since teens and young adults are one of the fastest-growing populations of HIV infection.

MILITARISM VERSUS HEALTH CARE

In September 1990, shortly after deployment of U.S. troops to Saudi Arabia, ACT UP demonstrated at the Army Recruiting Station in Times Square to protest severe cuts in appropriations for the Ryan White Care bill by Bush and Congress. A direct link between a war that would benefit only the wealthy and the war on AIDS was clearly made. As the antiwar movement grew, hundreds of ACT UP members marched in large coalition demonstrations across the nation. Day of Desperation (January 23, 1991) was a series of simultaneous actions across the country culminating in the shutdown of Grand Central Station in New York City for several hours. A balloon-lofted banner proclaimed "Money for AIDS, not for War."

The administration has now been caught in the lie that there isn't enough money or resources for AIDS. The Bush Administration mobilized human resources, private sector and public materiel, supplies, etc., and sent two million people to the middle of a desert virtually overnight. Despite bountiful resources, corporate profits and state security continue to prevail over public needs.

Some of the money needed for health care could come from the Pentagon's $100 million a day ($35 billion/year) so-called "black budget." Congress funds this ultrasecret budget largely ignorant of how the funds are spent. One "black budget" product, the Stealth bomber, originally designed at $250 million a plane, now costs around $850 million per plane. Nearly as much as was spent on AIDS in the first 10 years. The A-12 is a Navy plane which suffered budget overruns resulting in cancellation of the program and a taxpayer cost of $5 billion—for nothing. The federal government, at the behest of transnational corporate interests, is hell-bent on sustaining this economy of death.

City and state budgets have been slashed as a result of cuts in federal aid by the Bush Administration. Each federal tax dollar was spent as follows in Fiscal 1991: 52¢ to the military—29¢ to current military, and 23¢ to past military endeavors (i.e., WWII, Korea, Vietnam, Grenada, Panama); 9¢ was wasted on the savings and loan crisis and bank bailout; 10¢ of each tax dollar goes to general government. This leaves 29¢ of every dollar for everything else: education, homelessness, AIDS research, prenatal care, infrastructure, Medicaid, health care, energy research, mass transit, hospitals, the arts, etc. Specifically, 23¢ of that 29¢ goes to human resources, the other 6¢ to physical resources. This means 0.17 of 1¢ of each dollar goes to AIDS, according to 1991 spending levels.

In the war against AIDS, the media and politicians cite AZT—and now ddI—as the great treatment of modern science for AIDS. It is no wonder that these pathetic options are all that's available, considering 70 percent of all federal research and development money goes toward building weapons of mass destruction.

Initially AIDS reporting was nonexistent, then episodic, trendy, dismal, and outrageous. With the media's slavish acceptance of pools and military-issued, sanitized reports, media reporting on other issues was overwhelmed by such propaganda. In response, ACT UP members invaded Dan Rather's CBS News studios, evading security by dressing in network executive drag with CBS IDs. They burst into the live broadcast shouting "Fight AIDS, not Arabs!" Rather's response, rather than jump upon a news story in the making, was to refer to the activists as "rude people" after a few moments of expensive airtime.

Simultaneously, in the McNeil/Lehrer studios, activists chained themselves to desks. They arrived opportunely, during an interview concerning carpet bombing. The activists spoke for several minutes on the AIDS crisis and the work that needs to be done to save lives, not slaughter them. This was a leading topic of discussion at the January 26, 1991, rally in D.C. against the war that tens of thousands of people—including scores of ACT UP members—attended. Many remarked on these actions with grins and amazement. It was encouraging to see this recognition of ACT UP. It was personally encouraging to realize that I was not alone!

The videotaped beating of Rodney King and the subsequent nationwide rebellion highlighted police brutality and its toleration by the judicial system. Police forces, far from keeping order or being effective in fighting crime, too often serve the interests of government and the corporate elite as a tool of repression. Police brutality, largely directed against entire communities of color and militant activist groups perceived as a threat, has directly affected the AIDS activist movement. Physical and verbal abuse has been sustained by activists in Chicago, Philadelphia, Los Angeles, New York City, and elsewhere.

For example, at the end of a peaceful ACT UP/NY demonstration (itself protesting police violence!), the commanding officer ordered an unprovoked, nightstick charge. Several media people's cameras were intentionally smashed. One demonstrator, a pacifist and former seminarian, Chris Hennelly, was so severely beaten by police that he sustained permanent injuries, including epilepsy. As is typical when the police are in the wrong, he was arrested and charged with "assaulting an officer." The ludicrousness of this was reflected in Manhattan Criminal Court Judge Edgar Walker's strongly worded, nineteen-page opinion which threw out the City's charges against Chris as not only unsubstantiated but false, stating that Chris had been knocked to the ground without provocation. But no cop has yet been indicted for this crime. Incidents like this have resulted in ACT UP's raised awareness and chapters in many cities joining in broad coalition demonstrations against police brutality.

The FBI continues its surveillance and harassment of ACT UP members. The tactics employed are reminiscent of the COINTELPRO (Counter Intelligence Program) program that existed to "disrupt and destabilize" dissident political groups from the 1950s to the 1970s. These tactics included harassing phone calls, death threats, and other peculiar and bizarre acts. Some of these activities suggest access to phone company records. A Freedom of Information inquiry revealed FBI files on ACT UP across the country. As ACT UP broadens its base to be more inclusive of different views and people in true coalition, there is the potential for broad-based, radical change that threatens the inimical power base of both government and the giant pharmaceutical industry.

In his press statement about the Kennebunkport action, Bush stated that if the AIDS activists wanted "compassion, I got the message loud and clear." With his usual subtlety, he did not actually say he had any compassion for people with AIDS. In fact, his actions show that he does not, and he lies when he claims to have compassion for the American people. Perhaps dying Americans are also merely "collateral damage."

As many as two hundred thousand Iraqi children may be dead or dying as a direct result of Bush's bombing campaign. There are around twenty thousand children with AIDS in the United States alone. Nearly two thousand HIV-positive infants are born each year. The World Health Organization estimates there will be ten million HIV-infected children by the year 2000. Nonetheless, cuts in the Ryan White Care bill have had a direct impact on AIDS care for American children. Still Barbara Bush has the gall to hold AIDS babies, only to leave them to die.

SUCCESSES OF ACT UP

The following details some of the ways ACT UP, often in broad-based coalitions with many other people and groups, has had a direct impact on the AIDS crisis:

- The empowerment and active participation of patients in experimental treatments, input on policies and social needs and in the doctor/patient partnership.
- The initiation of clinical trials for a broad range of experimental AIDS drugs and alternative treatments.
- The initiation of parallel track. A patient can obtain unapproved drugs in a clinical trial that have shown efficacy, even though such patients may not be in the trial.
- The reduction in price of Burroughs Wellcome's drug, AZT and the illumination of pharmaceutical industry profiteering.
- The institution or review of needle exchange in stemming HIV infection in many areas.
- In the face of a media acquiescing to press-pool censorship during the Gulf war, ACT UP got the message out.
- Coalitions with health care workers, cancer and heart patient advocates, environmental, labor and other groups.
- Major demonstrations involving thousands of U.S. citizens focusing attention on shortcomings at the White House, the NIH in Bethesda, at the CDC in Atlanta and at the FDA in Washington, among other places.
- Demonstrations in Paris bringing forward the criminal, intentional use of tainted blood factor needed by hemophiliacs.

The genocidal indifference of the government to the AIDS crisis and its serious implications for health care, medical research and social problems require a reevaluation of the current system that controls the United States.

While some cheered the end of "Soviet Communism," capitalism nonetheless has not come out the winner. The failures include the numbers of uninsured, a frighteningly high infant mortality rate, the numbers of homeless and unemployed, the inestimable scandal of the savings and loans, and the increasing ownership of United States assets by a dwindling number of obscenely wealthy individuals, to name but a few. Society is only as strong as its weakest link.

Individual liberties are paramount in a democracy and must include among them the rights of housing, health care, education, and environmental protection. To achieve this end, the jobs of teachers, social workers, health care workers for the indigent and environmentally safe systems designers should be valued as highly as top corporate executives and attorneys. Energy utilization (i.e., solar, not oil/fission) and assurance of recyclability must be encouraged. This will only increase the incentive to take such jobs, solve social problems more swiftly and make such jobs more competitive.

Involvement in direct action groups is increasingly necessary considering the troubles our species faces. AIDS activism, environmental activism, and direct action include letters, calls and faxes to the President, mayors, state and federal statespeople, the various local and national media and corporate leaders. Direct action means demonstrations and civil disobedience, a willingness to be arrested. Direct action facilitates the changes that must take place in order for the species not only to survive but to thrive in harmony with one another and the life with which we share the planet. It requires coalition-building and communication with other people, persuasions, cultures—it requires solidarity. It is clear that we live in a world of interlocking systems; it is no longer possible to view the world solely on the basis of isolated problems.

Armed with information (or knowing where to get it), one is better able to address the systemic problems faced in the AIDS crisis. It is up to us to make changes philosophically, conceptually and through our actions and lives. Certainly, if we do nothing, if we do not speak, silence is death.

PART III

GREENING AMERICA

HELEN CALDICOTT

TOWARD A COMPASSIONATE SOCIETY

LECTURE—BOULDER, COLORADO, MARCH 19, 1991

It's lovely to be back in Boulder. Such a beautiful city. But I always feel pretty alarmed when I drive past Rocky Flats. That plant's just got to be closed down and finished forever, bang, like that! They have made the plutonium triggers for every single nuclear weapon in this country. thirty-five thousand hydrogen bombs. America is still pumping out five new bombs a day. The freeze movement and the nuclear weapons peace movement only achieved half our goal. Half our goal was to bring an end to the Cold War, and that was magnificent. But it's only half done. We didn't eliminate one nuclear weapon. There are still sixty thousand hydrogen bombs.

You have to know the buttons are still computerized, that it could occur tonight by a computer error, and we're damn lucky to still be here. The threat is not diminished. In fact, the danger is higher, because our perception of the risk is lower. We've heaved a sigh of relief because Gorbachev is there. The technology is still in place. Therefore the danger is higher. Get it? Because we've gone away and Bush proceeds apace, building more and more weapons. They're figuring that Gorbachev's going to be gone soon, and indeed he is, unless the United States works with him intensely to eliminate nuclear weapons within the next five years. That's the only thing that would give him back his credibility within the Soviet military establishment, the KGB and the Soviet people. He's in the middle of a catastrophe and chaos because he's unleashed the processes of democracy. It took Britain hundreds of years of chaos and civil war to get a Westminster system of government. It always takes time with a feudal nation, and they're a feudal nation. They've never had a democracy. They're a Third World country. It will take many years to get to a stable governmental situation. What he did was the most courageous thing any Warsaw Pact country leader has done this century. Unless he's supported by the U.S. government, he will go down. The opportunity is there, because he almost got Reagan to agree at Reykjavik about three or four years ago to eliminate nuclear weapons.

I went to Reykjavik, to that little house where they met. Reykjavik is in Iceland. There was a huge perimeter of safety around from which everyone was cleared. Armed guards were all around. The KGB were sitting in the basement. They got fairly full of vodka. They were watching television and accidentally the wastepaper basket started to burn. I suppose they'd thrown a match in it. They smoke incessantly, the Russians do. There was a fire in the basement, just underneath where Reagan and Gorbachev were meeting. Someone happened to find it; the KGB didn't notice it. That's number One. Number Two: the Russians came totally armed with the most magnificent strategies for bilateral nuclear disarmament. The Americans came, arrogantly thinking nothing would happen. Richard Perle—do you remember Richard Perle, the Prince of Darkness? Richard Perle was called by his colleagues in the Pentagon the Prince of Darkness. He was the architect of the first-strike nuclear war policy. He destroyed the "walk in the woods" proposal with Kitiwidzski and Rostow when they went to try to make peace. Remember the walk in the woods? Remember your history during the Reagan years? You really should know this. If you don't, read my book, *Missile Envy,* named after Freud, and you'll learn about the history of this. It's important that you know it.

Richard Perle, the Prince of Darkness, was up in the bathroom. It was a tiny house and there was nowhere for him to be except in the bathroom. A little lavatory there and a bath. He had a board over the bath. Reagan didn't know anything, you know. I know Reagan. I spent an afternoon with him. We quickly established a doctor-patient relationship. I was the doctor and he was the patient. I had to hold his hand frequently to reassure him because he was just flabbergasted. He really knew nothing about the nuclear arms race, period. He didn't know his numbers, his strategies, his technology—nothing. I went pretty flat out. I was all enthusiastic, full of numbers and figures, and everything he said was wrong. I'd let him talk for a while and then I'd interrupt him and stop him and correct him. He'd get this sort of flush on his cheeks and get really quite tense. I'd have to hold his hand to reassure him. He quoted to me from the *Reader's Digest,* which he told me was his "intelligence files." Altogether it was a fairly alarming procedure.

Gorbachev would give Reagan these proposals. He didn't understand what was going on, so he would go out to see the Prince of Darkness in the bathroom. The Prince of Darkness didn't even have any paper, so he's scribbling numbers on a piece of toilet paper. This is true. This is history. Then Reagan would run back to Gorbachev and have a little bit more semi-intelligent conversation and then run back again and see Perle. And indeed, they nearly made it. Until Reagan got stuck on Star Wars, which he saw from a Disneyland perspective. It was this big shield over America, and the missiles come in and it went "boink, boink, boink." Reagan, who really lived in Disneyland and Hollywood, believed that Star Wars was the way to go that would protect all of us. He was a nice guy, a decent guy, but he just didn't understand. It failed. And do you remember when Schulz came out of that meeting? Do you remember that press conference? Here was a man who had seen God. He came out shattered. It was an hour long. He said, "We did this, and then we got to this, and then we agreed to this and then we moved to this. And then it floundered." He talked about Star Wars. He had seen a miracle. He had seen it was possible for two mere mortals in a weekend to save the earth. It turned George Schulz, who used to be the head of Bechtel, which is now rebuilding Kuwait, into a statesman. He then worked with Shevardnadze, that wonderful Georgian, to help save the world. But then Bush got in and Baker got in, and now things are falling apart. This makes me cry, because we nearly made it. This was our work and everyone else's work in the world, to save the world.

Let's talk about this Gulf War. The peace dividends were working, and the popularity of the president was low. So, April Glaspie, the American ambassador, was called in five days before Hussein invaded Kuwait. Incidentally, Hussein was a very close ally of the United States right through the Iran-Iraq War, you know that, don't you? He gassed 50,000 Iranians, and that was OK. In fact, in Paris, just before he invaded Kuwait, the World Trust tried to pass a resolution against Hussein for using chemical weapons and America vetoed that resolution of condemnation, internationally. He gassed 5,000 Kurds, and now remember, pictures of gassed Kurds, these people lying in the gutters, their bodies rotting, in their saris, were on the front page of the *New York Times,* and no one turned a hair. It didn't matter, because he was a friendly despot.

Then April Glaspie went to see him and he said, "What would you do if I invaded Kuwait? I want to raise the price of oil. The Kuwaitis are stealing my oil. I feel very upset, and anyway, Kuwait used to be part of Iraq. Britain separated it in 1961." She said, "I am officially obliged to tell you that the State Department has no stand on Arab-Arab border disputes. James Baker told me to emphasize that." So he was given the green light to invade Kuwait. A setup. Why? They had all these terrific weapons. Immediately the United Nations admirably voted as a group for the first time to condemn the invasion of Kuwait, the day after America moved. She knew what was going to happen, and then she moved. Immediately James Baker set off, going around the world, persuading and bribing and coercing nations to support America to have a war. He paid off $14 billion of the Egyptian debt, gave Turkey $7 billion, gave the Soviet Union $7 billion—at a time when the United States is in a deep recession, when the savings and loan is probably going to cost U.S. taxpayers a trillion dollars, when many banks are on the verge of collapse and the insurance industry is on the verge of collapse because they invested in junk bonds and phony real estate deals. So America's in a mess, but there's always money if you want to have a war. The people who run the Congress, like General Dynamics and Raytheon—I know it because I stood at the Senate door seeing Teddy Kennedy and others come out straight into the welcoming arms of the lobbyists of the military-industrial complex, dressed in their green velvet jackets. They take them out to lunch, steak and kidney lunch, and they take them to hunting lodges over the weekend and they give them tickets to the ball games. I see it happening. They run the Senate and the Congress.

So they were all ready to go into Kuwait and it was OK if they used U.S. tax dollars to bribe other countries so they could have a war because the people who run the Congress and the White House would make more money ultimately and the taxpayer would lose out. So that's OK. Right? Let's get it really clear.

So the war started. Do you know why it started on January 15? Because there was no moon. The smart weapons work best, the heat-seeking guided missiles, when it's totally dark. So it was all planned with a brilliant strategy and by God did they have a ball! You'd think it was a Superbowl match! Who were the commentators? White male Americans. It went all over the world—to the Soviet Union, to our country, and were they excited! "Did you see that one? Look, Baghdad's lit up like a Christmas tree!" Christmas tree????? Carpet bombing. Carpets are nice and soft and homey and domestic. So carpet bombing must be OK. There were B52s flying so high that no one could see them and they each dropped seventy one-thousand-pound bombs. Seventy one-thousand-pound bombs. They flew in formations of four, wing to wing. It was great for the pilots. They got back and said, "We had a great mission." Totally hygienic. No blood, no guts, great. "Boy, did we perform our mission! Those weapons went really well!" They dropped more bombs on Kuwait and Iraq than we used in the whole of the Second World War. It was almost worse than what Hitler did. Do you know what war means? Descriptions of the First World War tell us of muddy pools of water with eyeballs floating in them. Men lying around with their intestines hanging out. Take it in and hear it, because the United States did it. Men lying around with half their brain blown away and flies covering the other section of it.

Remember when a little girl was trapped down a well in Texas about two years ago and the whole world stopped? One little girl? When you witness the birth of a baby, the baby comes out perfectly formed from this fat tummy. Ten fingers and ten toes, a beautiful thing. Would you say, "That's an Iraqi baby, that's not going to be worth very much. This is an American baby! This is sacred!"? Every child and every human life is sacred. If Hussein was mad, America has put in hundreds of mad dictators around the world, killing people like you can't believe in Guatemala, El Salvador, and until recently Chile. If a patient comes in to me who is a bit mad and needs treatment, I don't treat him by going out and killing his family. The numbers of dead are probably about four hundred thousand, as far as I can gather. Did you ever hear that? No. Remember that General Schwarzkopf said—and he's a great hero now, like Oliver North—that "we killed very, very, very many people." There were probably half a million troops, totally unprotected, not well fed, bombed out of existence, no weapons, no tanks, nothing, sitting there like trapped rats. And they used the verminization term, because if they're rats or cockroaches, you can obviously exterminate them. Half a million waiting to be slaughtered. They used near-nuclear weapons. Fuel air explosives. I write about this in my book, *Missile Envy.* They send out a cloud of propane and then they explode the propane gas and the explosion is so great that it sucks the oxygen out of the people's lungs and they suffocate. Great weapon. Then they use cluster bombs. That's one bomb breaking down into little bomblets that also explode. Some of them are made of plastic so that if shrapnel gets into a human you can't see it by X-ray. You can't find where the thing is. It's hard enough to find a bullet in the body, if you're a surgeon. It's pretty difficult. But to find a piece of plastic that you can't see on an X-ray is impossible. That foreign body stays in the patient. It becomes infected and abscessed and the patient dies. Fancy thinking like that to kill people. Cluster bombs that take out a hundred city blocks in area.

They used napalm. I heard they used liquid phosphorus. Phosphorus is such that if it gets on the skin it starts burning, smoldering and smoking and if you put your hand in water it makes it burn faster. It burns all the way through to the other side of the body. That's what they used. They probably killed, the figures are now, I hear, 250,000 troops. Remember they bombed those troops when they were running away? They slaughtered them. It's like *Guernica,* the painting that Picasso painted? The Spanish Civil War? It was worse, much worse. The most sophisticated weapons in the history of the human race were used.

There was a picture in the *New York Times* the other day. It got me. I kept turning back to it. It was one of those trucks that had been bombed escaping. I thought, "That's a leg." There was a leg hanging out the side. Then I thought, "That's an arm." There was an arm hanging over the side of the truck, two weeks old and swollen. It looked like a statue from the Jewish Holocaust that you'd see in Israel or at one of the concentration camps. It was on the pages of the *New York Times.*

As to civilians killed, we don't know how many—one hundred thousand, maybe two hundred thousand. Sixty percent were children. Sixty percent were children. Sixty percent were children.

I went to a medical clinic the other day and there were old women in there wearing pink nighties with yellow ribbons tied to them. The yellow ribbons were worn and displayed to show their support for the U.S. troops in the Gulf. Sixty percent were children. Where are we?

That's what Nazi Germany did. The Germans said, "We saw the cattle trucks going but we didn't know what was in them. We saw the smoke coming from the chimney. It smelled sort of funny, but we didn't know what it was." The good Germans, totally propagandized by that brilliant man Goebbels. The Nazis used the propaganda techniques learned during the First World War in the United States: How to move a nation from a state of total ignorance into a state of hatred. What did they call him? "Soddom." His name is not Soddom, it's Saddam. Sodomy. Soddom. That's propaganda. He is Mr. Hussein, like Mr. Bush. Did they say "George, George, George?" Soddom? See? He shouldn't have invaded Kuwait. He did some very bad things. But he'd been doing bad things for a long time. Lots of countries do bad things. The United States does dreadful things in Latin America and in the Philippines. It deposed my prime minister in 1975. That's the world, really. But it's great, because Bush is popular and defense starts going up and the Congress has just passed a bill to make sure that they can't transfer money directly from the Pentagon into social programs to look after you.

So let's talk about the environmental consequences of the war. Human beings are one thing, but let's talk about the environment. That's another thing. So Hussein said, "If you fight us I'll burn all the oil wells in Kuwait. I'll pump oil into the Gulf and I'll bomb Israel." So we did and he did. Equal and opposite reactions. So six hundred oil wells are burning. Apparently still in the middle of the day it's dark, and sometimes you'll see photographs they'll release. It's dark. They have to keep the lights on. Oily rain is falling over Iran. It's moving further east. It's thought that this oily smoke will block out the monsoons and prevent the monsoons on the Indian subcontinent, where over a billion people live, many of whom already are starving. If the monsoons fail because of this war millions more will starve. So we're not talking about 400,000 people dying. We're talking about millions. The military set no money aside for the environmental consequences of the war. Furthermore, before the war began ecologists got together and said, "If the oil wells burn what will happen?" The King of Jordan organized a conference. The scientists worked out that if the oil wells burn it could accelerate the greenhouse effect by thirty years. And this war was about oil, the Seven Sisters. Who are the Seven Sisters? Gulf, Texaco, Exxon, BP, Shell, Mobil, and AMOCO. We have got to stop burning oil because the world is dying. More money was spent in one day of this war than is spent on all the research and development for alternative energy systems each year. The war was about oil. And the earth is dying from global warming because we're driving cars all the time and burning oil and turning on the electricity. The way you make electricity is either you burn uranium and make toxic waste that lasts millions of years and kills millions by cancer or chemo and genetic diseases, or you burn coal, which pushes that carbon dioxide which hangs around the earth like a blanket, heating it up. We'll get into that in a minute.

So that's the oil wells. Some say it will take a year to put the fires out. Others say twenty years. Red Adair's over there with his Texas hat and his boots and everything to put it out. But with six hundred oil wells blazing they say that the ground is shaking three kilometers away from oil burning underground. That the sand around the oil wells is turning into glass. It's melting.

He emptied oil into the Gulf. Let's talk about the Gulf. I didn't know the Gulf was such an extraordinary wildlife area. Millions of birds, migratory birds, use the Gulf as a fly-over and they rest there on their way. The Gulf spill is ten to forty times larger than the Exxon-Valdez spill in Prince William Sound. Eighteen million people are dependent upon the desalinization plants in the Gulf. They're all closed down. They weren't designed to deal with oil. I don't know how they're getting their water. Water's a number one priority in the Middle East. There is none, or very little. There are the Euphrates and Tigris rivers. So water is a number one priority. The dike systems and irrigation channels were all bombed by the United States, like they bombed them in the ancient channels in Cambodia, which initiated the killing by Pol Pot of about three million Cambodians. And those secret bombings, initiated by Nixon and Kissinger, were code named Breakfast, Lunch, and Supper.

In the Gulf live mammals called dugongs. They're sea cows. They're sort of ugly, with tusks like elephants, but they're graceful and elegant and beautiful and curious. The legends of the mermaids were derived from the dugongs. They only live in the Gulf. There are only seven thousand left. They graze on beds of sea grass which can be killed by the toxic hydrocarbons leeching down from the oil on the surface. They themselves can be suffocated when the oil gets into their lungs. If they try and put detergent on the oil to break it up into smaller globules, that's even worse because it gets deep into their lungs. The origin of the mermaid legends is threatened and endangered. Why? Because we had to have a war about oil against someone who wasn't quite sane. You have to ask: Is Bush quite sane? The long-term consequences of this war are profound. Profound. The desert ecology is very fragile and sensitive. Do you know what they did? They drove their tanks all over it and just mashed it up. I often go to Europe and look at where the trenches from the First and Second World Wars were. It looks beautiful now, but by God, it must have been a dreadful sight, with those trenches and the fighting and the killing.

In the First and Second World Wars at least men saw other men with their entrails hanging out and their livers bleeding. At least they got it. These little boys who bombed Iraq didn't see it! They have no comprehension. They see the Ninja turtles and violence on television and sitcoms where one minute someone's grossly murdered and the next everyone's laughing. You see? But when one little girl gets trapped down a well . . . So people really care, but they are psychically numb to what feelings really are. You know? In so being, they're lonely and out of touch with their souls. That's why they can go and hygienically, absolutely lacerate two countries. One of the princes of the royal family of Kuwait said, "Why don't we drop nuclear bombs on Kuwait to liberate Kuwait?" He didn't care. The royal family was in London, living it up, discos, night clubs, and BMWs while the war went on and their people were massacred. That was OK. So, in November, before anyone thought there would be a war because negotiations were still going on, Bechtel, a huge American engineering company, was negotiating with the royal Kuwaiti family to rebuild their country. And they're doing it. It's great for the engineering and construction companies, and the shoveling companies, because they're just shoveling the dead bodies into ditches and shoveling down the buildings, and then they'll rebuild them. So the war's been an enormous success financially.

There's a biologist who went to the forest in Peru and found as many species of ants on one tree as are found in the whole of the United Kingdom. So the number of species in the tropical forests are enormous, and we're chopping them down. I would like to submit that we're not the most significant species on earth. I would like to submit that the elephants are more important than we are. There are only ten thousand elephants left. There used to be millions, when I was a child. They're endangered because we like to wear their tusks on our wrists and our ears. Imagine if I was a baby elephant. I'm standing there with my mother and this thing comes looking like a small ant and goes like that with a stick. The next thing I know my mother, who is one hundred years old, is lying on the ground. Then this man comes up with a chain saw and chops off her tusks. I try to drink milk from her breasts, but the milk's gone. I sit with her for a week as her huge carcass rots in the sun. They say it's OK because when the elephants are gone we'll put their genes in a gene bank. Have you ever heard of anything more arrogant, insensitive and out to lunch than that! If the elephants were killing us and we were almost extinct, they could say, "Well, it's OK if *Homo sapiens* disappears, because we'll put their genes in a gene bank. So one day we'll be able to look at their genes and maybe reconstruct a human being." Do you see what we're doing? The koalas are almost extinct. Do you know the koalas? Have you ever held a koala in your arms? They've got very long claws, but they only eat eucalyptus leaves, little tiny leaves. They don't drink. They've got very efficient kidneys that concentrate their uric acid. You put your nose in their fur and it smells of eucalyptus oil. Beautiful! They're marsupials. They have their babies in their pouches.

We're chopping down our forests. No, the Japanese are chopping down our forests. Because the Australian government started to deal with the Japanese to come in and take the last remaining forests in Australia. We don't have many left. The koalas are endangered. So when I ran for Parliament last year—and I nearly won, I'll tell you about that later—they chopped down a stand of eucalyptus trees beside a highway for "development." Never use the word "development." Never. It's a euphemism for destruction, like "collateral damage," like a "surgical strike," like "we had to destroy the village to save it." Use "destruction." Destruction. They chopped down a stand of trees for destruction to build some shops. The next day, staggering across the highway, were koalas and spiny anteaters, being hit by speeding cars. That's what development is. That's what we're doing in Australia and all over the world.

I think it's time we saw ourselves in the perspective of where we stand on the evolutionary scale. We should start valuing life forms other than ourselves—more than we love ourselves. Or, if we love them, really love them and see them as a creation, the creation of God, then we'll love ourselves enough to save them. Next time you see a beautiful butterfly, just look at it and think how many billions of years it took to evolve. That butterfly has as much right to live and survive as do we. They say the tropical rain forests are here because there are herbs and plants that we can use to cure cancer. Those plants were not put there for our benefit. They evolved to repel certain predators who would eat them. Not for us to cure cancer. We can use them, but not destroy the forest.

I went to the Amazon last year because I was so worried. I'd read about it for years, the Amazonian women and the Amazon jungle. So I went with my son and hired a dugout canoe. I was pretty brave because my husband had just left me and I was feeling pretty awful. But I thought, I'm going to do it. The dugout canoe was double the length of this room. We got on it. It had a plastic roof with a few leaves on it. As soon as we got in we started being bitten by things you couldn't see. These things produced a bite that was so itchy that you nearly went crazy for six weeks, and the more you scratched the more it itched. You got a subcutaneous hemorrhage underneath the bite. On every square inch we had hundreds of bites. We put on the most carcinogenic, anti-mosquito, Vietnam repellent, and it didn't work. There were bees ten times the size of any bee I've ever seen before.

We set off down the Amazon. In the morning we'd wake up at sunrise and go down the Amazon silently into this pink rising sun, in our hammocks, rocking as we went. I've never smelled air so perfumed. None of the perfumes we wear has anything on this air. That's what the Garden of Eden must have smelled like. That's what the earth must have been like before we got here and started destroying it. One-third of the fresh water in the world is in the Amazon. Every afternoon there would be a huge thunderstorm because the trees transpire thousands of gallons a day, each of them, to create their own climate. It rains. The leaves fall and create humus and the bacteria rot the humus. The trees lift up the rotting humus again as their nutrients. It's being chopped down by fast food joints here to grow cheap beef to give you lousy-tasting hamburgers which are no good for your health anyway because they produce hypercholesterolemia, arteriosclerosis, hypertension, strokes and heart attacks, and colonic cancer. A study in the *New England Journal* recently showed that women who eat red meat once a day have a higher incidence than other women of colonic cancer. It probably holds true for men, too. We didn't evolve eating meat. We evolved eating grain. In the 1920s Americans ate much lower on the food chain. That's what you've got to do, because it's much better for your health. The amount of grains that's used to feed the cows in this country would without doubt feed all the people in the world, and two-thirds of the world's children are malnourished and starving. So let's get down to it. Stop being greedy, and anyway it's bad for our health. But let's not think about our health. Let's think about compassion. Compassion for the other people. OK? So there's a big job. That's the number one big job.

The Amazon's being chopped down by McDonald's, who say they're not any more, but they were, and Wendy's. When you chop down the forest you get a bit of grass, and after two years nothing grows because the soil's rendered sterile, and without the rotting humus coming from the forest, ever recycling and regenerating, there's nothing and the grass dies. So they chop more trees down. There's a huge gold rush in the Amazon. The World Bank plans to build, I think, a hundred huge dams there. The World Bank put a road right down the center of the Amazon for "development." Open up a forest like that, then you get side roads and the whole thing goes. They chop down these huge, beautiful cathedral-like trees, giants, and they're left there to rot on the ground. They plant little spindly bananas between them. The Amazon is the lungs of this hemisphere.

The earth's dying. How? Simply because we are filling up the atmosphere with carbon dioxide. We have to drive cars because the auto companies and the oil companies in the 1930s bought up all the mass transit systems of this country and destroyed them on purpose and then they built freeways everywhere so you have to drive cars in order to live. You can't even work around the corner now because all the little corner shops are gone. They've built huge supermarkets in very lonely suburbs and you have to get in the car and drive five miles or so to the big supermarket to get a bottle of milk and a loaf of bread. When you get to the supermarket you go down the aisle with a cart and it's called impulse shopping. They strategically design it so they can advertise things. The staples are at the back of the store. You have to walk through all these aisles to get to the milk and the bread. The Ninja Turtles are at the level of the kids, so the kids are saying, "I want one of those, I saw it on television." Their mother's hair is standing on end. She takes this and that because she's seen it on television and it looks nice and it's packaged in a pink package. This sort of sugar because it's pink. Ten different varieties of sugar. Sugar is sugar is sugar, but it's all packaged to look different. She gets out with a big cart full of packaging and a little bit of food, with screaming kids and probably she's forgotten the milk anyway. She gets in the car and goes home. We add to global warming by getting our milk in little packages. We have to start living in communities. We have to chop down the fences in a city block, start growing our food together, start supporting and loving each other within our block so that we mind our children, get to know old Mrs. Smith and old Mr. Allen and we help the young mothers and start living with compassion and caring. We get a couple of cows and milk them. I was at a college recently in Schenectady. There's a biology professor who said he took the college students out to see where milk comes from. They didn't know. They thought it came from white cardboard cartons and plastic bottles and a girl fainted when the cow defecated because she'd never seen a cow defecate before. It was really disgusting, she said. Interesting, isn't it, how out of touch with nature we are. But we can form communities and start loving and caring for each other. Compassion starts at home and leads to compassion for the nation and compassion for the world. So we start at home. I'm seriously suggesting this. Huge shopping malls have to go. Huge shopping markets have to go. You need to have community stores where you have a big bag of sugar, a big bag of flour, a big bag of rice and we just get our stuff out of these bags. I'll tell you about packaging in a little while, some really neat things to do so that we can save the earth. Because packaging's killing the earth.

Back to the air for a minute. We're all driving cars and pumping out CO^2 and it's great because the oil companies give us cheap gas. Gasoline is less expensive than milk. Milk is a totally renewable product out of cows' breasts, and gasoline will run out in about forty-five years.

The oil supplies. What do we think we're doing driving around? Anyway, if we charged much more for gasoline, people would drive much less, use mass transit, we'd have money to build mass transit systems. Don't drive those stupid cars! One family should only have one car if they have to have a car, or get bicycles. I'm sure many of you do have bicycles. And use the mass transit systems. The more you use them, the more they'll build them. That's one way to go to save the earth. There are four hundred million cars on the earth, and you are in one-third of them. Five percent of the earth's population utilizing 25 percent of the earth's energy.

That's not right. How do you think other people in the world feel about this? What do you think? But George Bush said, in August, when he sent the troops in, "This is about maintaining our way of life." Our way of life? When two-thirds of the world's children are malnourished and starving? That's just not right.

We should all have solar houses. There should be a bill passed tomorrow that every building built in the United States is a solar building: high rises, houses, the lot. Solar panels for hot water. Solar electricity. The technology's here. It's cheap. And solar heating and cooling. Period.

Now how is the earth heating up? This CO^2 hangs around the earth like a big electrical blanket. The light from the sun gets in, heats up the earth and the heat gets trapped. It can't escape. So six out of the last seven years were the hottest on record.

The earth is heating up. I repeat: six out of the last seven years in the 140 years of record-taking have been the hottest on record. We think the worst-case possibility—I think this work comes from a couple of scientists here in Boulder—that with feedback mechanisms of lots of clouds trapping the heat, because as the earth heats there are more clouds which trap more heat, that the earth could heat up eighteen degrees Fahrenheit in fifty years. Jesus. The last ice age was about ten thousand years ago. The earth heated five degrees, but over thousands of years. Never has there been such a rapid gradient or change of temperature in such a short time. Never. What happened? We don't know. We're in the middle of a big experiment. As the oceans heat, the water rises maybe five feet, drowning maybe one-third of the cities on earth, because they're all on the coastline, like New York, Los Angeles, Sydney,

Venice, London, Amsterdam. There will be mass migrations of people which will create tremendous turmoil and disruption in all the other cities. Many will be drowned, because there will be massive tidal waves. There will be cyclones right up toward Canada, and the whole of the United States could turn into one great dustbowl, like in *The Grapes of Wrath* in the 1930s. Nothing will grow. The United States feeds the whole world now with its grain and cows, but if this happens it won't be able to feed itself.

The ozone layer is three kilometers thick up in the stratosphere. If you bring it down to the high pressures at the earth's level it's only three millimeters thick. Before there was ozone there was no oxygen-consuming life. Life created ozone when plankton appeared with chlorophyll. The plankton absorbed carbon dioxide, utilizing solar energy and created oxygen, which floated slowly up to the stratosphere, where it reacted with ultraviolet light to form ozone, O^3. The ozone then started filtering out, like a pair of sunglasses, the ultraviolet light from the sun. Then multicellular organisms could develop. Ultraviolet light is cytotoxic, it kills cells. We use it in medicine as a sterilizing agent. We think after a nuclear war that 80 percent of the ozone could disappear in the Northern Hemisphere. If that happened, and anyone survived and came out of a shelter six or ten weeks later, when the radiation had fallen, the ultraviolet light would be so intense that you would get a third-degree sunburn in half an hour. Then you would be blinded. It would blind every person's eyes on earth, every animal and every insect. In other words, without the ozone, there is no life.

Recently we discovered there's a hole in the ozone over the South Pole. The ozone over the North Pole is getting thinner. Why? Years ago they discovered this great, nifty gas, called CFC, chlorofluorocarbon, which was inert, didn't react with any other chemicals, it wasn't smelly, it didn't hurt us. We used it for refrigeration, air conditioners, and for spray cans—so we spray our hair, we spray our armpits, we spray other stupid parts, we spray spots on the carpet, we spray in ovens. All the furniture we use now is packed or stuffed with plastic full of holes with CFCs in them. Everywhere I travel I find planes full of styrofoam cups. Styrofoam has CFC in it. CFC when released rises slowly, like the oxygen. When it gets to the stratosphere, a chlorine atom breaks off and turns into a Pacman. It starts gobbling up the ozone molecules. As it eats them it's released to do another one. And so on for years and years. It's like nuclear waste. With chlorine in the stratosphere you can never get rid of it. Meanwhile we keep making more. For each one percent decrease in ozone there's a six percent increase in skin cancer. The dermatologists in Australia, who are usually a fairly depressed group, are getting hysterical. They have seen a doubling of malignant melanoma in the last ten years. The ozone's pretty thin in our part of the world. You have to wear a hat and be covered to go out in the sun. The friendly sun that gives life! When we were children we drew the sun with a smile on his face. It's now causing cancer. Malignant melanoma is when you get a black mole and it becomes cancerous. The cell will invade a blood vessel, go up in the blood into the brain and develop a second cancer. Another cell will break off and go to the liver. The cancer is a parasite, and as it grows, utilizing the nutrients of the body, the patient starts shriveling and becoming cachectic (emaciated) like a Belsen survivor and yellow. Then the cancers get into the bone marrow. There's no room to expand, and the bone pain is worse than toothache, dreadful. We really can't stop that pain. The brain is in a fixed box, the calvarium. There's nowhere to expand. So as the tumor grows the patient gets dreadful headaches and starts having seizures and mental aberrations. They become incontinent of urine and feces. They die, in their excreta, in their bed, in the most shocking pain, losing their mental faculties.

So these Australian students who are aware of this and scared about their future went to a conference in London last year where the men of the world gathered to talk about ozone and they said, "Please save our future." One of the men, probably who works for Dow or Monsanto Chemical, who make CFCs, came up to them and said, "Look. My attitude is, if you've got a berth on the Titanic, I want the best berth." That's the attitude of most of the men who run these corporations. Some are good, but most are totally numbed out psychically. They don't want to know, they don't want to hear. They're old anyway. I say, "What about your grandchildren," and they say, "I'm making money." They like the power and they like the money and they've lost their souls and they're killing their grandchildren, their children. The ozone is disappearing at a faster rate than we predicted. If we stop now, it would take eighty-five years to get the ozone back to 1985 levels. If we stop now producing CFCs. They said, "Let us reduce it by 50 percent production by 1995." They can't do it any faster because it's always too much money. That's like me saying to you, "You've got overwhelming septicemia, a bacterial blood infection. I can afford to get rid of half your bacteria, but no more because I'll lose my profits as a doctor. You'll die." The earth is dying. It's terminally ill. We've got an acute clinical emergency. You don't treat a biosystem like that. As the ozone goes the plankton get killed, and the plankton make the oxygen that replenishes the ozone. The trees die. The earth heats up and the plankton die further. Everything relates to everything else. If you get liver failure, the heart fails. If the heart fails, the kidneys fail. Every organ function is dependent upon every other organ. That's why we all have to be in good shape. That's why the earth, which is a living organism, also has to be protected. We thought it was infinite. It's not. Every launch of the space shuttle is for Star Wars. It's all militarily funded now. It's about the end of the earth. Every launch releases 240 tons of concentrated hydrochloric acid HCl, hydrogen, and chlorine. The chlorine breaks off and gets into the stratosphere. If the space program goes ahead as projected, the shuttle, within ten years will have destroyed ten percent of the ozone layer, which is a 60 percent increase in skin cancer. The medical profession has to start moving. We can't wait any more until people walk in with cancer.

Trees. I want you all to feel your neck. If you feel your trachea, you can feel it's sort of crackly. That's the main passage down into both lungs. It divides like branches of a tree and ends in the alveoli, where oxygen is absorbed into the blood and carbon dioxide is breathed out. Trees are upside down lungs. Lungs have a trunk, branches and leaves. The leaves absorb carbon dioxide that we create by burning electricity and gasoline. They breathe out oxygen that rises up to replenish the ozone. The trees are the lungs of the earth. We're taking out the lungs of the earth to pay back foreign debt, so the Japanese use the equivalent of one forest per day in disposable chopsticks, and we still think that wood is good. Wood is obsolete. We've got to stop using wood. It's like me coming to you and saying, "Look, I'm in the business of making glue, I've got to take both your lungs out, boil them up and make glue, because I need your lungs." And you say, "But without my lungs I'll die." And I say, "Too bad. I'm in the business of making glue and I need the money. Thanks a lot."

The trees: if we plant an area the size of the United States with billions of trees, we could use up all the CO^2 created since the beginning of the Industrial Revolution 150 years ago. That's how important they are. Yet we're chopping them down. There's a huge forestry commission in America, chopping them down. Look at the *New York Times* on Sunday. We can hardly carry it! It's a tree. And it's full of ads that no one ever reads, a whole lot of garbage. The papers are full of ads. They're not worth reading these days. They're like comic books. Who wants to read those silly ads? The newspapers should not be privately owned. The media are determining the fate of the earth, and the people who own the newspapers and networks are the people who build the weapons. General Electric owns NBC. They're not going to broadcast anything opposed to war, because they make weapons. That's the way they live. They make good things for life, like stoves, refrigerators, washing machines—and nuclear weapons. They've made every nuclear weapon.

Bill Casey, the ex-head of the CIA, bought ABC when he didn't like one of the programs. Capitol Cities bought it. If you have an uneducated public you can do what you've done about the Gulf war. I'm not saying you, but the powers that be totally brainwash and propagandize people. The people who own the media. Katherine Graham, who owns the *Washington Post,* sits on the board of General Electric. William French Smith, who was the Attorney General under Reagan, was on the board of General Electric. Reagan worked for General Electric for years. They built an all-electric house in the 1960s, and there's a picture of him and Nancy sitting there with their electric house. If we are not educated, then we'll die in ignorance. It's like in medicine. We use a language that no one understands. It's great. We can hide behind it. We go in disguise. We stand over a patient's bed and talk about them over their heads and they don't understand a word we're saying and then they die and they never know how they died. It's total arrogance. It's what the media are doing to the earth. It keeps us numbed with trivia. I go on the *Today* show. Gumbel says, "You've got three minutes to tell us about nuclear war." Thanks a lot. Then Donald Trump's girlfriend gets on, and she gets on for ten minutes. "Well, I don't know if he loves me. I think I love him. I don't know where the money's going. Do I have a good figure? Should I have a face lift?" The media are determining the face of the earth. They're using the trees and the lungs of the earth to give us a whole lot of garbage, mostly comic book stuff. It's all in color now, have you noticed? The *New York Times* has some good news. Read it every day. I don't know about the *Denver Post.* NPR is OK, but it is turning into National Petroleum Radio, isn't it, with Mobil and all sponsoring the ads, but they still do good work. But they're still being controlled by the sponsors of the ads. Think about it.

How do we use paper? We use trees to blow our noses on. I'll tell you what I blow my nose on. This! It's called a handkerchief. It's made of cotton. One handkerchief lasts me four weeks on a trip. It's a bit scungy, a bit stiff, but it's got no germs on it, because when mucus dries the bacteria and the viruses die, so it's fine. Sometimes I wash it, but I don't use trees to blow my nose. It's medically contraindicated to use trees to blow your nose because if we use trees to blow our noses we're killing the earth. It's medically contraindicated to kill the earth because then we'll die, and every other species on the earth.

I saw an ad the other day. Sometimes I can pluck just enough courage to watch television in the United States. I haven't watched much. There were these soft, beautiful, out of focus pictures of these young mothers with little babies drying their tears with Scott tissues. Drying the tears with the baby's future. I call that evil. Then we put trees on our baby's bottoms. When I was a young mother I had three babies under three and I used cloth diapers. I washed them and hung them under the sun. All of you must get rid of your clothes dryers. Hang your clothes out in the sun in the summer and in the winter hang them in the basement with clothespins and a line. That's what we do in Australia. If you all stopped using clothes dryers, the amount of electricity saved would mean you wouldn't need nuclear power in the United States. You don't need clothes dryers. I'm serious. Tomorrow I want you to take your clothes dryers out to the rubbish dump. Just dump them. Don't buy them any more. Boycott General Electric. There's a big boycott going on. Don't buy any of their goods.

I'm not being facetious. This is like washing your hands when you go to the bathroom. You all do, I know you do. You've been well taught since you were little children in kindergarten. I'm being really serious.

So we put trees on our babies' bottoms. They've got dioxin in them, because all white paper contains dioxins, which is almost as mutagenic and carcinogenic as plutonium from Rocky Flats. Baby's have very thin, delicate skin. You put Vaseline on the bottom to stop diaper rash from the urine. The dioxin can easily be absorbed into the blood stream, deposited in the fat tissue. Ten years later the child gets leukemia. It doesn't wear a little flag saying, "I was made by some dioxin that was absorbed from my diaper when I was a baby," because they don't identify their origins. It's got plastic on the outside that lasts four or five hundred years. Proctor & Gamble are making ads now in *Time* magazine with some beautiful, rich black dirt and a diaper beside it, which says, "In five weeks this turns into this," which is a total and absolute lie. A lie. They're lying, using our anxiety to make more money. America throws out fifteen billion diapers. How many trees is that per year? They're put in garbage dumps, packed down, no water gets on it. You can read papers from garbage dumps that are fifty years old. They don't rot because there's no air and no water. So they don't rot and they're not biodegradable. They would be if they were exposed to the air in a compost heap, but they're not.

We use tampons made of trees, with dioxin in them, and we put them in our vaginas. It's medically contraindicated to put dioxin in the vagina because it can be absorbed through the mecosal membrane into our blood and give us cancer. But what are we going to use? In Sweden they have unbleached tampons, but they're still made of trees. That's the most important thing, trees, remember trees. But you can buy cosmetic sponges at the pharmacists' and use those and when they get full you pull them out, rinse them in nice, clean cold water, squeeze them dry and put them back again. When I was a girl there weren't any tampons. I did fine. Didn't need them.

You use paper in the kitchen?—Trees. Don't use trees, use cloth, cotton tea towels. Don't buy unnecessary journals or papers. *Vogue* magazine is made of beautiful glossy paper from my eucalyptus trees, because it's short-fiber glossy paper. We used to think they had no use but now they make great paper. It's full of ads, hardly anything else, and they're all ads for people like me who are getting some wrinkles so if I just slap this thing on costing $50 a tube, which is really lanolin and really costs fifty cents to make, I'll live happily ever after and have great sex. Then I can see women in airplanes looking at these ads and they're thirteen-year-old girls without a blemish dressed up to look like thirty-year-old women and then fifty-year-old women like me stand in front of the mirror and do this trying to think, "Well, maybe I can look like that thirteen-year-old girl in *Vogue* magazine and I end up looking like Nancy Reagan, with all these facelifts." So the cosmetic industry makes billions of dollars on our vanity and aberrant values. It's better to nourish your soul and let that shine through your face. Then you have a beautiful face. So the magazines are full of garbage. Nothing to read. I see people sitting in planes flipping through that stuff. There's nothing there, but they're made of trees. Stop buying them. Junk mail: readdress it to the sender. I want you to think carefully about how you use paper in your lives, because it's trees, the lungs of the earth. Don't forget.

In your house, have one light on, one light bulb, where you are. If there are two people in one room—one light bulb. Never leave any lights on unnecessarily. Two people in two areas, two light bulbs. Throw away your hair dryer. Have your hair cut short. It looks nice. It feels good. We don't need all this puffed up hair anyway. You look better with short hair. I do, it makes me look younger. It's a better way to look younger, OK? Or let your hair dry naturally by blowing in the wind. I want you to know that every time you turn on a switch you're adding to global warming. Because it's carbon producing CO^2. No clothes dryers, no hair dryers, and be wise about the way you use washing machines. Sometimes wash by hand in the basement with soap.

Have you got it? Let's get on to plastic. When I was a child, there was no plastic, and I didn't suffer a severe case of plastic deprivation. I got through OK. I'm a bit traumatized, but I'm OK. I remember the first time I saw plastic. I was about eight. It was a nylon doorknob. They showed it to me like it was a diamond. Then they got laminex. "Wow, laminex, can we stop at the shop where there's laminex so we can have ice cream? It's so jazzy." Then I woke up and my whole world was full of plastic. Plastic is made out of oil, so this war was an oil war, a weapons war and a plastic war. When you make plastic you produce hundreds of toxic disposable carcinogenic compounds which are not necessary and they don't know what to do with them. So the corporations give them to the Mafia to dump in your lakes and sewage systems and ponds at night when no one is looking. That's Number One. Number Two: they put them in ships and sail them around the world and sell them to the Third World. How would you like a ship full of toxic waste? We'll pay you a little bit of money. And the Third World's starving, so they say, "Right." The Third World is the repository for the First World's toxic waste. And nuclear waste, it's getting to be now. We don't need plastic. This jug's plastic. It should be made of glass and rewashed. You can reuse that jug, but think about it . . .

. . . Now back to species extinction. I really hope you feel for the animals, the lion and tigers, the whales, the zebras. I surfed with the dolphins every morning in Byron Bay in Australia. They have brains as big as ours. Dolphins can count and speak in funny phonetics. They're as intelligent as we are, but they just can't communicate with us. They don't think, I'd like a nice human steak tonight. They don't go and kill a human and take out a filet steak from beside the vertebra and cook it up. By snagging dolphins in drift nets sixty kilometers long—to eat tuna fish sandwiches—we kill them. The tuna are being fished out. It's not your God-given right to eat tuna fish sandwiches, however delicious and moist and crunchy and beautiful they are. The seas are being fished out and polluted to death. My daughter's a vegetarian because one day she was in a train and she suddenly got a vision of all the animals she had ever eaten in her life on the field and she stopped.

I want to talk about the compassionate society. What we need is a compassionate society. I just had my gall bladder out and I'll show you my scar. It's really neat. Best surgeon in town. I'm proud of that scar. I stayed in the hospital ten days, and didn't pay a penny. The government paid for it. I go to the doctor and pay $90 to the doctor. I walk next door to the Medicare office and I'm given back $90 in cash. It's my money, it's my taxes, and I'm looked after. I pay forty-nine cents out of every dollar I earn in taxes and I'm proud of it! I don't want my taxes to be reduced. My daughter just finished medical school and it was free. I did medicine, free. Does that surprise you? That's called a compassionate society. That's what you need to have in your country. When American tax dollars are not used for GE or Rockwell International, or Rocky Flats, they're used for you. That's why they had that war, because you were getting a bit out of hand. So you'd all fly flags and wear yellow ribbons and get back into line again. Don't get in line! Get back to the Constitution and the Declaration of Independence! Remember Jefferson and Lincoln and the Gettysburg Address. They're your models, not Bush, I'm afraid to say.

Where are the Lincolns, the Jeffersons, the first woman U.S. president? In this room? Let's talk about women briefly. Fifty-three percent of the population is composed of women. We do two-thirds of the world's work, for which we earn only ten percent of the world's income, because we don't have external genitalia. We own one percent of the property of the world and we have all the babies. That's an absolute, unmitigated fact. And we have no power. And don't talk about Thatcher, because she wasn't a woman. What needs to happen is that a law needs to be passed, the Constitution changed, urgently, that 53 percent of the House and the Senate are women. All sorts of women! Black women, white women, Indian women, good women, bad women, fat women, thin women, old women, young women—the whole spectrum. Then our ethics will prevail. Fifty-three percent will prevail. I guarantee if that happened there will be no more wars, no more starving people in the streets of America, that you will have a free medical care system, that your educational system will be totally free and uniform, that there will be compulsory voting, as in Australia. We have to vote or we get fined $50. And when you vote you know why you're voting. Australians are very proud. It's an absolute privilege to vote, and we damn well know what we're voting for.

There will be compulsory registration. As soon as you register at an address, the post office has your number and your address, and you're automatically registered to vote. That campaigns are only four weeks long instead of two years or four years or six years. That the government funds your campaign. I ran for office and got $.91 from the government for every primary vote I received. It almost paid for my campaign. No funding from corporations—politicians who go into office like this are corporate prostitutes by the time they get elected. Because it costs $4 million to be in the House of Representatives, $6 million to be a senator, and $60 million to be the president. So you have to be a millionaire or you have to have received money like Reagan did from God knows who. But you are not your own person to constitutionally represent your electorate and your people. When I was nearly elected last year—I missed out by 500 votes out of 70,000—my campaign was three weeks long. I received no special money. It was incredible. I was going to—had I been elected—come back every week and hold public meetings in my electorate and say, look, the legislative agenda is this, I want your feedback, what do you want me to do? And I'd say, this is what I think. We would have worked it out together and I would have gone back and voted according to how I was dictated to vote by my people. That's called democracy. D-E-M-O-C-R-A-C-Y. Hands up those of you here who think you live in a true democracy. What was this war about? Who runs your country? See, you all know! You've got to take the power away! There's so few of them. Ten percent of the United States owns 90 percent of the wealth. They're the people who run your country. Do you want that to continue, or do you want access to your own money? Do you? You're the workers, you're the people of America. This is a democracy—make it so! But people say, what can I do? The United States is in a political vacuum, as it was in 1975, when I walked in. I was a woman, an Australian. I said we could get rid of nuclear weapons. People said, you're naïve, ignorant, stupid, foolish, you don't understand the scene and you're a woman. I didn't care. I just went straight through, through obstacles, over them, under them, through them, I didn't care. I wanted my kids to live.

You must be idealistic and you must be naïve and you mustn't be skeptical and you mustn't think of "but, but." Every time you put "but" at the beginning of a sentence you're procrastinating and saying no. Never say "but." I will. Bang. I can speak publicly. Some of you are journalists and writers. Some of you are good at working with the media or pressuring the media. I have a friend in Australia who went on talk shows. She disguised her voice. One time she was Mrs. Brown and the next time she was Mrs. Smith so they always thought it was a different woman. They might be talking about Donald Trump's ex-girlfriend or whatever, but she brings it back to uranium mining and nuclear war. See? It's easy! You can do that with all the talk shows in town. You can work out the agenda of the debate in the media. If you ever see anything that's wrong in a newspaper you ring them up and talk to the editor and say, "That's wrong. This is the data. You are supposed to be ethical journalists and I want the truth published." If you ever see anything wrong on TV you call ABC, call the producer and say, "That's wrong and I want to go on to refute it!" The reason that you're being mugged, mugged intellectually and psychologically by the media is that the right-wingers are incredibly aggressive with them. They are brutal with the media. And the media succumb. Many of the journalists are ethical. So you've got to be as strong as they are, but with love and compassion.

So women hold the gold key to the future, but so do all of you. So does every one of you. You were born for one reason, and so was I. We were born to save the creation. It's clear as the nose on my face. We've got ten years to do it. So now you've got to change your life. And after you go out tonight you might enter the stages of grief, like I've told you you've got cancer. The United States has got cancer. The first stage is shock and disbelief. Next stage is profound and deep depression. Feel it. Have the courage to feel it. Have the courage to feel uncomfortable and feel the pain for the earth. Because that's called love and compassion.

The next stage is anger, where you get really mad and it turns in the brain and you work out what you're going to do with your own special talents. Then you reach acceptance that the earth is dying, but I'm free now. Totally free to save it. And I will. If you stay on the side of hope, optimism and joy, you'll do it. Because the dark of control and deception and lying and self-doubt can't handle the light. We're really at a point now between the forces of evil and the forces of good. Light and dark. Which will prevail? It's us. We're going to prevail.

TOM ATHANASIOU

U.S. POLITICS AND GLOBAL WARMING

"A permanent modern scenario: apocalypse looms, and it doesn't occur . . . Apocalypse has become an event that is happening, and not happening. It may be that some of the most feared events, like those involving the irreparable ruin of the environment, have already happened. But we don't know it yet, because the standards have changed. Or because we do not have the right indexes for measuring the catastrophe. Or simply because this is a catastrophe in slow motion."

—Susan Sontag

The 1990 edition of the Worldwatch Institute's annual *State of the World Report* claims we have about forty years to establish a sustainable economy—or be engulfed in a self-perpetuating spiral of ecological and economic decline. It's an odd, precise figure, the sort usually discounted as a product of apocalyptic excess. These days, though, it seems to warrant extra consideration. For one thing, the elements of the projected catastrophe—from pollution, extinction, and population growth to deforestation and the ecological costs of energy production—have become depressingly familiar. For another, the power, inertia, and sheer dilapidation of the global economy have begun to sink in, as have the depth and power of institutionalized militarism.

More than two decades after the first Earth Day, we are then perhaps only forty years from the abyss. If the greenhouse theorists are right—and the bulk of the evidence suggests that they are—local ecological crises must be seen in the light of, and indeed as elements of, the even more threatening catastrophe of climatic destabilization. This aggregation offers the perverse satisfaction of rendering equivocation and half-measures absurd, but it may also set the stage for a tragic climax that has been centuries in the making.

Death, to misquote Samuel Johnson, concentrates the mind wonderfully, and it's for just this reason that global warming makes so potent a subject of reflection. The frames within which it is presented reveal, with rare clarity, the presumptions and prejudices of the framers. This is true in the media battle between those who emphasize the near-consensus among scientists on the warming and those whose stories abet equivocation and business-as-usual. And it's true in the environmental movement, where the warming, though unproven, is taken dead seriously, and the debate centers on its political and cultural significance.

THE SCOPE OF THE THREAT

The major consequences of a rapid greenhouse warming have been envisioned in detail: dying reefs, withering forests, seas of refugees (many of them leaving the United States), extinction, drought, and crushingly violent storms. Still, and despite the clarity of such foresights, uncertain and prospective events are difficult to force onto the policy agenda—especially in the United States, where much of the ruling elite regards the costs of prevention as a threat more dire than the warming itself.

The bulk of the greenhouse warming is caused by carbon dioxide (CO^2), chlorofluorocarbons (CFCs) and methane, gases which have been called "nontraditional" pollutants because they take their toll not by despoiling isolated regions but by accumulating globally and destabilizing the biosphere as a whole. Carbon dioxide, which because of its sheer abundance is the most damaging of the greenhouse gases, is an unavoidable product of fossil fuel consumption—and the cheap, easy energy available from fossil fuels has played a major and largely unappreciated role in the history of industrial capitalism. Now it seems imperative to drastically reduce the use not only of methane and CFCs, but of fossil fuels as well, even though this reduction implies a radical break with the energy economy that has underlain capitalism from its very earliest days. As subsequent events, the Gulf War and the Earth Summit to name but two, have shown, this break will not come easily.

There is—and this is crucial—much that can be done, though not an indefinite time to do it in. This is clear from the gap between "bad case" and "good case" scenarios, both supplied by the World Resources Institute. In the bad case, no substantive effort is made to slow CO^2

emissions, increase energy efficiency, or speed solar development, although CFC production and use is brought in line with the Montreal Protocol. The outcome? By 2020, an average global temperature of from 1.8 to 5.4 degrees Fahrenheit higher than it was a century ago, and by 2075 a rise of 5.8 to 17.5 degrees! If coal use increases as well—a real possibility, particularly in China—the warming could soon reach a truly staggering magnitude. (Even this isn't the worst case scenario, since there's a possibility of a "super greenhouse effect" set off by a relatively small warming and a series of "positive feedbacks" on it. Melting permafrost, for example, could release massive amounts of methane, an extremely powerful greenhouse gas.)

In the "good case" scenarios, such as they are, strong global efforts to reduce greenhouse-gas emissions allow the atmosphere to stabilize. Oil, gas, and coal prices are sharply increased, per capita energy use declines in industrialized countries, and support for solar development is radically increased. Tropical countries not only stop decimating their rain forests but begin large-scale reforestation efforts. And so on. The World Resources Institute model indicates that, even if all these heroic efforts had begun in 1988, there would still be a warming of 3 to 7 degrees Fahrenheit by 2075, when the temperature would level off. Such a temperature increase, over such a short period of time, is unprecedented in human history, and could well be large enough to cause massive ecological and social disruptions. According to the First Assessment Report of the scientific committee of the Intergovernmental Panel on Climate Change (IPCC), the U.N. agency chartered with the task of coordinating global warming policy, the "state of scientific knowledge" indicates that such a "stabilization" is the best that can be expected, and would require "an immediate reduction in global man-made [CO^2] emissions by 60 to 80%."

So, if greenhouse theory is valid, the whole global economy must be restructured, fundamentally and soon. The longer marketers push their phony optimism, the longer politicians dispute, equivocate, and lie, the longer technicians strain for faith in the viability of half-measures, the worse the odds will get. Not that these are the last days—humans are adaptable and will likely survive (which is more than can be said for lots of other species). But each moment wasted is another step along a path to an ugly and inauspicious future.

As the predictions of greenhouse theory have become familiar, they—like ecology in general—have emerged as key social metrics. We now know, for example, that ours is not a "sustainable" society, and as the ecological crisis worsens this charge becomes damning in a manner that somehow exceeds all prior accusations. It's no wonder, then, that ecological and climactic science are clotted with politics, or that the media frames imposed on greenhouse theory often emphasize "uncertainty," cost, and the putative dangers of "overreaction." The issues here are difficult, for science resists reduction to ideology, even as it can offer ideology its firmest ground. Witness the enduring influence of John Sununu, original architect of U.S. greenhouse policy and probably the first high U.S. official to hold a Ph.D in fluid dynamics, a Ph.D. he uses to disguise a corrupt and technocratic optimism as legitimate scientific skepticism. (It is worth noting that Sununu, who prided himself on his intelligence, was easily replaced as the Bush administration Science Officer by none other than Dan Quayle.)

The outlines of at least the immediate future are clear. The Bush administration, having consistently distinguished itself by the ideological vehemence of its opposition to meaningful antigreenhouse policies, and having forced its allies into line by holding the Earth Summit hostage, has ensured that there will will be no global antigreenhouse regime negotiated soon. Local initiatives will continue, of course, especially in Europe and Japan, which both plan on taking advantage of the widespread concern about global warming to polish their green facades and to increase the energy effiency of their domestic economies. But progress in the world as a whole is an altogether different matter. Absent a sudden, terrifying and very unlikely proof of rapid warming, the massive conversion and tech-transfer initiatives that could make a difference will never leave the drawing boards of the environmental institutes. In the South proper, and particularly in India and China, "development," as it is known, will continue, as will large-scale reliance on coal and other fossil fuels. In the former Soviet Union, rapid progress appears almost as unlikely—the energy crisis is now so bad that even dangerous Chernobyl-style reactors are being kept on line. All in all, it's fair to say that the politics of the greenhouse are inseparable from the politics of the larger world system—which suffers its fossil fuel dependency as only one element in a rich variety of debilitating legacies.

ENVIRONMENTAL OPTIMISM, ECOLOGICAL DESPAIR

The most compelling of the recent greenhouse books are probably Stephen Schneider's, *Global Warming: Are We Entering the Greenhouse Century?*, Michael Oppenheimer and Robert Boyle's, *Dead Heat: The Race Against the Greenhouse Effect*, and Bill McKibben's, *The End of Nature.* Taken together, they form a grim syllabus treating not only global warming but also the environmental movement's break with systemic political analysis. Each chooses, in its own manner and for its own reasons, to present the erosion of climatic stability by the fossil fuel economy—coal and oil!—with barely a nod to the political, economic, or ideological dynamics of the society within which it developed.

Stephen Schneider, head of Interdisciplinary Climate Systems at the National Center for Atmospheric Research, is among the most famous of the greenhouse scientists, and serves well to highlight the contours of mainstream environmentalism. Schneider cuts an interesting figure—the liberal public scientist as statesman of the greenhouse age. His world is big science and big government, and though he spends a good deal of time debating Reaganesque bureaucrats and politicians, he doesn't allow himself to lose hope. Trained in the habits of rationalism, he sees an emergency and thinks the need for a cooperative global response will soon be undeniable. He is a pragmatist, as he believes the times require.

In *Scientific American*'s special 1989 "Managing Planet Earth" issue, Schneider argued that conversion to a postgreenhouse economy would cost "hundreds of billions of dollars every year for many decades, both at home and in financial and technical assistance to developing nations," yet he was confident that this was a realistic possibility. Anticipating a pessimistic reading, he argued that pessimism was too easy, that not long ago "a massive disengagement of NATO and Warsaw Pact forces in Europe also seemed inconceivable." And so it did, to many. But today, with the flush of post–Cold War euphoria long past, the case for pessimism is again obvious. It is well known that world military expenditures, at almost a trillion dollars per year, could feed and educate the entire human race. They could also build a postgreenhouse economy. The question is whether they'll ever be spent doing so.

Optimism can be dangerous. When the Worldwatch Institute's ten-hour series, *The Race to Save the Planet*—which took five years and

$7 million to produce—was recently broadcast in the San Francisco Bay Area, one local critic remarked that it devoted so much time to upbeat segments (designed, presumably, to avoid spreading doom and gloom) that it left the impression that the situation wasn't that grim after all. The producers had stumbled in the precarious tug-of-war of ecological politics, which, despite widespread grass roots activism and an increasingly coherent analysis, is torn between radical despair on the one side and liberal optimism on the other.

Here's an extreme dose of inspirational liberal optimism, from *Dead Heat,* written by Michael Oppenheimer, a senior scientist at the Environmental Defense Fund, and Robert Boyle. This text was reprinted (as "Techno-Hope") in the 1990 Earth Day issue of *Mother Jones*:

> The change began in 1992 when the nations of the world, under the guidance of the United Nations Environmental Program, signed an agreement to limit greenhouse gases. Cynics scoffed at a "toothless" accord, but they failed to notice the underlying currents. Battered by foreign economic invasion and constrained by a limited budget, the United States canceled the Super Collider, the Space Station, and Star Wars and diverted billions to research and education. By the mid-1990s, it had concluded a series of treaties with the Soviet Union, which led gradually to a mutual reduction of forces. But the expected blow to the defense contractors never materialized because the government poured some of the billions of dollars saved into procurement of solar energy sources, and several large companies quickly converted to renewable-energy development. The trend accelerated when the Great Drought of the late 1990s struck and industry began the total phaseout of fossil fuels. Now rich nations compete to supply smaller countries with solar cells rather than weapons.

One must ask the purpose of such prose. Should it be excused as bad exhortatory fiction, or is it true to the dreams of Washington environmentalists? If this is the hope they can imagine, it's no wonder that "radical environmentalism," as it has emerged in the 1980s, chose pessimism.

Examples of radical pessimism are as easy to come by, but Bill McKibben's *The End of Nature* is distinguished by its vivid evocation of greenhouse crisis and by its relentless despair. McKibben is an apostle of deep-ecological radicalism. Not being a scientist, he need not posture at objectivity—yet neither does he accept political and economic explanations of the situation. To even name this society as "capitalist" and insist that the distinctions made thereby are significant strikes him as absurd. The warming is only the last in a long series of attacks on the environment, and politics too small a thing to place against the end of wilderness. We can and should resist—with direct action, by consuming less, wearing sweaters around the house, not having children—but it won't be enough, not really. Soon we'll find ourselves almost alone, with only the plants and animals we've chosen to save, on a desiccated and lonely world.

It's a view so tragic as to be almost absurd, were it not for its desire to face the whole grim truth. With the U.S. administration bent on resisting any real greenhouse treaty, there's a strong temptation to see the measures being taken elsewhere—like the European Community's insistence at the Rio Earth Summit, in the face of the United States' refusal to agree to any fixed targets and timetables for the reduction of CO^2 production, that it would nevertheless reduce its carbon output to 1990 levels by the year 2000—as substantial alternatives. But are they? The Third World is now well along on the road of fossil fuel industrialism—will the Europeans pay to help it go solar instead? In the next forty years? McKibben knows of the calls for massive military cuts and a crash campaign of conversion to a postgreenhouse economy; he just doesn't think it's going to happen.

"UNCERTAINTY" AS IDEOLOGY

In February 1990, when President Bush addressed the United Nation's climatic change panel, many environmentalists were bitterly disappointed. They had allowed campaign rhetoric about a "White House effect" to seduce them into hope for emergency initiatives, and now Bush, instead of giving voice to any spirit of emergency, had insisted that greenhouse policy "be consistent with economic growth and free market principles."

Just days before Bush delivered his speech, revisions had transformed it from one that emphasized the seriousness of global warming to one that emphasized scientific uncertainties and made no recommendations for action. In the preceding months, the media had taken the same turn, buzzing with reports that scientists (minus a few greenhouse radicals) in fact doubted the warming predictions. On December 13, 1989, for example, the *New York Times* ran a cover feature on the "greenhouse skeptics," and *Forbes*—which subsequently advertised itself as "The magazine that's not afraid to take a little heat"—ran an exposé on "The Global Warming Panic" (in its 1989 Christmas issue!).

The backstage maneuvering had been going on for some time, with both greenhouse theorists and skeptics pressing their arguments in Washington as the time for Bush's speech approached. In September 1989, for example, Richard S. Lindzen of M.I.T. and Jerome Namais of the Scripps Institute of Oceanography wrote the White House, arguing that current global warming forecasts "are so inaccurate and fraught with uncertainty as to be useless to policymakers." Sununu and Bush, according to press reports, "welcomed the input."

Lindzen and Namais are both noted meteorologists and members of the National Academy of Sciences. Lindzen, who is perhaps the leader of the antigreenhouse scientists, has made major contributions to atmospheric theory. Their views carry weight. Yet Lindzen's theories are, by his own words, of a "theological or philosophical" nature (*Science,* 12/1/89) and reduce to a faith in the existence of atmospheric dynamics, yet undiscovered, of sufficient magnitude to counter the known effects of the greenhouse gases. That such faith can be used to justify U.S. intransigence in U.N. greenhouse negotiations indicates how strong the political currents running below the surface of "objective" science can be. More specifically, it demonstrates the ideological uses, not only here but in a variety of debates over cancer and toxicity, of the "uncertainty" of scientific data. Incidentally, one of Lindzen's chief claims—that water vapor may diminish rather than amplify global warming—was refuted by research results published only a month after Bush's speech (*Scientific American,* March 1990).

Uncertainty plays such a key role in scientifically loaded policy debates because it converts the question, "What is to be done?" into "Should anything be done at all?" Witness Warren Brookes's *Forbes* article, which asks whether greenhouse warming is "the 1990s version of earlier scares: nuclear winter, cancer-causing cranberries and $100 oil?" and goes on to assert that "just as Marxism is giving way to markets, the political 'greens' seem determined to put the world economy back into the red, using the greenhouse effect to stop unfettered market-based expansion." All this is just a warmup, though, an ideological gloss. His real goal is to justify his claim that even though "60% of the public is convinced [global warming] will worsen," in reality "the evidence of that alleged trend is under increasingly sharp and solid attack."

This claim, common in the popular press, directly contradicts the scientific consensus and the conclusions of the U.N. IPCC's scientific committee. (The United States has its greatest veto power in the policy committee.) Yet because climatic dynamics are both complex and poorly understood, uncertainty can always be made to seem plausible simply by citing data selectively. Brookes, for example, is careful to focus on U.S. statistics, rather than the global statistics that contradict his chosen view.

All scientists acknowledge uncertainties in the atmospheric models. The real debate turns on the meaning of that uncertainty, and its ideological uses. These uses are both conscious and deliberate, as demonstrated by a White House memo to the U.S. IPCC delegation, which was leaked to the press in April 1990. The memo's list of "debates to avoid" included whether "there is or is not" global warming and how much warming could be expected. "In the eyes of the public," it went on, "we will lose this debate. A better approach is to raise the many uncertainties that need to be understood on this issue."

"Uncertainty" has a different meaning in the laboratory than in the White House press room. Though scientists argue over the details, the scientific community accepts the thrust of greenhouse theory for the simple reason that it dovetails with routine laboratory physics. Carbon dioxide, methane, and the CFCs do trap heat; that's why they're called greenhouse gases. The rising atmospheric concentrations of these gases are not in dispute; nor is the geological record, which indicates that increases in CO^2 correlate with increased temperatures. And though the earth's metabolism incorporates many buffers—ice sheets, forests, oceans, clouds—there's no scientific reason to believe that these buffers will neutralize the vast seas of CO^2 that will be spewed into the air in the coming century.

The summer of 1988, with its wilting heat wave and corresponding spike of greenhouse fear, was ages ago in ideological time. (Globally, 1990 was the hottest year on modern record books, but the heat wave will most likely flag these next few years, as high-atmosphere dust from the Mount Pinatubo eruption initiates a short-term cooling.) The U.S. antigreenhouse counter-revolution began in 1989, and today, having bred an absurdly weak but globally vetted greenhouse treaty, it would be wise to brace for a long wave of soothing rhetoric. Even if, by some electoral miracle, U.S. policy changes, it will likely change to match that of Europe—better than the U.S. status quo, but altogether inadequate in the face of the real challenge. The antigreenhouse counter-revolution began in 1989, and today, with militarism and recession pushing ecology and the "peace dividend" out of the news, it's wise to brace for a long wave of denial and lies. Even before the Gulf War, with ecology still in the media foreground, the greenhouse debate had begun to thicken with equivocation. Now, stonewalling is official U.S. policy.

The near future of the debate is reasonably predictable. It is only necessary to project current trends, and to review the history of another atmospheric crisis—the destruction of the ozone layer by chlorinated chemicals. Here, too, laboratory science predicted the threat. Here, too, the difficulty of proving atmospheric damage made it possible for interested powers to frame a scientific near-consensus as controversy—even though it was already clear in 1974 that CFCs damaged the ozone layer. Only the discovery of the Antarctic ozone hole finally turned the tide. (If indeed it has been turned at all: The 1990 revision to the Montreal Protocol allows half again the CFCs produced in the past fifty years to be produced in the next ten, yet, as recent findings have indicated, the ozone shield is thinning fast even over the temperate mid-latitudes.)

Sherwood Rowland, the scientist whose lab discovered the ozone-shredding properties of CFCs, once commented "It is quite common on the scientific side of industry to believe that there aren't any real environmental problems, that there are just public relations problems." It's an astute remark. Public relations, not physics, is the paradigm science of the modern age, and it's difficult to imagine it counting for more than it does today, when 76 percent of the American people describe themselves as environmentalists.

Why, finally, is prudence so difficult, even in the face of a more-than-plausible catastrophe? There are many answers, but rising above the mass is the insistence that the economy be left unfettered unless it can be "proved" that the ecological costs of inaction are absolutely intolerable. Meanwhile, 1990 was the hottest year to date, the year that dying coral reefs (global warming is the chief suspect) became big news, and the fourth straight record year for coal production.

FOSSIL-FUEL DEPENDENCY

The fossil fuel economy is expensive, very expensive. In the United States, subsidies to the automobile industry alone are about as large as the military budget—amounting to $2,200 per car per year, or $400 billion a year! (The U.S. truck and auto fleet now exceeds 180 million vehicles, up from 108 million in 1970. That's one vehicle for every 1.7 Americans, up from one for every 2.4 persons in 1970.) In fact, the real auto subsidy is much larger—although the $400 billion figure includes highway and road construction and repair, as well as other direct support services like police protection and paramedical aid, it omits indirect costs like the estimated $47 billion the United States has annually spent patrolling the Persian Gulf—a figure that has recently been substantially increased. And then there are the billions that go to Big Oil each year as tax shelters and depletion allowances, the health costs associated with the burning of fossil fuels, and the costs of the strategic petroleum reserve and oil spill cleanups. The cost of this last item alone vastly exceeds the entire solar energy budget. As for the ultimate costs of oil and coal dependence, these defy calculation.

The fossil fuels benefit from fantastic, almost unaccountable subsidies—paid in dependence, demoralization, and catastrophe, as well as in cash. In the 1970s, it seemed that a scarcity of oil might force a transition to a new energy economy, but in the last few years more fossil fuel has been discovered than has been extracted from the ground. This trend leaves government regulation standing alone, without increased energy prices to buttress environmental policies—a situation that will likely remain for the indefinite future. According to the *New York Times*, OPEC held a meeting just before the war that focused on Western European moves to reduce pollution by curbing the use of oil. Calling this "a serious challenge," a Saudi official said that OPEC economists would study the environmental concerns of Western Europe and the effects they might have on the use of oil. Now, after the Gulf War, price stability—at a level advantageous to the winners—is the order of the day, and there's little chance that the cost of oil will go high enough to, in the words of Albert T. Sommers, an economist at the Conference Board and something of an unconscious wag, "impair consumption."

The *New York Times Magazine* recently claimed that "many people, throughout the world, believe that the implications—scientific, economic, medical, social, technological and political—of Los Angeles's environmental confrontation foreshadow the showdown awaiting the entire world." It's a plausible claim. If even Los Angeles, one of the world's richest cities, can't control its air pollution, can there be any hope in the larger global "showdown"? At issue, of course, is the auto-industrial economy, or rather, the car. Cars mean individual freedom, and given the social and physical structure of the modern world, and especially of its cities, it's not hard to see why. Roads jam and commutes grow ever longer, but instead of real mass transit (which is hard to build for the low-density cities of the automobile age) we get "auto environments"—quieter cars, CD stereos, recorded novels, cellular phones, and even microwave ovens.

Even technical fixes, long scorned by eco-radicals as means of avoiding substantive changes, are considered threats—to the point where it's hard to imagine a technology as revolutionary as, say, insulation, being used to anything approaching its real potential. In late 1988, a mild EPA report on greenhouse policy became instantly controversial, recommending as it did auto efficiency standards of forty miles per gallon, plantation-grown wood as a fossil fuel substitute, and the aggressive pursuit of solar power. Such initiatives pose no threat to capitalism, at least not in the abstract, though they seem to threaten this particular capitalism, with all its ties—in history, ideology and infrastructure—to cheap fossil fuels.

If there is to be a conversion to a postgreenhouse economy, the power of the fossil fuel sector must be broken. This, obviously, is a tall order, for we inhabit a world in which "cheap" fossil fuels face us on every side, objectified as cities, factories, ruling elites. It will take work to get out of here, and luck, and planning. But, at least in the United States, free market ideology is so strong, and planning held in such ill esteem, that even government research-and-development funds for computer and networking technologies are threatened. With the now undeniable decline of the U.S. economy, this could change, but it will be a long, uphill battle. And even if "industrial policy" does make a comeback in the United States it is far more likely to be shaped by a trade war against Japan than designed to facilitate a social/ecological recovery.

PREVENTION VERSUS ADAPTATION

In greenhouse literature, conversion strategies aimed at reducing the production of greenhouse gases (i.e., carbon taxes aimed to phase out fossil fuels) go by the name of "prevention," while muddling along as the climate changes (i.e., building dikes against rising seas) is known as "adaptation." Environmentalists support prevention, while mainstream economists, following their own failing god, usually advocate "freeing" the market to reshape society (and nature) to the new climate. Usually, the debate is restrained, and the likely specifics of adaptation—political chaos, for example, or ferocious storms—disappear in a cloud of genteel generalization. And though everyone knows that some adaptation will be inevitable, environmentalists don't like to admit it, justifiably fearing that such an admission will help force prevention from the agenda. It's easier, after all, to breed drought-resistant crops (the Israelis are already doing so) than to convert to a sustainable economy; easier to insure against a possible rise in sea level by raising the height of offshore drilling platforms (Shell Oil is already doing so) than to reduce oil consumption.

Stephen Schneider has weighed into the prevention-versus-adaptation debate with the notion of "active adaptation," in which preventive measures are used to slow the warming and a planned postgreenhouse infrastructure is phased in as the existing infrastructure wears out. It's a fine idea, if a bit abstract, and he tries to make it practical as well by arguing that the adaptations necessary to stabilize the atmosphere—conservation, reforestation, and all the rest—would be economically beneficial in themselves, regardless of any threat of global warming.

The U.S. economics establishment, for its part, is wasting no time in combating moves to make prevention strategies appear reasonable. The *New York Times*, in a front page story by economics writer Peter Passell, titled "Cure for Greenhouse Effect: the Costs Will Be Staggering," sketched the drift of official opinion. "Crude initial estimates," Passell opines, indicate that for at least the next fifty years it will be cheaper to adapt to greenhouse warming than to attack its causes. He then presents a number of economists, all regally unconcerned by the "externalities" ignored by their models—storms, starvation, extinction—and suffering little strain extending their traditional views to emerging conditions. For example, Harvard's Thomas Shelling argues that increasing costs for irrigation and flood control will raise the price of food by only 20 percent, that the quality of life 100 years from now will depend as much on technology and capital as on the amount of CO^2 in the air, and that "if money to contain carbon dioxide emissions comes out of other investment, future civilizations could be the losers." In another article, Passell is even more sanguine. Citing Department of Agriculture estimates that a doubling of atmospheric CO^2 would cost $170 billion annually in reduced agricultural productivity, he concluded, "That's a lot of money. But it amounts to just one percent of current world income. As [Bush's Council of Economic Advisors] argues, it is in the same ballpark as the costs of government regulations that now distort food production and reduce its total value. To put it another way, freer markets in agriculture, the Council suggests, could more than offset greenhouse-effect losses."

There are more examples, equally appalling. The antiprevention economists tend to the political right, and generally see the economy as conforming to some idealized notion of free market efficiency. In reality, the economy is anything but efficient, as is shown by the work of physicist and alternative energy analyst Amory Lovins.

A "LEAST COST" ENERGY ECONOMY?

Lovins, best known for his Soft Energy Paths, takes a position so far from the traditional standard that it's hard to believe he's describing the same world. While many economists argue that conversion to a post-greenhouse world is unaffordable, especially in the Third World, Lovins insists that it would be far cheaper to cut greenhouse gas emissions by increasing energy efficiency than to continue along the present path. Further, he sees energy efficiency as a prerequisite for sustainable development, and believes that "far from being costly, abating global warming should, on the whole, be immensely profitable. Improving energy productivity can save the world upwards of a trillion dollars per year—as much as the global military budget."

Lovins isn't crazy. He's simply worked out the "inefficiencies" in world energy markets, in detail, and concluded that the world can be saved by being rationally frugal. In regard to a 1981 book, *Least Cost Energy: Solving the CO2 Problem*, which he co-authored, Lovins comments:

> We began by documenting the potential to save about three-fourths of the energy used in 1973 to run the West German economy. We then imagined, a century hence, an entire world industrialized to that level: a world of eight billion people, with a fivefold gross increase in the World Product and a tenfold increase in developing countries' economic activity. Yet if, in such a world, energy were used in ways that saved money with 1980 prices and technologies, total energy use would fall to a third of today's level . . . Of course, a world with eight billion people industrialized to a West German standard may be unrealistic or undesirable for other reasons. Our point was that an energy policy built on efficiency would enable the earth to support a prosperous civilization that was not plagued by acid rain, global warming, urban smog, nuclear proliferation and deforestation.

And what of Lovins' view that the market makes a good vehicle for such discipline? It makes his work interesting in two respects. First, by showing just how far today's economy diverges from one based on "least cost" energy, he proves the ideological nature of analyses that treat the existing economy as the product of "efficient" market forces. Second, his faith in the market prompts a key question: Why, after all, is our present society so monumentally inefficient? Is it, as Lovins believes, because powerful institutional forces prevent the market from imposing economic discipline? Or is it, as green radicals have long claimed, the very success of the market—in particular its success in "externalizing" social and ecological costs—that is to blame?

Certainly the captains of industry skip out on the bill whenever they can, but this doesn't prove the market compels them to do so, for today's economy is structured as much by militarism and state subsidy as by direct market force. What part, then, does the market play? Is this even an important question, or is it enough to know that countries and corporations alike find profit and comparative advantage in wasted energy? If some new energy policy could change the rules of the game, making it more profitable to pursue a solar transition than to continue along the present disastrous path, would that policy stand a chance of being implemented? Lovins believes that it would, and perhaps he's right. But is such an energy policy possible, given the degree to which the rich and powerful have bound their interests to the fossil fuels? Is it possible soon enough?

THE POLITICS OF EMERGENCY

Like ecological crisis in general, the greenhouse crisis compels us to ask, first of all, what will work. Unfortunately, this isn't a simple question, even in the best of cases—and judging by the rush to parlay the greenhouse crisis into a rebirth for nuclear power, it doesn't appear that much rational, clear-headed pragmatism will come of this emergency. Just how much room remains for cheap maneuvering is clear from the wave of articles we've suffered in the last few years on a "new generation" of "passively safe" reactors. The antinuclear battle, it seems, will have to be fought once again, and this time the battle lines will not be clearly drawn. Senator Wirth caught the spin of greenhouse nuclear boosterism just right when he argued, a few years back, that it's time for the country to get over the "nuclear measles." "The environmentalists will come around," he added. "They can't help but come around."

And some environmentalists have come around. William Reilly, director of the Environmental Protection Agency, is one of them, and so is Schneider, who finds himself compelled to advocate "inherently safe" nukes—in a book published by the Sierra Club! Thus, environmentalists take up the spirit of emergency, but sometimes only deepen the fogs of false necessity that obscure the real choices. Lovins, with his insistence on simple economics, is rather clearer, noting that "investing in nuclear power rather than in far cheaper energy-efficient technologies will make global warming worse." It's a point that alone justifies the end of the nuclear industry. It also shows how, amidst apocalyptic storms, the "least cost" argument can be a welcome tonic—the more you spend on nukes, the less you have for fluorescent bulbs, weatherstripping, solar research, and mass transit.

It's from the strength of such simple economics, ultimately, that "Third Wave Environmentalism" draws its charms. The Third Wavers, from the Worldwatch Institute to the Environmental Defense Fund to the Environmental Protection Agency, seek to yoke the market to the goal of ecological reform—and to avoid stickier political issues—by arguing that the best hope lies in modulating existing markets with new taxes (like carbon taxes) and in creating new markets in abstract goods like tradeable "pollution rights." With such markets in place, both companies and countries could profit by controlling pollution, since any unused space in their pollution allocations could be sold to the highest bidder. The goal of such devices is to "internalize" ecological costs into the economic calculus, and to thereby avoid the absurdities that occur when bureaucracies attempt to micromanage economies. In other words, Third Wavers want to use the market to force the larger economy to adapt to natural limits.

The historical background here is crucial—traditional pollution-control measures have failed, and just about everyone admits it. Further, in the wake of the Eastern Bloc catastrophe, state-centered "planning" is held in poor repute indeed. The Third Wavers, desperate and without faith in democratic forms of planning (if they have even heard of them) see the market as the sole alternative to bureaucratic command-and-control. These days, there are even radical Third Wavers, dreaming of markets that, though still capitalist, have become both ecologically efficient and democratically accountable. It's a desperate dream, to be sure, for it relegates popular opposition to the margins of a market-oriented politics. "Substantive democracy" is just not in the cards. Democracy may be possible, even necessary, but ecological realism demands that the old dream of liberation yield to the "socialization of the market."

Can Third Wave environmentalism work? The debate will last for decades, but the test must come in the real social world. Could a global market in CO^2-emissions rights reduce CO^2 production enough to make a difference? The first problem is determining just how much CO^2 each country would have the "right" to generate in the first place. If any matter was ever complicated, this is it, but it's fair to say that, in general, the issue is split between the North and the South—with the North preferring quotas based on GNP and the South preferring quotas based on population. This is a rather basic disagreement and it's hard to imagine it being overcome without social changes that go far beyond those imagined by Third Wave reformers.

In fact, it's difficult to be optimistic about the prospects for any kind of regulation, direct or market-mediated, as long as the core institutions of society—the market, militarism, property and wage relations, the fossil fuel economy—are taken as surface phenomena amenable to easy manipulation by bureaucratic agencies. Consider Los Angeles again, or any traffic-clogged U.S. city. What institutions were central to its construction? Well, there's the auto-industrial complex, for starters, and also the real-estate market. How shall they be regulated? The Alliance for a Paving Moratorium, a small but reasonably clear-sighted organization, proposes an end to new road construction. It's a simple, lovely idea, and we may perhaps measure our condition by checking to see if we can even take it seriously.

THE THIRD WORLD

The greenhouse debate has split the planet between the industrialized nations and Southern countries like China and India that claim that, since they currently generate only a fraction of the greenhouse gases, they should be substantially aided for cooperating in ways that will impede their development. As things stand, their claim is more than reasonable. The habits of the average North American release five tons of CO^2 into the atmosphere each year, while the global average, an average that includes North Americans, is only half a ton.

From an ecological perspective, everything depends on the Third World following a postgreenhouse path. If it doesn't, conservation gains in the industrialized countries will be swamped by deforestation and increased greenhouse gas production in the Third World—where the rate of growth of energy production, much of it based on burning dirty coal, is twice the global average. Unfortunately, helping the Third World carve out a radical new development path is no more than a rhetorical priority in the North, where all the real effort is going into the post–Cold War scramble for position.

At least environmentalists now understand this situation, something that was not true as recently as five years ago. In fact, both the left and the liberal wings of the environmental movement now see Third World debt as an ecological issue—along with pollution, population, energy production, agriculture, and the rest of it. Today, all serious reviews of the greenhouse crisis agree there's no real solution that doesn't define a new kind of development, one attractive enough to derail the considerable momentum of heavy-metal industrialism. This serves to complicate life for liberal politicians like Senate Majority

Leader George Mitchell, the first U.S. senator to write (with co-author Jack Waugh) a greenhouse book, *World on Fire: Saving an Endangered Earth.* Its most interesting moment comes when Mitchell tries to wedge "sustainable development" into the political agenda. He makes the main point, that "even dramatic improvements in energy efficiency will not be sufficient to protect the environment—if they are confined to the industrialized world," then goes on to call for "retiring the debt of developing countries" and for "technology-transfer, subsidies and loans" designed to "take developing counties beyond the levels of efficiency justified on the basis of free market prices." Brave words, these, from a senator who toured the Persian Gulf before the war, posing with Bush and adding a much-needed bipartisan gloss to his threats of war.

Public relations, as always, is part of the problem. The "development community"—the World Bank and its kin—is abuzz with talk of "sustainable development," but thus far the reality has been considerably less inspiring than the rhetoric. It's the same story with the debt crisis. Certainly the Brady Plan for "debt relief" aims not to lift the debt now crushing the Third World, but only to reduce it enough to avoid open revolt, and thus to continue the agonizing process by which the debt crisis is indefinitely, and profitably, protracted. The workings of the debt-management machinery are familiar enough—new loans and a new market, this time a market in discounted debt. The discounts reflect domestic austerity and international "confidence," and the debt market that sets them seems natural enough in a market-fixated society. Will it, however, ease the burden enough to allow humane development paths? This is an altogether different matter. Much of the Third World is sinking into ecological and social chaos, yet the international response is constrained by the prerogatives of the banks. The banks! This will change only when, in the words of one *New York Times* commentary, a Washington "consensus" develops that "the problems afflicting [the] debtors pose a threat to regional political and economic stability." How, under such conditions, can the Third World be asked to sacrifice for the common good?

The bottom line is that the Third World is profoundly constrained by economic and political dependency on the cores of international power. The industrial nations, with their control of capital and technology, hold the keys to a global postgreenhouse economy. If ecological disaster is to be avoided, they must act soon, decisively and in a way that doesn't simply seek to modernize the terms of Third World dependency. It's difficult to see this happening without a successful and radical campaign for ecological conversion here at home.

And where is that campaign? Stalled as usual, though conversion activists remain optimistic about "the long run." There are, to be sure, grounds for optimism—if the U.S. economy continues its decline, as is likely, pressure for a green "New Deal" of some sort will build. But will it be green enough to stop the warming? Think concretely. What authority would enforce the depreciation of oil company stocks? If this is politically impossible, then what politics and what market structure could motivate the redeployment of the capital now tied up in fossil fuels? Over what time period? What about the overall infrastructure, so much of which wouldn't fit into a postgreenhouse world? Who would take the loss? The government? Is the financing of a solar transition in the Third World really to be left to the World Bank, as indicated by the financing mechanism set up at the Rio Earth Summit? What, finally, will it take to get something more than fatal half-measures?

ECOLOGY AFTER THE COLD WAR

Earth Day 1990 brought a spasm of liberal self-congratulation, a "Good Earthkeeping Seal of Approval," and a victory in the dolphin battle—but little by way of structural reform. Still, 1990 will remain as a milestone, marking the passing of the Cold War as clearly as it marks a watershed in environmental history. The next decade may not be a happy one, but it will see the emergence of a new kind of ecological politics.

Not that there isn't already a radical green politics, or that it hasn't already marked the political landscape. But, far too often, the radicals place their faith in abstract ideals like "nature" and "personal responsibility," and are innocent of any coherent, sensible explanation for ecological crisis. Fortunately, a mature red/green politics is also, finally, emerging—"fortunately" because the need for it is acute. Why do we go to war for oil? Why is economic growth so chaotic and compulsive? Why does technology always seem to betray its promise? These questions simply find no good answers in the moral and biocentric categories of traditional environmentalism.

The green movement has been deeply marked by the silences and fears of Cold War culture, and it will take time for it to learn the significance (and understand the limits) of the socialist tradition. Many if not most ecological radicals still see "politics" as synonymous with self-serving compromise, and "capitalism" as merely an ideological category of a justly moribund left. Their view—that communism and capitalism are only variations on a system of exterminist industrialism—is not without merit, but it's hard to see it as the basis of an adequate politics, if only because its name for the beast, "industrialism," suggests inadequate correctives.

It is a measure of the times that, in the last few years, an essay called "The End of History" and a book called *The End of Nature* both took proud places in the march of literary events. In the first, a State Department functionary named Francis Fukuyama invoked Hegel's philosophy of history to claim the "triumph of liberal democracy" as an event of such significance that now "there will be neither art nor philosophy, just the perpetual caretaking of the museum of human history." In the second, a sensitive young man described the likely outcomes of greenhouse warming, then went on to dismiss all politics as insignificant, and to compose an ode to despair.

McKibben tells the tale of environmental radicals throughout the developed world, who can squeeze neither their fears nor their hopes into the old moulds. That they reject "socialism" along with official environmentalism is not altogether bad news, for the "real" socialism we have known has no just claim to our loyalty. But neither is it good news, for environmentalism—radical or otherwise—has a fair distance to go before it can reasonably hope to meet the challenges of the ecological crisis.

The distinctive culture and ideas of the greens—deep ecology, romantic naturalism, the claim to be "neither right nor left, but out front," animal rights, direct action, the too-simple Luddism that sees only evil in advanced technology—are easy to ridicule. But recall that the ecology movement evolved in a world where socialism, and left radicalism in general, were lost in the shadows of state communism, and that by virtue of its independence it has been able to claim key cultural and technological problems as its own, and to develop its own increasingly radical language. Left greens should remember this, even as they call upon their traditions to study the economic and political aspects of the crisis, deepen the notion of radical democracy, and mark the currents in these all-pervasive and almost invisible capitalist waters.

The coming devastation will breed a vast hatred. It may even be that the ideas of the green hard core—ecological misanthropy most notable among them—are poised for a breakout into larger domains. Fortunately, this is not the only possibility, and radical outrage is not likely to remain eternally constrained within the anticommunist frameworks of Cold War analysis. The ecology movement is full of those just now discovering the pleasures of romanticism, and believing it the essence of true revolution. Far more important than their illusions, though, is the probability that capitalism—like the atmosphere—may soon cease to seem a part of a natural, eternal world.

It's hard to be realistic about the ecological crisis without yielding to the formidable logic of a very grim situation. Still, it is wrong to follow McKibben in attributing the tragedy of the times to some inescapable trajectory toward an ecological holocaust. It is, rather, because our trajectory is not inescapable, because there is so much that could be done, and because so little of it is being done that this is such a dark time. This paralysis is the real tragedy.

A THOUSAND POINTS OF LIGHT

Race, Repression, and Resistance

HOWARD ZINN

COLUMBUS, THE INDIANS, AND HUMAN PROGRESS

George Orwell, who was a very wise man, wrote: "Who controls the past controls the future. And who controls the present controls the past." In other words, those who dominate our society are in a position to write our histories. And if they can do that, they can decide our futures. That is why the telling of the Columbus story is important.

Let me make a confession. I knew very little about Columbus until about twelve years ago, when I began writing my book *A People's History of the United States.* I had a Ph.D. in history from Columbia University—that is, I had the proper training of a historian, and what I knew about Columbus was pretty much what I had learned in elementary school.

But when I began to write *A People's History* I decided I must learn about Columbus. I had already concluded that I did not want to write just another overview of American history—I knew my point of view would be different. I was going to write about the United States from the point of view of those people who had been largely neglected in the history books: the indigenous Americans, black slaves, women, working people, whether native or immigrant.

I wanted to tell the story of the nation's industrial progress from the standpoint, not of Rockefeller and Carnegie and Vanderbilt, but of the people who worked their mines, their oil fields, and those who lost their limbs or their lives building the railroads.

I wanted to tell the story of wars, not from the standpoint of generals and presidents, not from the standpoint of those military heroes whose statues you see all over this country, but through the eyes of the G.I.s, or through the eyes of "the enemy." Yes, why not look at the Mexican War, that great military triumph of the United States, from the viewpoint of the Mexicans?

And so, how must I tell the story of Columbus? I concluded, I must see him through the eyes of the people who were here when he arrived, the people he called "Indians" because he thought he was in Asia.

Well, they left no memoirs, no histories. Their culture was an oral culture, not a written one. Besides, they had been wiped out in a few decades after Columbus's arrival. So I was compelled to turn to the next best thing: the Spaniards who were on the scene at the time. First, Columbus himself; he had kept a journal.

His journal was revealing. He described the people who greeted him when he landed in the Bahamas—they were Arawaks, sometimes called Tainos—and told how they waded out into the sea to greet him and his men, who must have looked and sounded like people from another world, and brought them gifts of various kinds. He described them as peaceable, gentle, and said: "They do not bear arms, and do not know them for I showed them a sword—they took it by the edge and cut themselves."

Throughout his journal, over the next months, Columbus spoke of the native Americans with what seemed like admiring awe: "They are the best people in the world and above all the gentlest—without knowledge of what is evil—nor do they murder or steal . . . they loved their neighbors as themselves and they have the sweetest talk in the world . . . always laughing."

And in a letter he wrote to one of his Spanish patrons, Columbus said: "They are very simple and honest and exceedingly liberal with all they have, none of them refusing anything he may possess when he is asked for it. They exhibit great love toward all others in preference to themselves." But then, in the midst of all this, in his journal, Columbus writes: "They would make fine servants. With fifty men we could subjugate them all and make them do whatever we want."

Yes, this was how Columbus saw the Indians—not as hospitable hosts, but as "servants," to "do whatever we want."

And what did Columbus want? This is not hard to determine. In the first two weeks of journal entries, there is one word that recurs seventy-five times: Gold.

In the standard accounts of Columbus what is emphasized again and again is his religious feeling, his desire to convert the natives to

Christianity, his reverence for the Bible. Yes, he was concerned about God. But more about Gold. Just one additional letter. His was a limited alphabet. Yes, all over the island of Hispaniola, where he, his brothers, his men, spent most of their time, he erected crosses. But also, all over the island, they built gallows—340 of them by the year 1500. Crosses and gallows—that deadly historic juxtaposition.

Columbus, seeing bits of gold among the Indians, concluded there were huge amounts of it. He ordered them to find a certain amount of gold within a certain period of time. And if they did not meet their quota, their arms were hacked off. The others were to learn from this and deliver the gold.

Samuel Eliot Morison, the Harvard historian who was Columbus's admiring biographer, acknowledged this. He wrote: "Whoever thought up this ghastly system, Columbus was responsible for it, as the only means of producing gold for export . . . Those who fled to the mountains were hunted with hounds, and of those who escaped, starvation and disease took toll, while thousands of the poor creatures in desperation took cassava poison to end their miseries."

Morison continues: "So the policy and acts of Columbus for which he alone was responsible began the depopulation of the terrestrial paradise that was Hispaniola in 1492. Of the original natives, estimated by a modern ethnologist at 300,000 in number, one-third were killed off between 1494 and 1496. By 1508, an enumeration showed only 60,000 alive . . . in 1548 Oviedo (Morison is referring to Fernandez de Oviedo, the official Spanish historian of the conquest) doubted whether 500 Indians remained."

But Columbus could not obtain enough gold to send home to impress the King and Queen and his Spanish financiers, so he decided to send back to Spain another kind of loot: slaves. They rounded up about twelve hundred natives, selected five hundred, and these were sent, jammed together, on the voyage across the Atlantic. Two hundred died on the way, of cold, of sickness.

In Columbus's journal, an entry of September, 1498 reads: "From here one might send, in the name of the Holy Trinity, as many slaves as could be sold . . ."

What the Spaniards did to the Indians is told in horrifying detail by Bartolome de las Casas, whose writings give the most thorough account of the Spanish-Indian encounter. Las Casas was a Dominican priest who came to the New World a few years after Columbus, spent 40 years on Hispaniola and nearby islands, and became the leading advocate in Spain for the rights of the natives. Las Casas, in his book *The Devastation of the Indies*, writes of the Arawaks: ". . . of all the infinite universe of humanity, these people are the most guileless, the most devoid of wickedness and duplicity . . . yet into this sheepfold . . . there came some Spaniards who immediately behaved like ravening beasts . . . Their reason for killing and destroying . . . is that the Christians have an ultimate aim which is to acquire gold . . ."

The cruelties multiplied. Las Casas saw soldiers stabbing Indians for sport, dashing babies' heads on rocks. And when the Indians resisted, the Spaniards hunted them down, equipped for killing with horses, armor plate, lances, pikes, rifles, crossbows, and vicious dogs. Indians who took things belonging to the Spaniards—they were not accustomed to the concept of private ownership and gave freely of their own possessions—were beheaded, or burned at the stake.

Las Casas's testimony was corroborated by other eyewitnesses. A group of Dominican friars, addressing the Spanish monarchy in 1519, hoping for the Spanish government to intercede, told about unspeakable atrocities, children thrown to dogs to be devoured, newborn babies born to women prisoners flung into the jungle to die.

Forced labor in the mines and on the land led to much sickness and death. Many children died because their mothers, overworked and starved, had no milk for them. Las Casas, in Cuba, estimated that seven thousand children died in three months.

The greatest toll was taken by sickness, because the Europeans brought with them diseases against which the natives had no immunity: typhoid, typhus, diphtheria, and smallpox.

As in any military conquest, women were subjected to especially brutal treatment. One Italian nobleman named Cuneo recorded an early sexual encounter. The "Admiral" he refers to is Columbus, who, as part of his agreement with the Spanish monarchy, insisted he be made an Admiral. Cuneo wrote:

> . . . I captured a very beautiful Carib woman, whom the said Lord Admiral gave to me and with whom . . . I conceived desire to take

> pleasure. I wanted to put my desire into execution but she did not want it and treated me with her finger nails in such a manner that I wished I had never begun. But seeing that, I took a rope and thrashed her well . . . Finally we came to an agreement.

There is other evidence which adds up to a picture of widespread rape of native women. Samuel Eliot Morison wrote: "In the Bahamas, Cuba and Hispaniola they found young and beautiful women, who everywhere were naked, in most places accessible, and presumably complaisant." Who presumes this? Morison, and so many others.

Morison saw the conquest as so many writers after him have done, as one of the great romantic adventures of world history. He seemed to get carried away by what appeared to him as a masculine conquest. He wrote:

> Never again may mortal men hope to recapture the amazement, the wonder, the delight of those October days in 1492, when the new world gracefully yielded her virginity to the conquering Castilians.

The language of Cuneo ("we came to an agreement"), and of Morison ("gracefully yielded") written almost five hundred years apart, surely suggests how persistent through modern history has been the mythology that rationalizes sexual brutality by seeing it as "complaisant."

So, I read Columbus's journal, I read las Casas. I also read Hans Koning's pioneering work of our time—*Columbus: His Enterprise*, which, at the time I wrote *A People's History* was the only contemporary account I could find which departed from the standard treatment.

When my book appeared, I began to get letters from all over the country about it. Here was a book of six hundred pages, starting with Columbus, ending with the 1970s, but most of the letters I got from readers were about one subject: Columbus. I could have interpreted this to mean that, since this was the very beginning of the book, that's all these people had read. But no, it seemed that the Columbus story was simply the part of my book that readers found most startling. Because every American, from elementary school on, learns the Columbus story, and learns it the same way: "In Fourteen Hundred and Ninety Two, Columbus Sailed the Ocean Blue."

How many of you have heard of Tigard, Oregon? Well, I didn't, until, about seven years ago, I began receiving, every semester, a bunch of letters, twenty or thirty, from students at one high school in Tigard, Oregon. It seems that their teacher was having them (knowing high schools, I almost said "forcing them to") read my *People's History.* He was photocopying a number of chapters and giving them to the students. And then he had them write letters to me, with comments and questions. Roughly half of them thanked me for giving them data which they had never seen before. The others were angry, or wondered how I got such information, and how I had arrived at such outrageous conclusions.

One high school student named Bethany wrote: "Out of all the articles that I've read of yours I found 'Columbus, the Indians, and Human Progress' the most shocking." Another student named Brian, seventeen years old, wrote: "An example of the confusion I feel after reading your article concerns Columbus coming to America . . . According to you, it seems he came for women, slaves, and gold. You say that Columbus physically abused the Indians that didn't help him find gold. You've said you have gained a lot of this information from Columbus's own journal. I am wondering if there is such a journal, and if so, why isn't it part of our history. Why isn't any of what you say in my history book, or in history books people have access to each day?"

I pondered this letter. It could be interpreted to mean that the writer was indignant that no other history books had told him what I did. Or, as was more likely, he was saying: "I don't believe a word of what you write! You made this up!"

I am not surprised at such reactions. It tells something about the claims of pluralism and diversity in American culture, the pride in our "free society," that generation after generation has learned exactly the same set of facts about Columbus, and finished their education with the same glaring omissions.

A schoolteacher in Portland, Oregon, named Bill Bigelow has undertaken a crusade to change the way the Columbus story is taught all over America. He tells of how he sometimes starts a new class. He goes over to a girl sitting in the front row, and takes her purse. She says: "You took my purse!" Bigelow responds: "No, I discovered it."

Bill Bigelow did a study of recent children's books on Columbus. He found them remarkably alike in their repetition of the traditional point of view. A typical fifth-grade biography of Columbus begins: "There once was a boy who loved the salty sea." Well! I can imagine a children's biography of Attila the Hun beginning with the sentence: "There once was a boy who loved horses."

Another children's book in Bigelow's study, this time for second graders reads: "The King and queen looked at the gold and the Indians. They listened in wonder to Columbus's stories of adventure. Then they all went to church to pray and sing. Tears of joy filled Columbus's eyes."

I once spoke about Columbus to a workshop of schoolteachers, and one of them suggested that school children were too young to hear of the horrors recounted by las Casas and others. Other teachers disagreed, said children's stories include plenty of violence, but the perpetrators are witches and monsters and "bad people," not national heroes who have holidays named after them.

Some of the teachers made suggestions on how the truth could be told in a way that would not frighten children unnecessarily, but that would avoid the falsification of history now taking place.

The arguments about children "not being ready to hear the truth" does not account for the fact that in American society, when the children grow up, they still are not told the truth. As I said earlier, right up through graduate school I was not presented with the information that would counter the myths told to me in the early grades. And it is clear that my experience is typical, judging from the shocked reactions to my book that I have received from readers of all ages.

If you look in an adult book, the *Columbia Encyclopedia* (my edition was put together in 1950 but all the relevant information was available then, including Morison's biography), there is a long entry on Columbus (about a thousand words) but you will find no mention of the atrocities committed by him and his men.

In the 1986 edition of the *Columbia History of the World*, there are several mentions of Columbus, but nothing about what he did to the natives. Several pages are devoted to "Spain and Portugal in America," in which the treatment of the native population is presented as a matter of controversy, among theologians at that time, and among historians today. You can get the flavor of this "balanced approach," containing a nugget of reality, by the following passage from that History:

> The determination of the Crown and the Church to Christianize the Indians, the need for labor to exploit the new lands, and the attempts of some Spaniards to protect the Indians resulted in a very remarkable complex of customs, laws, and institutions which even today leads historians to contradictory conclusions about Spanish rule in America . . . Academic disputes flourish on this debatable and in a sense insoluble question, but there is no doubt that cruelty, overwork, and disease resulted in an appalling depopulation. There were, according to recent estimates, about 25 million Indians in Mexico in 1519, slightly more than 1 million in 1605.

Despite this scholarly language—"contradictory conclusions . . . academic disputes . . . insoluble question"—there is no real dispute about the facts of enslavement, forced labor, rape, murder, the taking of hostages, the ravages of diseases carried from Europe, and the wiping out of huge numbers of native people. The only dispute is over how much emphasis is to be placed on these facts, and how they carry over into the issues of our time.

For instance, Samuel Eliot Morison does spend some time detailing the treatment of the natives by Columbus and his men, and uses the word "genocide" to describe the overall effect of the "discovery." But he buries this in the midst of a long, admiring treatment of Columbus, and sums up his view in the concluding paragraph of his popular book *Christopher Columbus, Mariner*, as follows:

> He had his faults and his defects, but they were largely the defects of the qualities that made him great—his indomitable will, his superb faith in God and in his own mission as the Christ-bearer to lands beyond the seas, his stubborn persistence despite neglect, poverty and discouragement. But there was no flaw, no dark side to the most outstanding and essential of all his qualities—his seamanship.

Yes, his seamanship!

Let me make myself clear. I am not interested in either denouncing or exalting Columbus. It is too late for that. We are not writing a letter of recommendation for him to decide his qualifications for undertaking another voyage to another part of the universe. To me, the Columbus story is important for what it tells us about ourselves, about our time, about the decisions we have to make for our century, for the next century.

Why this great controversy today about Columbus and the celebration of the quincentennial? Why the indignation of Native Americans and others about the glorification of that conqueror? Why the heated defense of Columbus by others? The intensity of the debate can only be because it is not about 1492, it is about 1992.

We can get a clue to this if we look back a hundred years to 1892, the year of the quadricentennial. There were great celebrations in Chicago and New York. In New York there were five days of parades, fireworks, military marches, naval pageants, a million visitors to the city, a memorial statue unveiled at a corner of Central Park, now known as Columbus Circle. A celebratory meeting took place at Carnegie Hall, addressed by Chauncey DePew.

You might not know the name of Chauncey DePew, unless you recently looked at Gustavus Myers's classic work, *A History of the Great American Fortunes.* In that book, Chauncey DePew is described as the front man for Cornelius Vanderbilt and his New York Central railroad. DePew traveled to Albany, the capital of New York State, with satchels of money and free railroad passes for members of the New York State legislature, and came away with subsidies and land grants for the New York Central.

DePew saw the Columbus festivities as a celebration of wealth and prosperity—you might say, as a self-celebration. He said that the quadricentennial event "marks the wealth and the civilization of a great people . . . it marks the things that belong to their comfort and their ease, their pleasure and their luxuries . . . and their power."

We might note that at the time he said this, there was much suffering among the working poor of America, huddled in city slums, their children sick and undernourished. The plight of people who worked on the land—which at this time was a considerable part of the population—was desperate, leading to the anger of the Farmers' Alliances and the rise of the People's (Populist) Party. And the following year, 1893 was a time of economic crisis and widespread misery.

DePew must have sensed, as he stood on the platform at Carnegie Hall, some murmurings of discontent at the smugness that accompanied the Columbus celebrations, for he said: "If there is anything I detest . . . it is that spirit of historical inquiry which doubts everything; that modern spirit which destroys all the illusions and all the heroes which have been the inspiration of patriotism through all the centuries."

So, to celebrate Columbus was to be patriotic. To doubt was to be unpatriotic. And what did "patriotism" mean to DePew? It meant the glorification of expansion and conquest—which Columbus represented, and which America represented. It was just six years after his speech that the United States, expelling Spain from Cuba, began its own long occupation (sporadically military, continuously political and economic) of Cuba, took Puerto Rico and Hawaii, and began its bloody war against the Filipinos to take over their country.

That "patriotism" which was tied to the celebration of Columbus, and the celebration of conquest, was reinforced in World War II by the emergence of the United States as the super power, all the old European empires now in decline. At that time, Henry Luce, the powerful president-maker and multimillionaire, owner of *Time*, *Life*, and *Fortune* (not just the publications, but the things!) wrote that the twentieth century was turning into the "American Century," in which the United States would have its way in the world.

George Bush, accepting the presidential nomination in 1988, said: "This has been called the American Century because in it we were the dominant force for good in the world . . . Now we are on the verge of a new century, and what country's name will it bear? I say it will be another American Century."

What arrogance! That the twenty-first century, when we should be getting away from the murderous jingoism of this century, should already be anticipated as an American century, or as any one nation's century. Bush must think of himself as a new Columbus, "discovering" and planting his nation's flag on new worlds because he called for a U.S. colony on the moon early in the next century. And forecast a mission to Mars in the year 2019.

The "patriotism" that Chauncey Depew invoked in celebrating Columbus was profoundly tied to the notion of the inferiority of the conquered peoples. Columbus's attacks on the Indians were justified by their status as subhumans. The taking of Texas and much of Mexico by the United States just before the Civil War was done with the same racist rationale. Sam Houston, the first governor of Texas, proclaimed: "The Anglo-Saxon race must pervade the whole southern extremity of this vast continent. The Mexicans are no better than the Indians and I see no reason why we should not take their land."

At the start of the twentieth century, the violence of the new American expansionism into the Caribbean and the Pacific was accepted because we were dealing with lesser beings.

In the year 1900, Chauncey DePew, by that time a U.S. senator, spoke again in Carnegie Hall, this time to support Theodore Roosevelt's candidacy for vice president. Celebrating the conquest of the Philippines as a beginning of the American penetration of China and more, he proclaimed: "The guns of Dewey in Manila Bay were heard across Asia and Africa, they echoed through the palace at Peking and brought to the Oriental mind a new and potent force among western nations. We, in common with the countries of Europe, are striving to enter the limitless markets of the east . . . These people respect nothing but power. I believe the Philippines will be enormous markets and sources of wealth."

Theodore Roosevelt, who appears endlessly on lists of our "great presidents," and whose face is one of the four colossal sculptures of American presidents (along with Washington, Jefferson, Lincoln) carved into Mount Rushmore in South Dakota, was the quintessential racist-imperialist. He was furious, back in 1893, when President Cleveland failed to annex Hawaii, telling the Naval War College it was "a crime against white civilization." In his book *The Strenuous Life*, Roosevelt wrote: "Of course our whole national history has been one of expansion . . . that the barbarians recede or are conquered . . . is due solely to the power of the mighty civilized races which have not lost the fighting instinct."

An Army officer in the Philippines put it even more bluntly: "There is no use mincing words . . . We exterminated the American Indians and I guess most of us are proud of it . . . and we must have no scruples about exterminating this other race standing in the way of progress and enlightenment, if it is necessary . . ."

The official historian of the Indies in the early 16th century, Fernandez de Oviedo, did not deny what was done to natives by the conquistadores. He described "innumerable cruel deaths as countless as the stars." But this was acceptable, because "to use gunpowder against pagans is to offer incense to the Lord." (One is reminded of President McKinley's decision to send the army and navy to take the Philippines, saying it was the duty of the United States to "Christianize and civilize" the Filipinos.)

Against las Casas's pleas for mercy to the Indians, the theologian Juan Gines de Sepulveda declared: "How can we doubt that these people, so uncivilized, so barbaric, so contaminated with so many sins and obscenities have been justly conquered?"

Sepulveda in the year 1531 visited his former college in Spain and was outraged by seeing the students there protesting Spain's war against Turkey. The students were saying: "All war . . . is contrary to the Catholic religion."

This led him to write a philosophical defense of the Spanish treatment of the Indians. He quoted Aristotle, who wrote in his *Politics* that some people were "slaves by nature," who "should be hunted down like wild beasts in order to bring them to the correct way of life."

Las Casas responded: "Let us send Aristotle packing, for we have in our favor the command of Christ: Thou shalt love thy neighbor as thyself."

The dehumanization of the "enemy" has been a necessary accompaniment to wars of conquest. It is easier to explain atrocities if they are committed against infidels, or people of an inferior race. Slavery and racial segregation in the United States, and European imperialism in Asia and Africa, were justified in this way.

The bombing of Vietnamese villages by the United States, the search-and-destroy missions, the My Lai massacre, were all made palatable to their perpetrators by the idea that the victims were not human. They were "gooks" or "Communists," and deserved what they received.

In the Gulf War, the dehumanization of the Iraqis consisted of not recognizing their existence. We were not bombing women, children, not bombing and shelling ordinary Iraqi young men in the act of flight and surrender. We were acting against a Hitler-like monster, Saddam Hussein, although the people we were killing were the Iraqi victims of this monster. When General Colin Powell was asked about Iraqi casualties he said that was "really not a matter I am terribly interested in."

The American people were led to accept the violence of the war in Iraq because the Iraqis were made invisible—because the United States only used "smart bombs." The major media ignored the enormous death toll in Iraq, ignored the report of the Harvard medical team that visited Iraq shortly after the war and found that tens of thousands of Iraqi children were dying because of the bombing of the water supply and the resultant epidemics of disease.

The celebrations of Columbus are declared to be celebrations not just of his maritime exploits but of "progress," of his arrival in the Bahamas as the beginning of that much-praised five hundred years of "Western civilization." But those concepts need to be re-examined. When Gandhi was once asked what he thought about Western civilization, he replied: "It's a good idea."

The point is not to deny the benefits of "progress" and "civilization"—by which are meant advances in technology, knowledge, science, health, education, and standards of living. But there is a question to be asked: progress yes, but at what human cost?

Is progress simply to be measured in the statistics of industrial and technological change, without regard to the consequences of that "progress" for human beings? Would we accept a Russian justification of Stalin's rule, including the enormous toll in human suffering, on the ground that he made Russia a great industrial power?

I recall that when my high school classes in American history came to the period after the Civil War, roughly the years between that war and World War I, it was looked on as the Gilded Age, the period of the great Industrial Revolution, when the United States became an economic giant. I remember how thrilled we were to learn of the dramatic growth of the steel and oil industries, of the building of the great fortunes, of the criss-crossing of the country by the railroads.

We were not told of the human cost of this great industrial progress: how the huge production of cotton came from the labor of black slaves, how the textile industry was built up by the labor of young girls who went into the mills at twelve and died at twenty-five; how the railroads were constructed by Irish and Chinese immigrants who were literally worked to death, in the heat of summer and cold of winter; how working people, immigrants and native-born, had to go out on strike and be beaten by police and jailed by National Guardsmen before they could win the eight-hour workday; how the children of the working class, in the slums of the city, had to drink polluted water and, and how they died early of malnutrition and disease. All this in the name of "progress."

And yes, there are huge benefits from industrialization, science, technology, medicine. But so far, in these five hundred years of Western civilization, of Western domination of the rest of the world, most of those benefits have gone to a small part of the human race. For billions of people in the Third World, they still face starvation, homelessness, disease, and the early deaths of their children.

Did the Columbus expeditions mark the transition from savagery to civilization? What of the Indian civilizations which had been built up over thousands of years before Columbus came? Las Casas and others marveled at the spirit of sharing and generosity which marked the Indian societies, the communal buildings in which they lived, their aesthetic sensibilities, the egalitarianism among men and women.

The British colonists in North America were startled at the democracy of the Iroquois—the tribes who occupied much of New York and Pennsylvania. The American historian Gary Nash describes Iroquois culture: "No laws and ordinances, sheriffs and constables, judges and juries, or courts or jails—the apparatus of authority in European societies—were to be found in the northeast woodlands prior to European arrival. Yet boundaries of acceptable behavior were firmly set. Though priding themselves on the autonomous individual, the Iroquois maintained a strict sense of right and wrong . . ."

In the course of westward expansion, the new nation, the United States, stole the Indians' land, killed them when they resisted, destroyed their sources of food and shelter, pushed them into smaller and smaller sections of the country, and went about the systematic destruction of Indian society. At the time of the Black Hawk War in the 1830s—one of hundreds of wars waged against the Indians of North America—Lewis Cass, the governor of the Michigan territory, referred to his taking of millions of acres from the Indians as "the progress of civilization." He said: "A barbarous people cannot live in contact with a civilized community."

We get a sense of how "barbarous" these Indians were when, in the 1880s, Congress prepared legislation to break up the communal lands in which Indians still live, into small private possessions, what today some people would call, admiringly, "privatization." Senator Henry Dawes, author of this legislation, visited the Cherokee Nation, and described what he found: ". . . there was not a family in that whole nation that had not a home of its own. There was not a pauper in that nation, and the nation did not owe a dollar . . . it built its own schools and its hospitals. Yet the defect of the system was apparent. They have got as far as they can go, because they own their land in common . . . there is not enterprise to make your home any better than that of your neighbors. There is no selfishness, which is at the bottom of civilization."

That selfishness at the bottom of "civilization" is connected with what drove Columbus on, and what is much-praised today, as American political leaders and the media speak about how the West will do a great favor to the Soviet Union and Eastern Europe by introducing "the profit motive."

Granted, there may be certain ways in which the incentive of profit may be helpful in economic development, but that incentive, in the history of the "free market" in the West, has had horrendous consequences. It led, throughout the centuries of "Western Civilization" to a ruthless imperialism.

In Joseph Conrad's novel *Heart of Darkness*, written in the 1890s, after some time spent in the Upper Congo of Africa, he describes the work done by black men in chains on behalf of white men who were interested only in ivory. He writes: "The word 'ivory' rang in the air, was whispered, was sighed. You would think they were praying to it . . . To tear treasure out of the bowels of the land was their desire, with no more moral purpose at the back of it than there is in burglars breaking into a safe."

The uncontrolled drive for profit has led to enormous human suffering, exploitation, slavery, cruelty in the workplace, dangerous working conditions, child labor, the destruction of land and forests, the poisoning of the air we breathe, the water we drink, the food we eat.

In his 1933 autobiography, Chief Luther Standing Bear wrote: "True the white man brought great change. But the varied fruits of his civilization, though highly colored and inviting, are sickening and deadening. And if it be the part of civilization to maim, rob, and thwart, then what is progress? I am going to venture that the man who sat on the ground in his tipi meditating on life and its meaning, accepting the kinship of all creatures, and acknowledging unity with the universe of things, was infusing into his being the true essence of civilization."

The present threats to the environment have caused a reconsideration among scientists and other scholars, of the value of "progress" as it has been so far defined. In December of 1991 there was a two-day conference at M.I.T., in which fifty scientists and historians discussed the idea of progress in Western thought. Here is part of the report on that conference in the *Boston Globe.*

> In a world where resources are being squandered and the environment poisoned, participants in an M.I.T. conference said yesterday, it is time for people to start thinking in terms of sustainability and stability rather than growth and progress . . . Verbal fireworks and heated exchanges that sometimes grew into shouting matches punctuated the discussions among scholars of economics, religion, medicine, history and the sciences.

One of the participants, historian Leo Marx, said that working toward a more harmonious coexistence with nature is itself a kind of progress, but different than the traditional one in which people try to overpower nature.

So, to look back at Columbus in a critical way is to raise all these questions about progress, civilization, our relations with one another, our relationship to the natural world.

You probably have heard—as I have, quite often—that it is wrong for us to treat the Columbus story the way we do. What they say is: "You are taking Columbus out of context, looking at him with the eyes of the 20th century. You must not superimpose the values of our time on events that took place 500 years ago. That is ahistorical."

I find this argument strange. Does it mean that cruelty, exploitation, greed, enslavement, violence against helpless people, are values peculiar to the fifteenth and sixteenth centuries? And that we in the twentieth century, are beyond that? Are there not certain human values which are common to the age of Columbus and to our own? Proof of that is that both in his time and in ours there were enslavers and exploiters; in both his time and ours there were those who protested against that, on behalf of human rights.

It is encouraging that, in this year of the quincentennial, there is a wave of protest, unprecedented in all the years of celebration of Columbus, all over the United States, and throughout the Americas. Much of this protest is being led by Indians, who are organizing conferences and meetings, who are engaging in acts of civil disobedience, who are trying to educate the American public about what really happened five hundred years ago, and what it tells us about the issues of our time.

There is a new generation of teachers in our schools, and many of them are insisting that the Columbus story be told from the point of view of Native Americans. In the fall of 1990 I was telephoned from Los Angeles by a talk-show host who wanted to discuss Columbus. Also on the line was a high school student in that city, named Blake Lindsey, who had insisted on addressing the Los Angeles City Council to oppose the traditional Columbus Day celebration. She told them of the genocide committed by the Spaniards against the Arawak Indians. The City Council did not respond.

Someone called in on that talk show, introducing herself as a woman who had emigrated from Haiti. She said: "The girl is right—we have no Indians left—in our last uprising against the government the people knocked down the statue of Columbus and now it is in the basement of the city hall in Port-au-Prince." The caller finished by saying: "Why don't we build statues for the aborigines?"

Despite the textbooks still in use, more teachers and students are questioning. Bill Bigelow reports on the reactions of his students after he introduces them to reading material which contradicts the traditional histories. One student wrote: "In 1492, Columbus sailed the ocean blue . . . That story is about as complete as Swiss cheese."

Another wrote a critique of her American history textbook to the publisher, Allyn and Bacon, pointing to many important omissions in that text. She said: "I'll just pick one topic to keep it simple. How about Columbus?"

Another student: "It seemed to me as if the publishers had just printed up some glory story that was supposed to make us feel more patriotic about our country . . . They want us to look at our country as great and powerful and forever right . . . We're being fed lies."

When students discover that in the very first history they learn—the story of Columbus—they have not been told the whole truth, it leads to a healthy skepticism about all of their historical education. One of Bigelow's students, named Rebecca, wrote: "What does it matter who discovered America, really?. . . But the thought that I've been lied to all my life about this, and who knows what else, really makes me angry."

This new critical thinking in the schools and in the colleges seems to frighten those who have glorified what is called "Western Civilization." Reagan's Secretary of Education, William Bennett, in his 1984 "Report on the Humanities in Higher Education," writes of Western civilization as "our common culture . . . its highest ideas and aspirations."

One of the most ferocious defenders of Western civilization is philosopher Alan Bloom, who wrote *The Closing of the American Mind* in a spirit of panic at what the social movements of the 1960s had done to change the educational atmosphere of American universities. He was frightened by the student demonstrations he saw at Cornell, which he saw as a terrible interference with education.

Bloom's idea of education was a small group of very smart students, in an elite university, studying Plato and Aristotle, and refusing to be disturbed in their contemplation by the noise outside their windows of students rallying against racism or protesting against the war in Vietnam.

As I read him, I was reminded of some of my colleagues, when I was teaching in a black college in Atlanta, Georgia, at the time of the civil rights movement, who shook their heads in disapproval when our students left their classes to sit-in, to be arrested in protest against racial segregation. These students were neglecting their education, they said. In fact, these students were learning more in a few weeks of participation in social struggle than they could learn in a year of going to class.

What a narrow, stunted understanding of education! It corresponds perfectly to the view of history which insists that Western civilization is the summit of human achievement. As Bloom wrote in his book: ". . . only in the Western nations, i.e., those influenced by Greek philosophy, is there some willingness to doubt the identification of the good with one's own way." Well, if this willingness to doubt is the hallmark of Greek philosophy, then Bloom and his fellow idolizers of Western civilization are ignorant of that philosophy.

If Western civilization is considered the high point of human progress, the United States is the best representative of this civilization. Here is Alan Bloom again: "This is the American moment in world history . . . America tells one story: the unbroken, ineluctable progress of freedom and equality. From its first settlers and its political foundings on, there has been no dispute that freedom and equality are the essence of justice for us . . ."

Yes, tell black people and Native Americans and the homeless and those without health insurance, and all the victims abroad of American foreign policy that America "tells one story . . . freedom and equality."

Western civilization is complex. It represents many things, some decent, some horrifying. We would have to pause before celebrating it uncritically when we note that David Duke, the Louisiana Ku Klux Klan member and ex-Nazi says that people have got him wrong. "The common strain in my thinking," he told a reporter, "is my love for Western civilization."

We who insist on looking critically at the Columbus story, and indeed at everything in our traditional histories, are often accused of insisting on political correctness, to the detriment of free speech. I find this odd. It is the guardians of the old stories, the orthodox histories, who refuse to widen the spectrum of ideas, to take in new books, new approaches, new information, new views of history. They, who claim to believe in "free markets," do not believe in a free marketplace of ideas, any more than they believe in a free marketplace of goods and services. In both material goods and in ideas, they want the market dominated by those who have always held power and wealth. They worry that if new ideas enter the marketplace, people may begin to rethink the social arrangements that have given us so much suffering, so much violence, so much war these last five hundred years of "civilization."

Of course we had all that before Columbus arrived in this hemisphere, but resources were puny, people were isolated from one another, and the possibilities were narrow. In recent centuries, however, the world has become amazingly small, our possibilities for creating a decent society have enormously magnified, and so the excuses for hunger, ignorance, violence, racism, no longer exist.

In rethinking our history, we are not just looking at the past, but at the present, and trying to look at it from the point of view of those who have been left out of the benefits of so-called civilization. It is a simple but profoundly important thing we are trying to accomplish, to look at the world from other points of view. We need to do that, as we come into the next century, if we want this coming century to be different, if we want it to be, not an American century, or a Western century, or a white century, or a male century, or any nation's, any group's century, but a century for the human race.

MIKE DAVIS

LOS ANGELES WAS JUST THE BEGINNING

Urban Revolt in the United States: A Thousand Points of Light

BURNING ALL ILLUSIONS

LOS ANGELES—The armored personnel carrier squats on the corner like *un gran sapo feo*—"a big ugly toad"—according to nine-year-old Emerio. His parents talk anxiously, almost in a whisper, about the *desaparecidos*: Raul from Tepic, big Mario, the younger Flores girl, and the cousin from Ahuachapan. Like all Salvadorans, they know about those who "disappear"; they remember the headless corpses and the man whose tongue had been pulled through the hole in his throat like a necktie. That is why they came here—to ZIP code 90057, Los Angeles, California.

Now they are counting their friends and neighbors, Salvadoran and Mexican, who are suddenly gone. Some are still in the county jail on Bauchet Street, little more than brown grains of sand lost among the 12,545 other alleged *saqueadores* (looters) and *incendarios* (arsonists) detained after the most violent American civil disturbance since the Irish poor burned Manhattan in 1863. Those without papers are probably already back in Tijuana, broke and disconsolate, cut off from their families and new lives. Violating city policy, the police fed hundreds of hapless undocumented *saqueadores* to the INS for deportation before the ACLU or immigrant rights groups even realized they had been arrested.

For many days the television talked only of the "South Central riot," "black rage," and the "Crips and Bloods." But Emerio's parents know that thousands of their neighbors from the MacArthur Park district—home to nearly one-tenth of all the Salvadorans in the world—also looted, burned, stayed out past curfew, and went to jail. (A sheriff's department analysis of riot-related arrests revealed that 45 percent were Latino, 41 percent African American and 12 percent Anglo. Sixty percent lacked prior criminal records.) They also know that the nation's first multiracial riot was as much about empty bellies and broken hearts as it was about police batons and Rodney King.

The week before the riot was unseasonably hot. At night the people lingered outside on the stoops and sidewalks of their tenements (MacArthur Park is L.A.'s Spanish Harlem), talking about their new burden of trouble. In a neighborhood far more crowded than mid-Manhattan and more dangerous than downtown Detroit, with more crack addicts and gangbangers than registered voters, *la gente* know how to laugh away every disaster except the final one. Yet there was a new melancholy in the air.

Too many people have been losing their jobs: their *pinche* $5.25-an-hour jobs as seamstresses, laborers, busboys and factory workers. In two years of recession, unemployment has tripled in L.A.'s immigrant neighborhoods. At Christmas more than twenty thousand predominantly Latina women and children from throughout the central city waited all night in the cold to collect a free turkey and a blanket from charities. Other visible barometers of distress are the rapidly growing colonies of homeless *compañeros* on the desolate flanks of Crown Hill and in the concrete bed of the L.A. River, where people are forced to use sewage water for bathing and cooking.

As mothers and fathers lose their jobs, or as unemployed relatives move under the shelter of the extended family, there is increasing pressure on teenagers to supplement the family income. Belmont High School is the pride of "Little Central America," but with nearly forty-five hundred students it is severely overcrowded, and an additional two thousand students must be bused to distant schools in the San Fernando Valley and elsewhere. Fully seven thousand school-age teenagers in the Belmont area, moreover, have dropped out of school. Some have entered the *la vida loca* of gang culture (there are one hundred different gangs in the school district that includes Belmont High), but most are struggling to find minimum-wage footholds in a declining economy.

The neighbors in MacArthur Park whom I interviewed, such as Emerio's parents, all speak of this gathering sense of unease, a perception of a future already looted. The riot arrived like a magic dispensation. People were initially shocked by the violence, then mesmerized by the televised images of biracial crowds in South Central L.A. helping themselves to mountains of desirable goods without interference from the police. The next day, Thursday, April 30, the authorities blundered twice: first by suspending school and releasing the kids into the streets; second by announcing that the National Guard was on the way to help enforce a dusk-to-dawn curfew.

Thousands immediately interpreted this as a last call to participate in the general redistribution of wealth in progress. Looting spread with explosive force throughout Hollywood, Mid-Wilshire and MacArthur Park, as well as parts of Echo Park, Van Nuys, and Huntington Park. Although arsonists spread terrifying destruction, the looting crowds were governed by a visible moral economy. As one middle-aged lady explained to me, "Stealing is a sin, but this is like a television game show where everyone in the audience gets to win." Unlike the looters in Hollywood (some on skateboards) who stole Madonna's bustier and all the crotchless panties from Frederick's, the masses of MacArthur Park concentrated on the prosaic necessities of life like cockroach spray and diapers.

One week later, MacArthur Park entered a state of siege. A special "We Tip" hotline invited people to inform on neighbors or acquaintances suspected of looting. Elite LAPD metro Squad units, supported by the National Guard, swept through the tenements in search of stolen goods, while border patrolmen from as far away as Texas prowl the streets. Frantic parents search for missing kids, like mentally retarded fourteen-year-old Zuly Estrada, who is believed to have been deported to Mexico.

Meanwhile, thousands of *saqueadores*, many of them pathetic scavengers captured in the charred ruins the day after the looting, languish in County Jail, unable to meet absurdly high bails. One man, caught with a packet of sunflower seeds and two cartons of milk, is being held on $15,000 bail; hundreds of others face felony indictments and possible two-year prison terms. Prosecutors demand thirty-day jail sentences for curfew violators, despite the fact that many of those are either homeless street people or Spanish-speakers who were unaware of the curfew. These are the "weeds" that George Bush said we must pull from the soil of our cities before it can be sown with the regenerating "seeds" of enterprise zones and tax breaks for private capital.

There is rising apprehension that the entire community will become a scapegoat. An ugly, seal-the-border nativism has been growing like crabgrass in southern California since the start of the recession. A lynch mob of Orange County Republicans, led by Representative Dana Rohrabacher of Huntington Beach, demands the immediate deportation of all the undocumented immigrants arrested in the disturbance, while liberal Democrat Anthony Beilenson, sounding like the San Fernando Valley's son-of-Le-Pen, proposes to strip citizenship from the U.S.-born children of illegals. According to Roberto Lovato of MacArthur Park's Central American Refugee Center, "We are becoming the guinea pigs, the Jews, in the militarized laboratory where George Bush is inventing his new urban order."

A Black Intifada?

"Little Gangster" Tak can't get over his amazement that he is actually standing in the same room of Brother Aziz's mosque with a bunch of Inglewood Crips. The handsome, twenty-two-year-old Tak, a "straight up" Inglewood Blood who looks more like a black angel by Michelangelo than one of the *Boyz 'N the Hood,* still has two Crip bullets in his body, and "they still carry a few of mine." Some of the Crips and Bloods, whose blue or red gang colors have been virtual tribal flags, remember one another from school playground days, but mainly they have met over the barrels of automatics in a war that has divided Inglewood—the pleasant, black-majority city southwest of L.A. where the Lakers play—by a river of teenage blood. Now, as Tak explains, "Everybody knows what time it is. If we don't end the killing now and unite as black men, we never will."

Although Imam Aziz and the Nation of Islam have provided the formal auspices for peacemaking, the real hands that have "tied the red and blue rags together into a 'black thang'" are in Simi Valley. Within a few hours of the first attack on white motorists, which started in Eight-Tray (83rd Street) Gangster Crip territory near Florence and Normandie, the insatiable war between the Crips and Bloods, fueled by a thousand neighborhood vendettas and dead homeboys, was "put on hold" throughout Los Angeles and the adjacent black suburbs of Compton and Inglewood.

Unlike the 1965 rebellion, which broke out south of Watts and remained primarily focused on the poorer east side of the ghetto, the 1992 riot reached its maximum temperature along Crenshaw Boulevard—the very heart of black Los Angeles's more affluent west side. Despite the illusion of full-immersion "actuality" provided by the minicam and the helicopter, television's coverage of the riot's angry edge was even more twisted than the melted steel of Crenshaw's devastated shopping centers. Most reporters—"image looters" as they are now being called in South Central—merely lip-synched suburban clichés as they tramped through the ruins of lives they had no desire to understand. A violent kaleidoscope of bewildering complexity was flattened into a single, categorical scenario: legitimate black anger over the King decision hijacked by hard-core street criminals and transformed into a maddened assault on their own community.

Local television thus unwittingly mimed the McCone Commission's summary judgment that the August 1965 Watts riot was primarily the act of a hoodlum fringe. In that case, a subsequent UCLA study revealed that the "riot of the riffraff" was in fact a popular uprising involving at least fifty thousand working-class adults and their teenage children. When the arrest records of this latest uprising are finally analyzed, they will probably also vindicate the judgment of many residents that all segments of black youth, gang and non-gang, "buppie" as well as underclass, took part in the disorder.

Although in Los Angeles, as elsewhere, the new black middle class has socially and spatially pulled farther apart from the deindustrialized black working class, the LAPD's Operation Hammer and other antigang dragnets that arrested kids at random (entering their names and addresses into an electronic gang roster that is now proving useful in house-to-house searches for riot "ringleaders") have tended to criminalize black youth without class distinction. Between 1987 and 1990, the combined sweeps of the LAPD and the county sheriff's office ensnared fifty thousand "suspects." Even the children of doctors and lawyers from View Park and Windsor Hills have had to "kiss the pavement" and occasionally endure some of the humiliations that the homeboys in the flats face every day—experiences that reinforce the reputation of the gangs (and their poets laureate, the gangster rappers like Ice Cube and NWA) as the heroes of an outlaw generation.

Yet if the riot had a broad social base, it was the participation of the gangs—or, rather, their cooperation—that gave it constant momentum and direction. If the 1965 rebellion was a hurricane, leveling one hundred blocks of Central Avenue from Vernon to Imperial Highway, the 1992 riot was a tornado, no less destructive but snaking a zigzag course through the commercial areas of the ghetto and beyond. Most of the media saw no pattern in its path, just blind, nihilistic destruction. In fact, the arson was ruthlessly systematic. By Friday morning 90 percent of the myriad Korean-owned liquor stores, markets, and swapmeets in South Central L.A. had been wiped out. Deserted by the LAPD, which made no attempt to defend small businesses, the Koreans suffered damage or destruction to almost two thousand stores from Compton to the heart of Koreatown itself. One of the first to be attacked (although, ironically, it survived) was the grocery store where fifteen-year-old Latasha Harlins was shot in the back of the head last year by Korean grocer Soon Ja Du in a dispute over a $1.79 bottle of orange juice. The girl died with the money for her purchase in her hand.

Latasha Harlins. A name that was scarcely mentioned on television was the key to the catastrophic collapse of relations between L.A.'s black and Korean communities. Ever since white judge Joyce Karlin let Du off with a $500 fine and some community service—a sentence which declared that the taking of a black child's life was scarcely more serious than drunk driving—some interethnic explosion has been virtually inevitable. The several near-riots at the Compton courthouse this winter were early warning signals of the black community's unassuaged grief over Harlins's murder. On the streets of South Central Wednesday and Thursday, I was repeatedly told, "This is for our baby sister. This is for Latasha."

The balance of grievances in the community is complex. Rodney King is the symbol that links unleashed police racism in Los Angeles to the crisis of black life everywhere, from Las Vegas to Toronto. Indeed, it is becoming clear that the King case may be almost as much of a watershed in American history as Dred Scott, a test of the very meaning of the citizenship for which African Americans have struggled for four hundred years.

But on the grass-roots level, especially among gang youth, Rodney King may not have quite the same profound resonance. As one of the

Inglewood Bloods told me: "Rodney King? Shit, my homies be beat like dogs by the police every day. This riot is about all the homeboys murdered by the police, about the little sister killed by the Koreans, about twenty-seven years of oppression. Rodney King just the trigger."

At the same time, those who predicted that the next L.A. riot would be a literal Armageddon have been proved wrong. Despite a thousand day-glo exhortations on the walls of South Central to "Kill the Police," the gangs have refrained from the deadly guerrilla warfare that they are so formidably equipped to conduct. As in 1965, there has not been a single LAPD fatality, and indeed few serious police injuries of any kind.

In this round, at least, the brunt of gang power was directed toward the looting and destruction of the Korean stores. If Latasha Harlins is the impassioned pretext, there may be other agendas as well. I saw graffiti in South Central that advocated "Day one: burn them out. Day two: we rebuild." The only national leader whom most Crips and Bloods seem to take seriously is Louis Farrakhan, and his goal of black economic self-determination is broadly embraced. (Farrakhan, it should be emphasized, has never advocated violence as a means to this end.) At the Inglewood gang summit, which took place on May 5, there were repeated references to a renaissance of black capitalism out of the ashes of Korean businesses. "After all," an ex-Crip told me later, "we didn't burn our community, just their stores."

In the meantime, the police and military occupiers of Los Angeles give no credence to any peaceful, let alone entrepreneurial, transformation of L.A.'s black gang cultures. The ecumenical movement of the Crips and Bloods is their worst imagining: gang violence no longer random but politicized into a black intifada. The LAPD remembers only too well that a generation ago the Watts rebellion produced a gang peace out of which grew the Los Angeles branch of the Black Panther Party. As if to prove their suspicions, the police have circulated a copy of an anonymous and possibly spurious leaflet calling for gang unity and "an eye for an eye. If LAPD hurt a black we'll kill two."

For its part, the Bush administration has federalized the repression in L.A.—the most sweeping since the Nixon era—with an eye to the spectacle of the president marching in triumph, like a Roman emperor, with captured Crips and Bloods in chains. Thus, the Justice Department has dispatched to L.A. the same elite task force of federal marshals who captured Manuel Noriega in Panama, as well as prosecutor William Hogan from Chicago, who led the federal task force that crushed the Windy City's famous El Rukn gang. The FBI, which has assigned one hundred agents to track down the supposed gang instigators of the riot, acknowledges that "this is, frankly, the biggest effort ever, federally."

Crucial to the Justice Department's strategy in South Central L.A. is the application of RICO, the federal anti-racketeering law, that allows the government to indict street gangs as criminal organizations. U.S. Attorney Lourdes Baird has promised that RICO will be used unsparingly against "street terrorists." Some Bush supporters, meanwhile, are smacking their lips over the appetizing electoral fallout of a big federal victory over L.A.'s street gangs. But as a veteran of the 1965 riot said while watching SWAT teams arrest some of the hundreds of rival gang members trying to meet peacefully at Watts's Jordan Downs Housing Project: "That ole fool Bush think we as dumb as Saddam. Land Marines in Compton and get hisself reelected. But this ain't Iraq. This is Vietnam, Jack."

The Great Fear

A core grievance fueling the Watts rebellion and the subsequent urban insurrections of 1967–68 was rising black unemployment in the midst of a boom economy. What contemporary journalists fearfully described as the beginning of the "Second Civil War" was as much a protest against black America's exclusion from the military-Keynesian expansion of the 1960s as it was an uprising against police racism and de facto segregation in schools and housing. The 1992 riot and its possible progenies must likewise be understood as insurrections against an intolerable political-economic order. As even the *Los Angeles Times*, main cheerleader for "World City L.A.," now editorially acknowledges, the "globalization of Los Angeles" has produced "devastating poverty for those weak in skills and resources."

Although the $1 billion worth of liquor stores and mini-malls destroyed in L.A. may seem like chump change next to the $2.6 trillion recently annihilated on the Tokyo Stock Exchange, the burning of Oz probably fits into the same Hegelian niche with the bursting of the Bubble Economy: not the "end of history" at the seacoast of Malibu but the beginning of an ominous dialectic on the rim of the Pacific. It was a hallucination in the first place to imagine that the wheel of the world economy could be turned indefinitely by a Himalaya of U.S. trade deficits and a fictitious yen.

This structural crisis of the Japan-California "co-prosperity sphere," however, threatens to translate class contradictions into inter-ethnic conflict on both the national and local level. Culturally distinct "middleman" groups—ethnic entrepreneurs and the like—risk being seen as the personal representatives of the invisible hand that has looted local communities of economic autonomy. In the case of Los Angeles, it was tragically the neighborhood Korean liquor store, not the skyscraper corporate fortress downtown, that became the symbol of a despised new world order.

On their side, the half-million Korean-Americans in L.A. have been psychologically lacerated by the failure of the state to protect them against black rage. Indeed, several young Koreans told me that they were especially bitter that the South Central shopping malls controlled by Alexander Haagen, a wealthy contributor to local politics, were quickly defended by police and National Guard, while their stores were leisurely ransacked and burned to the ground. "Maybe this is what we get," a UCLA student said, "for uncritically buying into the white middle class's attitude toward blacks and its faith in the police."

The prospects for a multicultural reconciliation in Los Angeles depend much less on white knight Peter Ueberroth's committee of corporate rebuilders than upon a general economic recovery in southern California. As the *Los Angeles Business Journal* complained (after noting that L.A. had lost one hundred thousand manufacturing jobs over the past three years), "The riots are like poison administered to a sick patient." Recent forecasts from the Southern California Association of Governments paint a dark future for the Land of Sunshine, as job growth, slowed by the decline of aerospace as well as manufacturing shifts to Mexico, lags far behind population increase. Unemployment rates—not counting the estimated forty thousand jobs lost from the riot, and the uprising's impact on the business climate—are predicted to remain at 10 to 13 percent (and 40 to 50 percent for minority youth) for the next generation, while the housing crisis, already the most acute in the nation, will spill over into new waves of homelessness. Thus, the "widening divide" of income inequality in Los Angeles County, described in a landmark 1988 study by UCLA Professor Paul Ong, will become an unbridgeable chasm. Southern California's endless summer is finally over.

Affluent Angelenos instinctively sensed this as they patrolled their Hancock Park estates with shotguns or bolted in their BMWs for white sanctuaries in Orange and Ventura counties. From Palm Springs poolsides they anxiously awaited news of the burning of Beverly Hills by the Crips and Bloods, and fretted over the extra set of house keys they had foolishly entrusted to the Latina maid.

Was she now an *incendario*? Although their fears were hysterically magnified, tentacles of disorder did penetrate such sanctums of white life as the Beverly Center and Westwood Village, as well as the Melrose and Fairfax neighborhoods. Most alarmingly, the LAPD's "thin blue line," which had protected them in 1965, was now little more than a defunct metaphor, the last of Chief Gates's bad jokes.

L.A. IGNITES LAS VEGAS

Las Vegas's frenzied Memorial Day weekend was winding down with the promise of a big storm. Spring lightning danced in the dark clouds above Charleston Peak and the Valley of Fire. As raindrops the size of silver dollars intermittently splattered the sidewalks outside, weary casino tellers counted a quarter-billion dollars in holiday revenue. Across the Mojave, fifty thousand homebound revelers were strung out almost bumper to bumper, from Ivanpah Dry Lake to the outskirts of L.A., 250 miles away.

In a small park in the northwest part of town, several hundred Crips and Bloods, ignoring the storm warnings, were merrily barbequing pork ribs and passing around forty-ounce bottles of beer. Earlier in the day, dozens of formerly hostile sets with names like Anybody's Murderers (ABM), Donna Street Crips, and North Town Bloods had joined at a nearby cemetery to mark a gang truce and place flowers on the graves of their homeboys (there were twenty-seven local gang-related deaths in 1991). Now these erstwhile enemies and their girlfriends were swapping jokes and new rap lyrics.

But gatherings of three or more people, however amicable, have been banned since May 17 by sheriff's order throughout Las Vegas's black Westside as well as in the neighboring blue-collar suburb of North Las Vegas. To enforce this extraordinary edict, Metro Police pulled up in front of Valley View Park in three V-100 armored personnel carriers borrowed from a nearby Air Force base. When defiant picnickers refused to disperse, the cops opened up with tear gas and concussion grenades. The Las Vegas "riots" had resumed for the fourth weekend in a row since the Rodney King verdict had ignited a tinderbox of black grievances.

The Rules Have Changed, Nigger

I caught up with some of the casualties in the parking lot of a burned-out market an hour later. As a fascinated crowd watched, Yolanda, who said she was seventeen, exhibited the bloody gash in her leg, while her boyfriend, David, hopped around excitedly with a crumpled olive-green canister in his hand. "Check this out!" he commanded somewhat menacingly as he shoved the offending projectile in my face. I read the label out loud: "Model 429, Thunderflash, Stun Grenade."

"We were just having a picnic, a goddamn peaceful picnic," David repeated. Several kids stared hard, unblinking, in my direction. Someone lobbed an empty Colt 45 bottle into the sagebrush. Then a tall figure in a Georgetown sweatshirt grabbed my arm. "You'd better split, man. If you want an interview, come back tomorrow. I'll tell you anything you want to know about Lost fuckin' Vegas. " I asked his name. He laughed: "Just call me Nice D., Valley View Gangster Crips. O.K.?"

I went looking for D. the next day. West Las Vegas (population 20,000) is the antipode to the pleasure domes of downtown and the Strip. Grit without glitter, it has no hotels, casinos, supermarkets, banks or even regular bus service. Yet, like South Central L.A., it scarcely resembles the Frostbelt stereotype of a ghetto. Its detached homes lack the verdant, Astroturf-like lawns and backyard swimming pools of the white neighborhoods, but they appear to be lovingly tended, with groves of shade trees to protect against the blast-furnace desert heat. Even the spartan public housing units in Gerson Park have a tidy ambience that belies their poverty.

I met up with D., who is twenty, near the ruins of Nucleus Plaza—the closest thing on the Westside to a shopping center. He recalled the night of April 30, the day after the L.A. verdict, when protest turned to riot and gang members looted and firebombed buildings, including the Korean-owned Super 8 Market in the middle of the plaza. "A young brother [high school senior Isaiah Charles, Jr.] went in to rescue a little girl. She managed to get out, but he was trapped when the roof collapsed. The fire department had already run away, so the fire just burned for a long time." He showed me the charred remains of an adjacent NAACP office and an AIDS clinic.

Although the scale of arson damage in West Las Vegas ($5 million) was minute compared with that of Los Angeles (about $1 billion), the sheer fury of confrontation was, if anything, more intense. Accounts of that first day's events have a Rashomon-like ambiguity, only here no third party emerges to resolve the contradictions. Everyone agrees that rioting did not begin until about 7:30 the evening of the 30th, after police used tear gas to turn back several hundred young blacks trying to march from the Westside to downtown. From that point the stories dramatically diverge: the local newspapers' version, almost totally reliant on police reports, versus the street-level perspective of young African Americans like D.

According to Metro Police Lieut. Steve Franks (who would shoot a teenager during the second weekend of disturbances), "Our intelligence was that if that group had reached downtown, they were ready to set fire to the hotels. Had it not been for our officers this town would have gone up in flames." D. says, "This is total bullshit. We were only trying to demonstrate against the Rodney King verdict and apartheid right here in Las Vegas. The police just wanted an excuse to attack us."

Having broken up the march, the police cordoned off most of West Las Vegas and drew weapons on anyone who approached their barricades. Hundreds of young people, meanwhile, had regrouped near the Gerson Park projects, where the local Kingsmen Gang was hosting an impromptu party for the various Crip and Blood sets who had agreed the previous day—apparently influenced by news from L.A.— to stop fighting. According to D., a Metro squad car drove straight into the festive crowd. "People went crazy. They started throwing rocks and bottles; then one of the homies opened up with his gat [gun]." The angry crowd burned down a nearby office of the Pardon and Parole Board, while other groups attacked stores and gas stations with Molotov cocktails.

Lieutenant Franks claimed that snipers "hid in trees and rooftops, and used human targets when they came out in the open to fire. These yellow-bellied rats stood with young children around them and then opened fire on police cars." Another police spokesman claimed that gang members tried to kidnap an infant from a white family living on a predominantly black street. I found no one who could confirm either of these lurid stories, which the city's two daily papers disseminated uncritically to a horrified white public. Nor were there follow-up reports of suspects in such crimes from among the 111 people arrested.

At the same time, the media, as in Los Angeles, studiously avoided any reference to police misconduct during the disturbances. D., however, has vivid recollections. "Me and my friends left after the shooting started," he said. "Our car was pulled over a few blocks later. When we asked what we had done wrong, a big redneck cop said, 'The rules have changed, nigger' and hit me in the face with his pistol. I was held five days in jail for 'obstruction.' The cops threw away my ID and health card, so I lost my job at Carl's Junior."

D. got out of jail just in time to witness the renewal of violence on Sunday, May 10. Once again kids gathered near Gerson Park to play softball and party. Metro police called in an armored personnel carrier and began shooting wooden bullets at the crowd. The following weekend was a virtual rerun, as a gang picnic at the Doolittle Community Center disintegrated into a wild all-night melee between cops in their V-100s and hundreds of angry youths.

D. thinks these now-ritual confrontations will only grow more violent over the summer. Like other black youths with whom I spoke, he believes that Clark County Sheriff John Moran "will do anything, however extreme, to break up the [gang] unification process." Indeed, D. and the others are convinced that a recent drive-by shooting that wounded four members of the Rollin' 60s (a local branch of the famous L.A. Crip set) was actually organized by the police. They also speak derisively of the "reverse buy" program, in which undercover cops pose as drug dealers to entrap crack addicts whom they then coerce into becoming police informants. D. warned me that Las Vegas is on the verge of what he calls "an underground holocaust." Why?

Mississippi West

Although Las Vegas's mythographers (most recently, Warren Beatty in *Bugsy*) typically elide race, black entertainers and laborers played decisive roles in the transformation of a sleepy desert railroad town into a

$14-billion-a-year tourist oasis. But the sensational rise of the modern casino economy went hand in hand with the degradation of black rights. Glitter Gulch was built by Jim Crow.

As exiled L.A. gamblers began to buy up the old Fremont Street casinos in downtown Las Vegas in the late 1930s, local black residents were barred from the blackjack tables and slot machines. When Tom Hull opened his El Rancho in 1941—the Strip's pioneer casino and resort hotel—restrictive covenants were being used to evict black families from downtown and force them across the Union Pacific tracks into West Las Vegas, a wasteland without paved roads, utilities or fire protection. Thus, by the time Meyer Lansky's gunmen ruined Bugsy Siegel's good looks in 1947, segregation in Las Vegas was virtually total. Blacks could wash dishes, make beds, even entertain, like Lena Horne and Sammy Davis Jr., but they could not work as dealers or bartenders, stay in a hotel, live in a white neighborhood or go to a white school.

An all-white police department, with a national reputation for brutality, enforced the color line in a town that African Americans began to call *Mississippi West.* When in 1944 black GIs guarding nearby Boulder Dam tried to defy the racist rules that kept them out of downtown bars and casinos, they were attacked by police. In the full-fledged riot that erupted, one soldier was killed. A quarter-century later, in October 1969, heavy-handed police tactics, together with disgust over continuing job discrimination, again ignited a riot. Two people died and Governor Paul Laxalt called in the National Guard to seal off the Westside. For nearly a year afterward, Clark County's schools, only partially integrated, were rocked by battles between white and black students.

While racism was building in the premier city of the Silver State, those with power could ignore its ugly features, but now racial turmoil was tarnishing its image. The major hotels and their complacent unions reluctantly signed a consent decree in 1971 guaranteeing open employment. In the same year the Nevada legislature passed a long-delayed fair housing law. Clark County schools followed a year later with an integration scheme that overrode white resistance to busing. After thirty years of wandering in the wilderness, black Las Vegans thought they could see equality ahead.

Like so much else in the desert, this has turned out to be a cruel mirage. Although token integration is the rule, the majority of blacks are locked out of Las Vegas's boom economy. In recent years, as the rest of the Sunbelt has slipped into recession, Clark County's population has increased at warp speed (one thousand new residents per week), and Nevada, the "most fortunate state in the nation," according to the local AFL-CIO, has repeatedly led in job creation (8 percent annually between 1987 and 1990). Employment on the Strip has soared with the construction of mega-hotels like the four-thousand-room Excalibur—soon to be followed by the five-thousand-room MGM Grand, the biggest in the world—while the so-called South Nevada Industrial Revolution has seduced dozens of high-tech computer and military aerospace firms from California.

But only a handful of black families have found their way into affluent new-growth suburbs like Winchester and Green Valley. Despite the twenty-year-old consent decree, blacks remain vastly under-represented in the higher-paying hotel jobs and construction trades as well as in the new science parks. Although minorities make up 20 percent of Nevada's labor force (25 percent in Clark County), they hold only 14 percent of public-sector jobs, and Governor Robert Miller recently acknowledged the bankruptcy of the state's affirmative action efforts. Concurrently, the growth in the metropolitan area's Latino population—from 578 in 1960 to 82,904 in 1990—and a huge influx of jobless whites from nearby states have severely crimped traditional black employment in the low-wage service industries.

Not surprisingly, black Las Vegans of all classes worry about creeping "Miamization," with their community, despite impressive political gains, becoming more socially and economically peripheral. For too many "native sons" like D., the recent boom has been an embittering "prisoner's dilemma," offering equally futureless choices between menial labor and the underground economy. As in Los Angeles, the shortfall between the spectacle of profligate consumption and the reality of ghetto life has been made up by street gangs and rock cocaine. The first Crip set, transplanted from Watts, took root in Gerson Park in 1978–79; crack hit the streets of West Las Vegas in 1984, shortly after its arrival in South Central L.A. Now an estimated four thousand Crips and Bloods (together with three thousand Latino and Asian gang members) are locked in a grim twilight struggle with police a few dozen blocks from the Liberace Museum and Caesar's Palace.

Lynching, 90s Style

Chan Kendrick is a scraggy, angular Southerner with a jaw-line beard who looks like he might have stepped out of a Civil War daguerreotype. A veteran civil liberties activist, he headed the Virginia ACLU for many years before moving to Las Vegas to run the organization's Nevada chapter. He makes no bones about which area is morally farthest below the Mason-Dixon line: "Police abuse here is worse than anywhere in the contemporary urban South. In an average month I get more complaints about police misconduct in Las Vegas than I received altogether during twelve years in Richmond. The situation is just incredible."

According to Kendrick and other critics, the Metro Las Vegas Police Force, headed by Sheriff Moran (whom a local reporter described as being "as accessible as the King of Nepal"), is little more than a mean guard dog for the casinos and the Nevada Resort Association. Kendrick is constantly challenging the use of nuisance, loitering and vagrancy laws to keep "undesirables," especially young blacks and homeless people, off the Strip. Likewise, he fights to force the police, particularly its rogue narcotics squads, to respect the constitutional constraints on search and seizure.

In a notorious 1989 incident reported by the Las Vegas *Review-Journal*, ten policemen, presumably looking for illegal narcotics, raided the home of fifty-eight-year-old Barbara Melvin. They announced their arrival by tossing two powerful concussion grenades through her bedroom window, then broke down her front door. While her fifth-grade grandson cowered in terror, they called her "nigger" and "bitch," tore off her nightgown, knocked her to the floor and kicked her between the legs. After trashing the house and finding nothing, they seized $4,500 in cash and left. Melvin was not charged with any offense. She filed a complaint with the police, but it was dismissed with a form letter. According to the *Review-Journal*, the cops also kept $4,001 of the confiscated money.

The case that most haunts West Las Vegas today, however, is the killing of casino floorman Charles Bush in July 1990. Bush was asleep when three plainclothes police, wanting to question him about the arrest of his pregnant girlfriend for prostitution, broke into his apartment without a warrant and choked him to death. The official police explanation was that Bush, surprised in his sleep, had fought with them.

At the coroners' inquest, attorneys representing Bush's family were prevented from asking questions, and the strangulation was ruled "justifiable"—the forty-fourth time in a row since 1976 that the police had been exonerated in the death of a suspect.

Despite a storm of criticism over the coroner's verdict, the Clark County D.A. would not indict the three cops. Six months later the Nevada Attorney General's office brought them to trial for manslaughter, but the all-white jury deadlocked eleven to one for acquittal and the case was dropped. The local U.S. Attorney ignored the ACLU's petition for prosecution under federal civil rights statutes. As Kendrick points out, "The legacy of the Bush case is even more disastrous than the Rodney King verdict. It shows that the Las Vegas police are allowed, on the flimsiest of pretexts, to break into black people's homes and kill them when they resist."

For D. and his friends, meanwhile, the Bush case "is just another lynching, Las Vegas–style." They point to the hypocrisy of a new state law that doubles sentences for gang-related felonies while local law enforcement "plays patty-cake with the Mafia up on the Strip." They complain about the humiliation of being strip-searched in the street in front of girlfriends and neighbors. And they acidly contrast the Feds' apathy in the Bush case with their zeal to crush "Killa" Daniel and the other ABM Crips from North Las Vegas—"really small-time hoods," according to D.—who were recently indicted on federal conspiracy charges of distributing twelve grams of cocaine.

But their bitterest feelings are reserved for the politicians who think black Las Vegas's grievances can be swept under the rug with a few more token gestures, like liberal Mayor Jan Laverty Jones's grandiloquent promise of forty-two new jobs in the casinos, or Sheriff Moran's offer of "better communication" with the Westside. For D.—who feels the only people "telling the truth about radical-level reality" in America are rappers like Ice Cube and Chuck D—"things are already near the ultimate edge. The time for lies is past. We built Las Vegas for them, and without equality, we will tear this motherfucker down."

CASTING THE FIRST STONE

LOS ANGELES—"The black man is an intelligence test the white man is taking." The Reverend Albert Cleage, a Detroit civil rights leader, said this in the wake of the ghetto uprisings of 1967. If the test still applies, the three white guys in the booth next to me are flunking badly.

I am eating breakfast in a retro-fifties diner favored by minor writers and itinerant Euro-trash. Ever since the looting of a nearby camera shop, the entire neighborhood has suffered from increasingly bizarre hallucinations. Although this is the edge of Beverly Hills and not Sarajevo, the locals complain about "post-riot stress" and greet each other as "fellow survivors."

My neighbors are discussing the beating of white truckdriver Reginald Denny near the corner of Florence and Normandie on April 29. KCOP-Channel 13's lurid newscopter view of Denny being dragged from his rig and hammered senseless has become the definitive image of the Los Angeles rebellion. Like an aching toothache in the the electronic void, it has been shown and reshown a hundred times on local television.

The trio are particularly riveted by the vision of a young powerful black man smashing Denny over the head with a rock or piece of concrete. With strange familiarity, they refer to him as "Football." "I just bought a pistol," I overhear one guy boasting, "no 'Football' is gonna come through my front door." "You'd have been smarter to have bought a shotgun," says the second. "Or a bazooka," adds the third.

There is a new self-righteousness on this side of the barricades. The near-lynching of Rodney King has faded from moral focus. Just as Reginald Denny has now become *everyman's* urban victim, so has Damian "Football" Williams—charged with nineteen counts of attempted murder, torture, aggravated mayhem and robbery—become the all-purpose Monster in white L.A.'s self-serving nightmare.

Mother Courage and Her Children

Most of the tired little bungalows on 71st Street east of Normandie could use a slap of fresh paint, but the lawns are tidy and well-tended. Thirty years ago, the last whites—some of them with Okie drawls—surrendered this part of blue-collar South Central L.A. to black immigrants from the South. Now, aging black homeowners watch with a measure of irony as young Mexican families supplant them in turn.

Georgiana Williams has raised four children by herself in number 1315. Most of her neighbors hail from Texas or Louisiana, but Georgiana is grass-roots Mississippi. She grew up with twelve brothers and sisters on a hardscrabble tenant farm across Highway 61 from the Vicksburg Civil War memorial. Her people were poor but resourceful and self-sufficient. "Before I was ten I knew how to plow as well as sew. I could chop cotton, harness a mule, even make moonshine. We wore homemade dresses and went barefoot."

Although she speaks proudly of her mother and grandmother ("beautiful, strong ladies"), Georgiana did not want to become another sharecropper's wife trapped for life in a shotgun shack. Nor did she want to end up in a grim Westside Chicago tenement like so many thousands of other Mississippi emigrants of her generation. Instead, in 1960, at age twenty, she headed west to California. After a brief spell with her sister in Vallejo, she married and moved to Los Angeles. The marriage didn't work (nor did a second), but with her earnings as a vocational nurse, Georgiana was able to buy the little house on 71st Street.

Damian Monroe, nineteen, is the youngest of the Williams's children and the apple of his mother's eye. "He is a very caring person. The little kids in this neighborhood look up to him because he has always taken care of them. He has fed them and bought them shoes. Put twenty dollars in his hand and he will give it away to someone more needy. That is how I raised him: not to be wrapped up in worldy possessions but to look after others."

Although Georgiana bridles at the nickname "Football" ("His name is *Damian*"), she points to one of the many sports trophies scattered throughout the house. "He runs so lovely, like one of those African deer, like a gazelle." Through sports, Damian has also built many friendships outside the neighborhood, including whites and Latinos. "I taught him always to look for the good in people, to judge everyone equally."

Damian's older siblings went to neighborhood schools, but he was sent to private schools as Georgiana struggled to keep him out of harm's way. As he was entering junior high school in 1985, crack was flooding the streets of South Central and 'Crippin' was at the height of its popularity. The Eight-Tray Gangster Crips, locked in a spiraling blood feud with the Rolling Sixties Crips, had become the invisible government in the Williams's neighborhood near Florence and Normandie.

Ultimately Georgiana decided that she could best protect Damian by moving back to Vicksburg. The boy from the 'hood adapted with gusto to the hardy routine of his rural kinfolk. "My God how Damian loved Mississippi. He explored the woods, learned to hunt and fish, soaked up lore from the older men. I never saw him happier."

But eventually, wracked by financial difficulties, Georgiana had to move back to 71st Street. To her distress Damian, like many of his friends, became disenchanted and dropped out of school. Although he promised to finish his diploma, he fathered a child and acquired a weighty new obligation. Working with his older brother out of the family garage, he scraped a living together installing car alarms and stereos.

In an aging neighborhood with few young blacks left at home, Damian—working in the garage or playing pickup basketball—was the most visible teenager. Increasingly he fell afoul of the tough street cops from the LAPD's 77th Street Division. Over Georgiana's vehement protests, they added his name to their roster of active Eight-Tray Crips. As she says with a bitterness gone acid, "they marked him."

The Big Fix

Unlike many of her neighbors glued to their TV sets, Georgiana paid scant attention to the trial of Rodney King's assailants. "Why raise my blood pressure? I knew those cops would never be convicted. I knew *personally.*"

Georgiana recalls her own encounter with suburban bigotry. In the 1970s she had been sent to Simi Valley by a private nursing service to tend a terminally ill cancer patient. His irate neighbors complained to the agency about her presence. "They wanted a white nurse for their lily-white neighborhood. I didn't fit into the decor."

Thus Georgiana was hardly surprised when the radio announced the King case acquittals while she was driving home from the beauty shop late in the afternoon of April 29. But as she approached the corner of Normandie and Florence—a block from her house—she was shocked by the scene of chaos. Police cars with sirens screaming charged down streets while angry knots of youth cursed and threw stones. As she pulled into her driveway, excited neighbors told of a confrontation earlier that afternoon.

As word of the verdict spread, a large crowd of local kids and unemployed young adults had gathered at the corner. Some began to throw rocks at passing white motorists. (LAPD logs record that the initial emergency call from the vicinity of Florence and Normandie was received at 4:17 p.m.) As the first patrol units from the 77th Division arrived on the scene they too were pelted with stones and bricks. One of the rock-throwers, sixteen-year-old Shandal Tate who lives across the street from the Williamses, was cornered by a group of pissed-off cops.

Georgiana's neighbors described how the police threw him across a fence, twisted his arms and beat him. When Damian's older half-brother, Mark Jackson (age thirty), yelled at the cops to stop, he too was pummeled, then arrested for "inciting a riot" and "resisting arrest." At this point, Shandal's mother, Aileen Tate (known affectionately to everyone on the block as 'Baby') arrived on the scene. "Don't take my child," she shrieked before a cop promptly put a chokehold on her.

Folks on 71st Street generally agree that police brutality toward the Tates was like throwing gasoline on a fire. Simmering anger was set ablaze, and, shortly before 6:00 p.m., as the police suddenly began to withdraw from the neighborhood, the inflamed crowd resumed attacks on passing whites. The LAPD made no effort to warn unsuspecting motorists of the dangerous situation at Normandie and Florence, and at 6:45 p.m. Channel 13's hovering newscopter began broadcasting live coverage of the beating of Reginald Denny.

Although the *Los Angeles Times* knew from the beginning about the earlier roughing-up of the Tates, the story was not reported until May 15 (in an admiring piece about the rank-and-file cops of the 77th Street Division), and was depicted without causal connection to the attacks on Denny and others. Yet Georgiana and most of her neighbors are convinced that it is impossible to understand what happened at 6:45 except as a consequence of the earlier incident. She believes the media have deliberately disguised the logic of events and emotions in order to conjure an image of irrational black malevolence.

And she is tormented that her son, out of the tens of thousands of participants in the rebellion, has been arraigned before the entire world as the incarnation of that malevolence. She remembers Damian's outrage at the police on Wednesday, but equally she recalls how he spent the next day (April 30) helping neighbors water their roofs with garden hoses as flames leaped menacingly close from burning storefronts on Florence. She had no inkling that he would be arrested or charged with any crime.

"Two weeks later I was working overnight in Huntington Beach when I received a beeper call early in the morning from my sister-in-law. I was scared that momma had died in Mississippi. But my sister-in-law said that Damian had been arrested by a whole army of police including old, lying Daryl Gates." Indeed, Chief Gates, clad in a bullet-proof vest and with a backup of two hundred cops and FBI agents, personally arrested Damian, whom he taunted as "Football."

Gates claimed that Damian had been identified from Channel 13 footage as the person who hit Denny with a rock. Two other alleged Eight-Tray Gangster Crips, Antonine Miller (twenty) and Henry Watson (twenty-seven), were charged as co-assailants. In contrast to the simple assault count filed against the cops who devastated Rodney King, Williams, Miller and Watson were each charged with attempted murder, torture, aggravated mayhem, and robbery. Three additional suspects—separately accused of attempted robbery, misdemeanor battery (spitting on Denny), and assault with a deadly weapon—were also eventually arrested.

Heroic efforts by Georgiana, her family and supporters to extricate Damian have only resulted in the judicial vise being turned tighter. The authorities have consistently undermined his chances for a fair trial with one melodramatic escalation after another. At his arraignment, for example, Chief Gates placed the entire LAPD on full tactical alert: a move that seemed to imply that Damian was as dangerous as Manuel Noriega or Pablo Escobar. Then the Judge set the bail at a staggering $195,000, or $165,000 more than Rodney King's LAPD assailants. When Georgiana heroically raised the money, the U.S. Attorney promptly placed a federal "hold" on the case preventing Damian's release.

While defense lawyers were contesting this, District Attorney Ira Reiner filed thirty-seven new felony charges against Damian and his two principal co-defendants. Bail soared to $580,000. When Georgiana, with widespread support from an outraged black community, seemed on the verge of scraping this new fortune together, the court ordered a special hearing to determine whether the property used to secure the bail was "acquired legally." The D.A. began videotaping Damian's family and supporters as they gathered in the courtroom.

Georgiana feels like she is spending time on the cross. "Why do I have to go through this? They're treating me like I'm a drug dealer. I'm not a drug dealer. I'm just a working mother from South Central, and they are trying to lynch my son. Lynch him just as sure as if this was Dixie in the 1950s."

The Hate Factory

The system is still figuring out new charges to hang on Damian Williams. At time of writing (August 1), he faces possible life imprisonment for nineteen felony counts. In the prosecution's scenario, he has been promoted from simply bashing Reginald Denny in the head to being the grand conductor of the entire whirlwind of violence that engulfed the corner of Florence and Normandie on April 29. He is accused of having "directed" the beating of nearly a dozen whites and Asians. While the district attorney weighs further assault counts, the FBI reportedly is investigating violations of federal racketeering statutes (RICO), presumably for membership in the Eight-Tray Crips. Damian's attorneys, meanwhile, have filed a $10 million lawsuit claiming that "Williams was charged with the panoply of crimes so as to become the focus of the riots."

Like hundreds of other young blacks and Latinos charged with felonies for their participation in the L.A. uprising, Damian waits for trial at the Peter Pitchess Honor Rancho located near the Six Flags Magic Mountain amusement park in northern L.A. County. The Rancho—still known to inmates and their families by its old name of "Wayside"—was established in the 1930s by Sheriff Eugene Biscailuz as a "revolutionary experiment" in rehabilitating minor offenders. Biscailuz, a legendary outdoorsman with "an inborn dislike of confinement," ran Wayside as a working ranch where prisoners could experience the rugged life of cowboys and farmhands in "the unbounded hills."

Cattle still graze in the meadows at Wayside, but everything else has changed for the worse. The benign "honor rancho" has evolved into a giant prison with 9,000 inmates shoehorned into facilities designed for less than 6,000. Only a handful of sentenced inmates still enjoy Biscailuz's outdoor life; most of the population is claustrophobically confined twenty-three hours a day in pressure-cooker-like dormitories. Formerly Wayside raised alfalfa, now its main product is hate.

During the last year hundreds of inmates have been seriously injured in virtually constant racial warfare. Although most of the twenty-five major melees have broken out as a result of an intractable power struggle between blacks and Latinos (since 1989 the new majority at Wayside), there have also been brutal clashes between blacks and whites. Indeed, it can be argued that the L.A. Rebellion actually began at Wayside, where, within minutes of the original announcement of the King case verdict, black inmates were fighting whites. The whites, in turn, retaliated in late July when thirty black inmates were ambushed and slashed with jail-made shanks.

Although racial violence is now epidemic throughout Wayside's five wings, the most sustained conflict has occurred in the high-security facility where Damian Williams, Antonine Miller, and Henry Watson are imprisoned together with 300 other black and Latino youth charged with murder. Bitter inmates complain that the sheriffs take grim delight in fanning the flames of racial hatred. One Crip, o.g., who almost had his ear cut off in the latest clash with white prisoners, told me that guards had ignored black protests about shank knives being made and concealed by white prisoners. Then when the blacks were ambushed, the guards refused to intervene until the whites had finished their handiwork.

Georgiana says that Damian has so far avoided being sucked into the maelstrom of the hate factory. "He remains proud and generally confident, though we had to get a court order to ensure that he would be fed regularly and allowed to bathe. And, of course, he misses sports." I asked Georgiana what she talks about with Damian during her regular visits to Wayside.

"Mostly we talk about Mississippi, and family memories, especially my grandmother who died last December at age 100. She was Damian's favorite. He really loved that old lady. A tiny woman—only four foot eleven inches—she wore long old-fashioned dresses and was constantly singing. She'd go from room to room in the sharecroppers' shacks putting the kids to sleep with a prayer and a song. I can hear her sweet voice always."

Georgiana smiles and softly sings a few emphatic lines: "I shall not, I shall not be moved . . . just like a tree standing by the water, I shall not be moved."

MANNING MARABLE

BLACK AMERICA

Multicultural Democracy in the Age of Clarence Thomas, David Duke, and the Los Angeles Uprisings

UPRISING IN LOS ANGELES

The recent racial uprising in Los Angeles revealed a fundamental division which separates two Americas along a race and class fault line. The responses to the violence on the "white" side of this race/class division help to illustrate why more urban unrest is inevitable.

In a shameful display of political cowardice, President George Bush's initial instinct was to attribute blame for the Los Angeles revolt on the liberal "Great Society" programs of Lyndon Johnson, a quarter century ago. But when pressed for specific programs which contributed to the racial crisis of today, White House press secretary Marlin Fitzwater could only mumble, "I don't have a list with me."

Did Bush mean the 1964 Civil Rights Act, which had outlawed racial discrimination in public accommodations? Was the president blaming the National Housing Act of 1968, which established the National Housing Partnership to promote the construction of houses for low- to middle-income people? Or maybe the reason blacks rioted was due to the 1965 Voting Rights Act, which had established the principle of "one person, one vote" a century after the abolition of slavery. Bush's pathetic effort to rewrite history, to blame the victim, was yet another example of his Willie Horton racial politics. The current agony of our inner cities is a direct and deliberate consequence of Reagan-Bush policies, and no amount of historical distortion can erase that fact.

On different sides of the race/class fault, each group tends to perceive issues in radically different ways. The vast majority of all Americans—black, Latino, Asian American and white—believed that the innocent verdict in the King case was wrong. But according to one poll in *USA Today*, 81 percent of all African Americans stated that the criminal justice system was clearly "biased against black people." Sixty percent of all blacks agreed that there was "very much" police brutality against people of color, and another 33 percent believed that such violence was "considerable." Conversely, only 36 percent of all whites responded that the justice system was racially biased. Only 17 percent of whites stated that there was excessive police brutality against minorities. The unanticipated eruption of rage stripped away the façade of black progress in the central cities, boiling with the problems of poverty, drugs, gang violence, unemployment, poor schools and deteriorating public housing. The white media tried desperately to turn attention away from these issues, in part by arguing that the Los Angeles uprising was merely a "riot" which was opposed by most African Americans. This ignores the historical evidence about the dynamics of all civil unrest. After the Watts racial rebellion of 1965, for example, sociologists later determined that only 15 percent of all black ghetto residents had actually participated in the arson and violence. However, between one-third to one-half of all residents later expressed support for those who had destroyed white-owned property and attacked symbols of white authority. About two-thirds later agreed that "the targets of the rebellion got what they deserved." So although the majority of African Americans in South Central L.A. didn't take to the streets, that doesn't mean that they aren't alienated and outraged by race and class oppression.

The same race/class fault line which trembled and shook across impoverished South Central Los Angeles also runs directly beneath the affluent white suburbs as well. This time, young black and Latino rebels weren't content to destroy the symbols of ghetto economic exploitation. Violence and arson unexpectedly struck against white-owned property across Los Angeles county. The Bloods and Crips street gangs established a fragile peace pact, announcing to the media that the current street violence was a "slave rebellion, like other slave rebellions in black history." One local Samoan rap group declared that the rebellion was "great," but that the violence against property should have been directed not against the Korean stores, but at the "rich people in Beverly Hills." For the black middle-class professionals, many of whom had come to believe the mythology about racial progress under the Reagan-Bush era, the King verdict was like a "fireball in the night." They were jolted into the realization that they, like Rodney King, could be halted by the police, brutalized, kicked, and possibly killed—and that their assailants in police uniforms would probably walk away free. They were awakened by the haunting fear that their college-bound sons and daughters could be stopped for minor traffic violations, and later be found dead or dying in the city streets. This is what Representative Floyd Flake of Brooklyn meant when he explained why the hopes of millions of African Americans in the inherent fairness of the legal system were shattered: "When Rodney King was on the ground getting beat, we were all on the ground getting beat."

But if we listen carefully to young African Americans in the streets, this generation is telling us more than just its dissatisfaction with the King verdict. The violence was not directly generated by reactions to courtroom decisions. What our young people painfully realize is that the entire "system"—the government and its politicians, the courts and the police, the corporations and the media—has written them off. They recognize that Bush had virtually no coherent policies addressing urban problems, until he was confronted by massive street violence. They feel instinctively that American businesses have no intention of hiring them at real "living wages," that the courts refuse to treat them as human beings, and that the politicians take their votes and ignore their needs. By taking to the streets, they are crying out to a society: "We will be heard! We will not be ignored, and we will not go away quietly. And if the system and society refuses to listen to us, we intend to burn it to the ground." That is the meaning of Los Angeles.

THIS IS DEMOCRACY?

One of the most striking things about the 1980s and 1990s is how the nature of racism has transmuted and transformed. In the 1950s and 1960s, the struggle against racial discrimination was very clear to everyone. Racism was embodied in the reality of "white" and "colored" signs that relegated African Americans to go into second-class positions, whether in lunchrooms, schools, toilets, or hotels. Racism was simply a form of legal segregation—Jim Crow. The racist renaissance of the 1980s and 1990s has ushered in a transformation in the character and essence of institutional bigotry. Think back—in the wake of the civil rights movement, it was no longer possible or viable for white elected officials, administrators, or corporate executives to attack African

Americans as "niggers." At least not openly. The Ku Klux Klan and other violent racist groups still existed, but they did not represent a mass movement among white Americans. But over the past ten years a neo-racist presence has emerged that attributes the source of all racial tensions to the actions of people of color themselves.

Consider the presence of David Duke. According to voter surveys, about 55 percent of all Louisiana whites supported Duke over three-term former Governor Edwin Edwards. Duke's greatest concentration of support was registered among whites who had suffered most in the state's economic recession. Sixty-eight percent of all whites with a high school education or less voted for Duke; 69 percent of the white "born-again Christians" and 63 percent of all whites with incomes between $15,000 to $30,000 favored Duke. Conversely, only 30 percent of whites who earn more than $75,000 annually voted for the former Klansman. This illustrates that race can be highly effective in mobilizing white working class discontent.

Both the Democrats and the Republicans are aware that race will be the crucial factor in determining the 1992 election. The Democratic candidates go into the election as distinct long-shots for several reasons. First, despite Bush's decline in popularity, incumbent presidents of either party rarely lose. The only incumbent presidents who were defeated seeking reelection since World War I were Hoover, Ford, and Carter, the victims of the Great Depression, Watergate, and the oil/hostage crisis.

Second, Republicans have received a majority of whites' votes in every presidential election except one since 1948. No matter who the Democrats nominate for the presidency, any candidate will have the same difficult task: pulling together northern white ethnics and many white workers from the South while courting African-American and Latino voters. The only recent Democratic candidate who achieved such a coalition was Jimmy Carter back in 1976. But even Carter failed to gain a majority of the white vote nationally.

The Republicans and Bush have already begun to respond by playing the "race card," the deliberate manipulation of racial prejudices for partisan political purposes. By first vetoing and later signing a weakened civil rights bill, Bush postured in the shadow of Duke. Bush's counsel, C. Boyden Gray, attempted to force the president to sign a policy statement which would have ended the use of racial preferences in federal government hiring policies. Although Gray's statement was repudiated, the controversy it provoked among civil rights and congressional leaders illustrated once again that Bush has absolutely no principles or commitment to the fight against discrimination.

Bush knows that if 66 percent of all white Americans support him in 1992—exactly the same percentage of whites who backed Reagan eight years before—that he would win the White House without a single black or Latino vote. By pandering to white racism, Bush solidifies his support among fearful, frustrated whites. Millions of jobless, discouraged whites are searching for simplistic answers to explain their poverty and economic marginality.

But all speculation concerning the demise of Duke as a national presence due to his recent electoral loss in Louisiana is highly exaggerated. Duke flourishes because Bush has prepared the ideological and cultural terrain by his own pandering to racism. In political terms, Duke is Bush's "illegitimate son" and heir. Duke is the child whom the president desperately desires to disown, but his political features of hatred and hostility to civil rights bear too striking a resemblance to those of his "father."

The "race card" will continue to be decisive in American politics, so long as white Americans vote according to their perceived racial interests, and not in concert with their basic material interests. Millions of white Americans are unemployed, just like Latinos and African Americans. Millions of white women do not receive equal pay for equal work, and experience discrimination on the job like minorities. If a Democratic presidential candidate had the courage and vision to attack the lies behind the "race card," and carried an aggressive message of social justice, the Republicans could be defeated.

RACISM AND STEREOTYPES

What is racism? How does the system of racial discrimination that people of color experience today differ from the type of discrimination that existed in the period of Jim Crow, or legal racial segregation? How is the rich spectrum of cultural groups affected by practices of discrimination within America's so-called "democratic society" today? What parallels can be drawn between sexism, racism and other types of intolerance, such as anti-Semitism, anti-Arabism, homophobia and handicapism? What kinds of national and international strategies are needed for a multicultural democracy in the whole of American society and throughout the Western world? And finally, what do we need to do to not just see beyond our differences, but to realize our commonalities and deepen one another's efforts to seize our full freedom and transform the nature of society?

Let's begin with point one: Racism is the system of ignorance, exploitation, and power used to oppress African Americans, Latinos, Asians, Pacific Americans, Native Americans, and other people on the basis of ethnicity, culture, mannerisms, and color. Point two: When we try to articulate an agenda of multicultural democracy, we run immediately into the stumbling block of stereotypes—the device at the heart of every form of racism today. Stereotypes are at work when people are not viewed as individuals with unique cultural and social backgrounds, with different religious traditions and ethnic identities, but as two-dimensional characters bred from the preconceived attitudes, half-truths, ignorance and fear of closed minds. When seen through a stereotype, a person isn't viewed as a bona fide human being, but as an object onto which myths and half-truths are projected. There are many ways that we see stereotypes degrade people, but perhaps the most insidious way is the manner in which stereotypes deny people their own history. In a racist society like our own, people of color are not viewed as having their own history or culture. Everything must conform to the so-called standards of white bourgeois society. Nothing generated by people of color is accepted as historically original, dynamic, or creative. This even applies to the way in which people of color are miseducated about their own history. Indeed, the most insidious element of stereotypes is how people who are oppressed themselves begin to lose touch with their own traditions of history, community, love, celebration, struggle, and change.

If we don't have a sense of where we've been and what we've experienced, how do we know where we want to go? This is crucially important, and one can see this as a form of political crippling, a type of historical amnesia that exists for a whole generation of young Americans who did not individually participate in the national ordeal to demolish Jim Crow, who did not participate in the social struggles in the streets against the war in Vietnam or for black empowerment, who did not participate in the mighty democratic movements of the 1960s. Many of us have a type of historical amnesia whereby we perpetuate the stereotypes, internalize them and project them upon others within our community.

If we don't have a sense of those who have contributed to democratic struggles and how those struggles relate to us now, how can we deepen the patterns of social change and continue to create greater vistas of democracy for our children and for their children? My grandmother, who never went to college or high school, who never finished elementary school, is far more articulate than I am. She used to say, "Manning, if you don't know where you're going, any road will get you there." So we need to understand the road that we're traveling. Where we're going is a function of where we've been.

THE RACISM OF REAGAN AND BUSH

The Ronald Reagan/Bush administration was unquestionably the fountainhead of much of the new racist upsurge. Remember: When Reagan won the Republican Party's presidential nomination, the very first place he chose to speak was a small town named Philadelphia, Mississippi. The day Reagan arrived the people of this town were holding a county fair, and Reagan got up before a crowd of several thousand white people who were waving Confederate flags and he said, "I have always been and I will always be for states' rights." Question one: Why Philadelphia, Mississippi? Question two: What does states' rights mean in the context of Mississippi? It means white supremacy. The crowd understood that. The president's speechwriters understood that. Even though Ronald Reagan had an IQ lower than a rock, even he understood that.

Question three: What happened in Mississippi in the town of Philadelphia in 1964? Remember: Three civil rights workers were brutally murdered; two whites, one black. The crowd knew that instinctively. It was red meat for them. Of course Reagan's speechwriters knew it too. It was an incredulous kind of posthumous affirmation of the hatred, closure, and violence of the murderers, and a nauseating attack against the democracy and freedom for which the three slain men were struggling. We have to understand that there is a correlation between racism and the absence of democracy in all this. That's really the thesis guiding my research and much of the thesis of my whole life. To understand the absence of democracy in this country, to understand the absence of equality and a decent life for millions of Americans, to understand the reasons why over two million Americans sleep in the filth of gutters and streets of this country, we must begin by understanding the odious structures of institutional racism. Racism will not answer all of our questions, but it does put us on the path to understanding why we have not achieved the reality of democracy in this country.

In the 1980s we saw a proliferation of racist violence, most disturbingly on college campuses. Several years ago at Purdue University a cross was actually burned in front of a black cultural center. A week later someone carved into a black employee's door: "Death to you, nigger." At the University of Texas, Austin, there was the formation of the Aryan Collegiates, who have the goal of the elimination of "all outspoken minorities" from the campus. There have been a whole series of racist incidents over a three- or four-year period at the University of Michigan at Ann Arbor. At Columbia University in the spring of 1988 there was an assault against several African-American students by a group of whites, prompting an anti-racist rally of over 1,000 students denouncing racism on campus. These are only a few of countless incidents occurring across the nation.

Why the upsurgence of racism? Why was it occurring in the 1980s and why does this disease continue to spread into the 1990s? How is it complicit with other systemic crises that we now face within the political, economic, and social structures of our society?

First we need to be clear about how we recognize racism. Racism is never accidental within a social structure or institution. It is the systematic exploitation of people of color in the process of production and labor, the attempt to subordinate our cultural, social, educational, and political life. The key concepts here are subordinate and systemic. The dynamics of racism attempt to inflict a subordinate position for people of color—Latinos, Native Americans, Arabs, Asians, African Americans, and other people of color within the society.

The people and policies working for Bush and Reagan have consolidated the process of inequality in the legal system, because the real legacy of Reagan is not what occurred in the White House over an eight-year period. Along with leaving us an insurmountable national debt and an obese military arsenal, the real legacy of Reagan, I believe, is going to be the 425 judges that he appointed to federal district courts and circuit courts of appeals. Through these appointments he ensured that the discrimination of Reaganism would continue long after his presidency had ended. The average age of the judges Reagan appointed to the federal level is only forty-six years. Reagan ensured that his ideology would permeate the legal apparatus, and this ideology bears definite racist dimensions. Remember: During Reagan's first term in office, the percentage of black appointments to the federal district court and the U.S. circuit court of appeals fell below one percent. By comparison, Jimmy Carter made fifty-six appointments to the U.S. circuit court of appeals from 1977 to 1981. These included eleven women, ten African Americans, two Latinos, and one Asian American. Reagan's appointments were slightly different: one woman, one black, one Hispanic, and probably all the same person.

The Reagan/Bush administration was openly contemptuous of African-American rights; it nominated virtually no people of color to the federal courts, and it openly supported the apartheid regime in South Africa through Reagan's policy of "constructive engagement." George Bush pursued the presidency in 1988 by employing Reagan's racial strategy. His campaign cited the infamous example of black convict Willie Horton as an example of the Democrat's "softness on crime." Even without openly appealing to white supremacy, Bush nevertheless benefited from a racist backlash against the gains achieved by racial minorities since the 1960s. As president, Bush continues to pursue a racist agenda while employing a public style and discourse of racial harmony. He openly courts black middle-class leaders. He invites them to the White House for lunch. He said, OK. Thurgood Marshall, the only African American on the Supreme Court, is leaving the court, but I believe in racial equality. I'm going to give you another black justice. So he produces a black justice who's against women's right of choice. It's a black justice, Clarence Thomas, who clearly is antithetical and hostile toward the civil rights agenda. This is a black justice who is opposed to affirmative action, opposed to workers' rights and trade union rights, a so-called black justice who has carried out in his personal and public life an attitude of contempt for women and particularly for African American women! But that's the one Bush has given us. This is a kind of "slick" racism, as one of my students once put it. In fact, Malcolm X developed a term for it: he called it *tricknology.* It gives us something without giving us anything—an appearance that diverts attention away from the real and malignant social impact.

Racism in the 1990s means lower pay for equal work. It means a process that sustains inequality within the income structure of this country. Institutional racism in America's economic system today means that the rhetoric of equal opportunity in the marketplace remains, in effect, a hoax for most people of color. Between 1973 and 1986 the real average earnings for black males between the ages of twenty and twenty-nine actually fell 50 percent. When thousands of African-American families struggle to save enough for home mortgages and loans to start small businesses, they are frequently denied these loans from banks. There was a recent study in the *Rocky Mountain News* and other newspapers over the last several months, commissioned by the Federal Reserve Bank of Boston, indicating that the percentage of loans made to predominantly black communities is substantially lower than those granted to white neighborhoods. From 1982 to 1988 mortgages were issued on 7 percent of properties in white areas and only 2.5 percent in areas that were virtually black. By denying African Americans credit, and by denying credit to other people of color in the central cities, the process of gentrification accelerates, permitting thousands of middle-class whites to seize minority-owned property at bargain basement prices inside the central cities.

CRACK

What else intensifies racism and inequality in the 1990s? Drugs. We are witnessing the complete disintegration of America's inner cities, the home of millions of Latinos and blacks. We see the daily destructive impact of gang violence inside our neighborhoods and communities which is directly attributable to the fact that for twenty years the federal government has done little to address the crisis of drugs inside the ghetto and the inner city. It seems as if there is no drug epidemic in this country so long as young black and Latina women and men are the primary victims. It seems as if there is no drug epidemic in this country so long as the drug disease is quarantined to low-income neighborhoods and voiceless ghettos. How many more of our people will we allow to be shattered by drugs? How many more of our homes can we allow to be torn and destroyed? How many daughters and sons will we allow our families and friends to lose? For people of color, crack addiction has become part of the new urban slavery, a method of disrupting lives and regulating masses of young people who would otherwise be demanding jobs, adequate health care, better schools and control of their own communities. Is it accidental that this insidious cancer has been unleashed within the very poorest urban neighborhoods, and that the police concentrate on petty street dealers rather than those who actually control and profit from the drug traffic? How is it possible that thousands and thousands of pounds of illegal drugs can be transported throughout the country, in airplanes, trucks and automobiles, to hundreds of central distribution centers with thousands of employees, given the ultra high-tech surveillance and intelligence capacity of law enforcement officers? How, unless crack presented a systemic form of social control?

Some of you may say, "Manning, this is a type of conspiratorial theory." This is no conspiracy. This is a fact. If you were living in an inner-city community in the mid-1980s you saw the appearance of crack and felt it seep into your neighborhood and sap the will and resistance of thousands of young women and men. The struggle that we have now is not simply against the system. It's against the kind of insidious violence and oppressive behavior that people of color carry out against each other. What I'm talking about is the convergence between the utility of a certain type of commodity—addictive narcotics—and economic and social problems which are confronting the system. That is, the redundancy, the unemployment of millions of people of color, young women and men, living in our urban centers. The criminal justice system represents one type of social control. Crack and addictive narcotics represent another type. If you're doing organizing work within the black community it becomes impossible to get people and families to come out to your community center when there are crack houses all around the building. It becomes impossible to continue political organizing when people are afraid for their own lives. This is the new manifestation of racism in which we see a form of social control existing in our communities, the destruction of social institutions, and the erosion of people's ability to fight against the forms of domination that continuously try to oppress them.

WOMEN'S FREEDOM

How do we locate the connections between racism and sexism? There are many direct parallels, in both theory and practice, between these two systems of domination. A good working definition of sexism is the subordination of women's social, cultural, political and educational rights as human beings, and the unequal distribution of power and resources between women and men based on gender. Sexism is a subsocial dynamic, like racism, in that the dynamic is used to subordinate one part of the population to another.

How does sexism function in the economic system? Women experience it through the lack of pay equity—the absence of equal pay for comparable work performed by women versus men on the job. Sexism exists in the stratification of the vocational hierarchy by gender, which keeps women disproportionately at the bottom. The upper levels of the corporations are dominated by white, wealthy males, as is the ownership of productive forces and property largely that of white males. Women consequently have less income mobility, and frequently are defined as "homemakers," a vocation for which there is absolutely no financial compensation, despite sixty to eighty hours of work per week.

Sexism within cultural and social institutions means the domination of males in decision-making positions. Males control the majority of newspapers, the film industry, radio and television. Sexist stereotypes of both males and females are thus perpetuated through the dominant cultural institutions, advertising, and broadcast media.

In political institutions, sexism translates into an unequal voice and influence within the government. The overwhelming majority of seats in the Congress, state legislatures, courts, and city councils are controlled by white men. The United States has one of the lowest percentages of women represented within its national legislature among Western democratic societies.

And finally, like racism, the wire that knots sexist mechanisms together, which perpetuates women's inequality within the fabric of the social institutions, is violence. Rape, spouse abuse, sexual harassment on the job, are all essential to the perpetuation of a sexist society. For the sexist, violence is the necessary and logical part of an unequal, exploitative relationship. To dominate and control, sexism requires violence. Rape and sexual harassment are therefore not accidental to the structure of gender relations within a sexist order. This is why progressives must first target the issue of violence against women, in the struggle for human equality and a nonsexist environment. This is why we must fight for women's rights to control their own bodies and not submit to the demagogues of the rabid right who would return us to the back alley abortionists, to those who destroy young women's lives. Those who oppose the woman's right to choose express so much love for the rights of the fetus, yet too frequently express contempt for child nutrition programs, child care and education after the child has come into the world.

Sexism and racism combine with class exploitation to produce a three-edged mode of oppression for women of color. Economically, African American, Latina, and Native American women are far below white women in terms of income, job security, and job mobility. The median income of a black woman who is also a single parent with children is below $10,000 annually. Thirty-six percent of all black people live below the federal government's poverty line. And more than 75 percent of that number are black women and their children.

Black and Latina women own virtually no sizeable property; they head no major corporations; they only rarely are the heads of colleges and universities; they hold no massive real estate holdings; they are not on the Supreme Court; few are in the federal court system; they are barely represented in Congress, and they represent tiny minorities in state legislatures or in the leadership of both major parties. Only a fractional percentage of the attorneys and those involved in the criminal justice system are African American women. It is women of color, not white women, who are overwhelmingly those who are harassed by police, arrested without cause, and who are the chief victims of all types of crimes.

Sexism and racism are not perpetuated biologically like a disease or drug addiction; both behaviors are learned within a social framework and have absolutely no ground in hereditary biology. They are perpetuated by stereotypes, myths, and irrational fears that are rooted in false sense of superiority. Both sexism and racism involve acts of systemic coercion—job discrimination, legal domination, and political under-representation. And both sexism and racism may culminate in acts of physical violence.

What correlations can be established between racism, sexism, homophobia, anti-Semitism, handicapism, and other manifestations of intolerance and violence? It is unfortunately true that people who are victimized by one form of prejudice or social intolerance sometimes fail to appreciate the oppression of other victims. There are blacks who are unfortunately anti-Semitic, and Jews who are racist; there are white women who are racist and oppressive to sisters of color; there are Latinos who are homophobic and oppressive to gays and lesbians; there are people of color who are insensitive to whites who are physically challenged. Yet for many of us, the experience of oppression gives us some insights into the pain and discrimination of others. I am a scholar of the civil rights movement, and I write about lynching, political franchisement, and Jim Crow. But I also lived through this experience. I personally know what it is like to go to the back of the bus. I know what it is like not to be served at a restaurant. I know what it is like not to be permitted to sit inside a heated bus terminal, but be forced to stand outside in the cold. I know what it is like not to be permitted to try on a cap or a pair of pants because you are black. When you experience this, you can never forget it.

And I believe that the experience of oppression, if properly understood, can be universalized. Because I have felt the pain of oppression, I can understand and feel the pain of my sisters, victimized by violence, harassment, and sexist discrimination. I can understand the anger of my Jewish sisters and brothers who must confront the hatred and bigotry of the anti-Semite. I can express my sympathy and support for lesbians and gays who experience discrimination because of their sexual preference.

EDUCATION

What are some other characteristics of the new racism that we are now encountering? What we see in general is a duplicitous pattern that argues that African Americans and other people of color are moving forward while their actual material conditions are being pushed back. Look at America's education system. The number of doctoral degrees being granted to blacks, for example, is falling. Between 1977 and 1987 the total number of students who received doctorates in American universities increased by about 500, to 32,278 students. In 1977, the number of African Americans receiving doctorates was 1,116. By 1987, that figure had declined to barely 700. By 1980, the year Reagan was elected, there were 1.1 million African Americans enrolled in American colleges and various types of professional schools, and the number of black doctorates had fallen slightly to 1,032 students. The Reagan administration initiated budget cuts in education, replacing government grants for loans, and deliberately escalated unemployment for low-income people, making it difficult to afford tuition at professional schools. By 1983, the number of black doctorates dropped to 921; and by 1987 only 765 black women and men were awarded doctorates. By 1987, there were nearly 100,000 fewer black Americans enrolled in college than there were ten years ago. We're seeing the vision of equality moving away from us.

A similar story exists for the overall enrollment of African Americans in institutions of higher education. In 1980, 1,107,000 black men and women were enrolled in a college or post-secondary institution. Six years later, that figure had declined slightly, down to 1,081,000 students. Since, however, the population base for blacks of college age (18 to 26 years) had increased significantly during these years, the decline was actually far greater than it appeared when considered as a percentage of that population group. By contrast, white college enrollment between 1976 and 1986 increased by nearly one million students—almost the total number of all African Americans currently enrolled.

We can think about the problem of educational under-development at the collegiate level if we backtrack the progress of young people of color from kindergarten through to their senior year in college. According to the California Post-secondary Education Commission Director's Report, the 1988 black kindergarten enrollment in California was approximately 35,290 students. Of this number, the director's report projects that only 17,645 black students from this 1988 kindergarten class, roughly 50 percent, will graduate from high schools. About 6,800 will enter community colleges, approximately 20 percent; 1,235 are projected to enter campuses of the California State University system; and another 706 will enroll in the University of California, which is only 2 percent of the original kindergarten class. How many will graduate? Only 363 black students will ultimately receive college diplomas from either California State University or the University of California, one percent of the initial group.

The basic pattern of elitism and racism in colleges conforms to the dynamics of Third World colonialism. At nearly all white academic institutions, the power relationship between whites as a group and people of color is unequal. Authority is invested in the hands of a core of largely white male administrators, bureaucrats, and influential senior faculty. The board of trustees or regents is dominated by white, conservative, affluent males. Despite the presence of academic courses on minorities, the vast majority of white students take few or no classes which explore the heritage or cultures of non-Western peoples or domestic minorities. Most courses in the humanities and social sciences focus narrowly on topics or issues from the Western capitalist experience and minimize the centrality and importance of non-Western perspectives. Finally, the university or college divorces itself from the pressing concerns, problems and debates which relate to blacks, Hispanics or even white working class people. Given this structure and guiding philosophy, it shouldn't surprise us that many talented nonwhite students fail to achieve in such a hostile environment.

THE COLOR OF OUR PRISONS

There are over 2.2 million arrests of black people every year in the United States; one-half million blacks are currently incarcerated in a federal or state prison or a penal institution. At least one-half of the black prisoners are less than thirty years of age, and over one thousand are not even old enough to vote. Most black male prisoners were unemployed at the time of their arrests; the others averaged less than $8,000 annual income during the year before they were jailed. And about 45 percent of the over twenty-two hundred people currently awaiting execution are African Americans. As Lennox S. Hinds, former National Director of the National Conference of Black Lawyers, has stated, "someone black and poor tried for stealing a few hundred dollars has a 90 percent likelihood of being convicted of robbery with a sentence averaging between 94 and 138 months. A white business executive who embezzled hundreds of thousands of dollars has only a 20 percent likelihood of conviction with a sentence averaging about 20 to 48 months." Justice is not color blind when black people are the accused.

The American economic and political system promises equality, but has never delivered for the African American. In fact, the system uses the rhetoric and myth of equality to hide the process of oppression. Both through legal and illegal means blacks are being subordinated, marginalized, and oppressed.

TOWARD A MULTICULTURAL DEMOCRACY

So what do we need in this country? How do we begin to redefine the nature of democracy? Not as a thing, but as a process. Democracy is a dynamic concept. African Americans twenty-five years ago did not have the right to eat in many restaurants, we couldn't sit down in the front seats of buses or planes, we couldn't vote in the South, we weren't allowed to use public toilets or drink from water fountains marked "For Whites Only." All of that changed through struggle, commitment, and an understanding that democracy is not something that you do once every four years when you vote, it's something that you live every single day.

What can we do to create a more pluralistic, democratic society in America? Before the end of this decade, the majority of California's total population will consist of people of color—Asian Americans, Latinos, Arab Americans, Native Americans, African Americans, and others. By the year 2030, the majority of the working class between the ages of twenty and forty will consist of people of color. And not long after the midpoint of the next century, no later than 2056, we will live in a country in which Caucasian people will be a distinct minority of the total population, and people of color will be the numerical majority. Over the next fifty years there will be a transition from a white majority society to a society which is far more pluralistic and diverse, where multilingualism is increasingly the norm, where different cultures, different spiritualities, and different philosophies are a beautiful mosaic of human exchange and interaction. This is the emerging multicultural majority.

People of color are radically redefining the nature of democracy. We assert that democratic government is empty and meaningless without active social justice and cultural diversity. Multicultural political democracy means that this country was not built by and for only one group—Western Europeans; that our country does not have only one language—English; or only one religion—Christianity; or only one economic philosophy—corporate capitalism. Multicultural democracy means that the leadership within our society should reflect the richness, colors and diversity expressed in the lives of all of our people. Multicultural democracy demands new types of power-sharing and the reallocation of resources necessary to create economic and social development for those who have been systematically excluded and denied. Multicultural democracy enables all women and men to achieve full self-determination, which may include territorial and geographical restructuring, if that is the desire of an indigenous group, community, or oppressed nation. Native Americans can no longer be denied their legitimate claims of sovereignty as an oppressed nation, and we must fight for their right to self-determination as a central principle of democracy.

Multicultural democracy articulates a vision of society which is feminist or, in the words of Alice Walker, "womanist." The patterns of subordination and exploitation of women of color—including job discrimination rooted in gender, race and class, rape and sexual abuse, forced sterilizations, harassment and abuse within the criminal justice system, housing discrimination against single mothers with children, the absence of pay equity for comparable work, political under-representation, and legal disfranchisement—combine to perpetuate a subordinate status for women within society. No progressive struggles have ever been won for people of color throughout history without the courage, contributions, sacrifices and leadership of women. No political agenda of emancipation is possible unless one begins with the central principle of empowerment and full liberation for all women, at every level of organization and society. Men must learn from the experiences and insights of women if we are to liberate ourselves from the political, cultural and ideological restraints which deny us our rights as Americans and free human beings.

What else is multicultural democracy? Multicultural democracy includes a powerful economic vision which is centered on the needs of human beings. We each need to go out into the community and begin hammering out an economic vision of empowerment that grass roots people can grasp and understand and use. We need to break the media monologues that talk at us through the TV and begin talking with one another in the terms of our practical life experiences. What kinds of questions should we raise? Is it right for a government to spend billions and billions for bailing out fat cats who profited from the savings and loan scam while millions of jobless Americans stand in unemployment lines desperate for work? Is it fair that billions of our dollars are allocated for the Pentagon's permanent war economy to obliterate the lives of millions of poor people from Panama to Iraq to Grenada to Vietnam, while two million Americans sleep in the streets and 37 million Americans lack any form of medical coverage? Bush and the Democrats recently came up with a compromise on the permanent war economy. They called for a $291 billion military budget for the next fiscal year! Figure that out. It's equivalent to spending one trillion dollars on military in the next three years. This is supposed to be the post–Cold War era? Who is the military-industrial complex gearing up to fight? Is the war going to be in the Soviet Union? There is already a war going on, and the war is between them and us. We're losing the war as we see millions of people slide into hunger and poverty. We're losing the war when we see children go to elementary schools throughout thousands of cities and towns across America without adequate food and clothing, while no one stands up and advocates an economics of empowerment and social justice. Is it a democracy that we have when we have the right to vote but no right to a job? Is it a democracy when people of color have the freedom to starve, the freedom to live in housing without adequate heating facilities, the freedom to attend substandard schools? Democracy without social justice, without human rights, without human dignity is no democracy at all.

We can unite by pooling our resources and energies around progressive projects designed to promote greater awareness and protest among national communities of people of color. This could mean joint mobilizations against the 1992 Columbus Quincentennial. Any "celebration" of the so-called conquest of the Americas and the Caribbean is a sick insult to the millions of Native Americans, Latinos, Asians and Africans who died at the sword of capitalism, the trans-Atlantic slave trade, and colonialism. We have the opportunity to denounce 500 years of invasion, war, genocide, and racism by holding teach-ins, demonstrations, and collective protest actions while bringing greater strength and momentum to the multicultural movement. We could initiate "Freedom Schools," liberation academies which identify and nurture young women and men with an interest in community-based struggles—a curriculum which teaches young people about their own protest leaders, which reinforces their identification with our collective cultures of resistance, and which deepens our solidarity by celebrating rather than stifling our cultural differences. The new majority must build progressive research institutes, bridging the distance between activists, community organizers, and progressive intellectuals who can provide the policies and theoretical tools useful in the empowerment of grassroots constituencies and national communities.

Finally, we must infuse our definition of politics with a common sense of ethics and spirituality which challenges the structures of oppression, power, and privilege within the dominant social order. Part of the historic strength of the Black Freedom Movement were the deep connections between political objectives and ethical prerogatives. This connection gave the rhetoric of Frederick Douglass, Sojourner Truth, W. E. B. Du Bois, Paul Robeson, and Fannie Lou Hamer a clear vision of the moral ground that was simultaneously particular and universal. It spoke to the uplifting of African Americans, but its humanistic imperative continues to reach far further.

Multicultural democracy must perceive itself in this historic tradition, as a critical project which transforms the larger society. We must place humanity at the center of our politics. It is not sufficient that we assert what we are against; we must affirm what we are for. It is not sufficient that we declare what we want to overturn, but what we are seeking to build, in the sense of restoring humanity and humanistic values to a system which is materialistic, destructive to the environment, and abusive to fellow human beings. We need to enact policies which say that the people who actually produce society's wealth should control how it is used.

The moral bankruptcy of contemporary American society is found, in part, in the vast chasm which separates the conditions of material well being, affluence, power and privilege of a small elite from the whole spectrum of America's communities. The evil in our world is politically and socially engineered, and its products are poverty, homelessness, illiteracy, political subservience, race discrimination, and gender domination. The old saying from the sixties—we either are part of the solution or part of the problem—is simultaneously moral, cultural, economic, and political. Paul Robeson reminds us that we must "take a stand," not simply dare to dream, if our endeavors are to have lasting meaning. We cannot be disinterested observers as the physical and spiritual beings of millions of people are collectively crushed.

Can we believe in certain inalienable rights that go beyond Jefferson's terminology of "life, liberty, and the pursuit of happiness"? What about the inalienable right not to go hungry in a land of agricultural abundance? The human right to decent housing? The human right to free public medical care for all? The human right to an adequate income in one's old age? Democracy must believe in freedom, but that freedom in my terminology is something different from what "freedom" has come to mean in this country in the age of Ronald Reagan and George Bush, Clarence Thomas and David Duke. Freedom now means, unfortunately, the freedom of corporations to raise prices, the wealthy to evade taxes, or the freedom of the unemployed to dwell at the edge of starvation and desperation. Can we believe in a freedom to build a new society without racism and sexism, to work and live in our neighborhoods without fear of police repression and brutality, to live in a neighborhood and have access to free public medical care and decent shelter for all? If we can achieve such a democracy, if we can believe in the vision of a dynamic democracy in which all human beings, women and men, Latinos, Asian Americans, African Americans, Native Americans, coming to terms with each other, we can perhaps begin to achieve Martin Luther King, Jr.'s vision when he said, "We shall overcome."

PART V

STORMING OZ

NOAM CHOMSKY

MEDIA CONTROL

The Spectacular Achievements of Propaganda

EXCERPTS FROM A LECTURE,
KENTFIELD, CALIFORNIA—MARCH 17, 1991

The role of the media in contemporary politics forces us to ask what kind of a world and what kind of a society we want to live in, and in particular in what sense of "democracy" do we want this to be a democratic society? Let me begin by counterposing two different conceptions of democracy. One conception of democracy has it that a democratic society is one in which the public has the means to participate in some meaningful way in the management of their own affairs and the means of information are open and free. If you look up "democracy" in the dictionary you'll get a definition something like that.

An alternative conception of democracy is that the public must be barred from managing their own affairs and the means of information must be kept narrowly and rigidly controlled. That may sound like an odd conception of democracy, but it's important to understand that it is the prevailing conception. In fact, it has long been, not just in operation, but even in theory. There's a long history that goes back to the earliest modern democratic revolutions in seventeenth century England which largely expresses this point of view. I'm just going to keep to the modern period and say a few words about how that notion of democracy develops and why and how the problem of media and disinformation enters within that context.

EARLY HISTORY OF PROPAGANDA

Let's begin with the first modern government propaganda operation. That was under the Woodrow Wilson Administration. Woodrow Wilson was elected President in 1916 on the platform "Peace Without Victory." That was right in the middle of World War I. The population was extremely pacifistic and saw no reason to become involved in a European war. The Wilson administration was actually committed to war and had to do something about it. They established a government propaganda commission, called the Creel Commission, which succeeded, within six months, in turning a pacifistic population into a hysterical, war–mongering population which wanted to destroy everything German, tear the Germans limb from limb, go to war and save the world. That was a major achievement, and it led to a further achievement. Right at that time and after the war the same techniques were used to whip up a hysterical Red Scare, as it was called, which succeeded pretty much in destroying unions and eliminating such dangerous problems as freedom of the press and freedom of political thought. There was very strong support from the media, from the business establishment, which in fact organized, pushed much of this work, and it was, in general, a great success.

Among those who participated actively and enthusiastically in Wilson's war were the progressive intellectuals, people of the John Dewey circle, who took great pride, as you can see from their own writings at the time, in having shown that what they called the "more intelligent members of the community," namely, themselves, were able to drive a reluctant population into a war by terrifying them and eliciting jingoist fanaticism. The means that were used were extensive. For example, there was a good deal of fabrication of atrocities by the Huns, Belgian babies with their arms torn off, all sorts of awful things that you still read in history books. Much of it was invented by the British propaganda ministry, whose own commitment at the time, as they put it in their secret deliberations, was "to direct the thought of most of the world." But more crucially they wanted to control the thought of the more intelligent members of the community in the United States, who would then disseminate the propaganda that they were concocting and convert the pacifistic country to wartime hysteria. That worked. It worked very well. And it taught a lesson: state propaganda, when supported by the educated classes and when no deviation is permitted from it, can have a big effect. It was a lesson learned by Hitler and many others, and it has been pursued to this day.

SPECTATOR DEMOCRACY

Another group that was impressed by these successes was liberal democratic theorists and leading media figures like Walter Lippmann, who was the dean of American journalists, a major foreign and domestic policy critic and also a major theorist of liberal democracy. If you take a look at his collected essays, you'll see that they're subtitled something like "A Progressive Theory of Liberal Democratic Thought." Lippmann was involved in these propaganda commissions and recognized their achievements. He argued that what he called a "revolution in the art of democracy," could be used to "manufacture consent," that is, to bring about agreement on the part of the public for things that they didn't want by the new techniques of propaganda. He also thought that this was a good idea, in fact, necessary. It was necessary because, as he put it, "the common interests elude public opinion entirely" and can only be understood and managed by a "specialized class" of "responsible men" who are smart enough to figure things out. This theory asserts that only a small elite, the intellectual community that the Deweyites were talking about, can understand the common interests, what all of us care about, and that these things "elude the general public." This is a view that goes back hundreds of years. It's also a typical Leninist view. In fact, it has very close resemblance to the Leninist conception that a vanguard of revolutionary intellectuals take state power, using popular revolutions as the force that brings them to state power, and then drive the stupid masses toward a future that they're too dumb and incompetent to envision for themselves. The liberal democratic theory and Marxism–Leninism are very close in their common ideological assumptions. I think that's one reason why people have found it so easy over the years to drift from one position to another without any particular sense of change. It's just a matter of assessing where power is. Maybe there will be a popular revolution, and that will put us into state power; or maybe there won't be, in which case we'll just work for the people with real power: the business community. But we'll do the same thing. We'll drive the stupid masses toward a world that they're too dumb to understand for themselves.

Lippmann backed this up by a pretty elaborate theory of progressive democracy. He argued that in a properly functioning democracy there are classes of citizens. There is first of all the class of citizens who have to take some active role in running general affairs. That's the specialized class. They are the people who analyze, execute, make decisions, and run things in the political, economic, and ideological systems.

That's a small percentage of the population. Naturally, anyone who puts these ideas forth is always part of that small group, and they're talking about what to do about *those others*. Those others, who are out of the small group, the big majority of the population, they are what Lippmann called "the bewildered herd." We have to protect ourselves from "the trampling and roar of a bewildered herd." Now, there are two "functions" in a democracy: the specialized class, the responsible men, carry out the executive function, which means they do the thinking and planning and understand the common interests. Then, there is the bewildered herd, and they have a function in democracy too. Their function in a democracy, he said, is to be "spectators," not participants in action. But they have more of a function than that, because it's a democracy. Occasionally they are allowed to lend their weight to one or another member of the specialized class. In other words, they're allowed to say, "We want you to be our leader" or "We want *you* to be our leader." That's because it's a democracy and not a totalitarian state. That's called an election. But once they've lent their weight to one or another member of the specialized class they're supposed to sink back and become spectators of action, but not participants. That's in a properly functioning democracy.

And there's a logic behind it. There's even a kind of compelling moral principle behind it. The compelling moral principle is that the mass of the public are just too stupid to be able to understand things. If they try to participate in managing their own affairs, they're just going to cause trouble. Therefore, it would be immoral and improper to permit them to do this. We have to tame the bewildered herd, not allow the bewildered herd to rage and trample and destroy things. It's pretty much the same logic that says that it would be improper to let a three-year-old run across the street. You don't give a three-year-old that kind of freedom because the three-year-old doesn't know how to handle that freedom. Correspondingly, you don't allow the bewildered herd to become participants in action. They'll just cause trouble.

So we need something to tame the bewildered herd, and that something is this new revolution in the art of democracy: the manufacture of consent. The media, the schools, and popular culture have to be divided. The political class and decision makers have to provide some tolerable sense of reality, although they also have to instill the proper beliefs. Just remember, there is an unstated premise here. The unstated premise—and even the responsible men have to disguise this from themselves—has to do with the question of how they get into the position where they have the authority to make decisions. The way they do that, of course, is by serving people with *real* power. The people with real power are the ones who own the society, which is a pretty narrow group. If the specialized class can come along and say, *I can serve your interests,* then they'll be part of the executive group. You've got to keep that quiet. That means they have to have instilled in them the beliefs and doctrines that will serve the interests of private power. Unless they can master that skill, they're not part of the specialized class. So we have one kind of educational system directed to the responsible men, the specialized class. They have to be deeply indoctrinated in the values and interests of private power and the state-corporate nexus that represents it. If they can achieve that, then they can be part of the specialized class. The rest of the bewildered herd basically just have to be distracted. Turn their attention to something else. Keep them out of trouble. Make sure that they remain at most spectators of action, occasionally lending their weight to one or another of the real leaders, who they may select among.

This point of view has been developed by lots of other people. In fact, it's pretty conventional. For example, the leading theologian and foreign policy critic Reinhold Niebuhr, sometimes called "the theologian of the establishment," the guru of George Kennan and the Kennedy intellectuals, put it that rationality is a very narrowly restricted skill. Only a small number of people have it. Most people are guided by just emotion and impulse. Those of us who have rationality have to create "necessary illusions" and emotionally potent "oversimplifications" to keep the naïve simpletons more or less on course. This became a substantial part of contemporary political science. In the 1920s and early 1930s, Harold Lasswell, the founder of the modern field of communications and one of the leading American political scientists, explained that we should not succumb to "democratic dogmatisms about men being the best judges of their own interests." Because they're not. *We're* the best judges of the public interests. Therefore, just out of ordinary morality, *we* have to make sure that they don't have an opportunity to act on the basis of their misjudgments. In what is nowadays called a totalitarian state, or a military state, it's easy. You just hold a bludgeon over their heads, and if they get out of line you smash them over the head. But as society has become more free and democratic, you lose that capacity. Therefore you have to turn to the techniques of propaganda. The logic is clear. Propaganda is to a democracy what the bludgeon is to a totalitarian state. That's wise and good because, again, the common interests elude the bewildered herd. They can't figure them out.

PUBLIC RELATIONS

The United States pioneered the public relations industry. Its commitment was "to control the public mind," as its leaders put it. They learned a lot from the successes of the Creel Commission and the successes in creating the Red Scare and its aftermath. The public relations industry underwent a huge expansion at that time. It succeeded for some time in creating almost total subordination of the public to business rule through the 1920s. This was so extreme that congressional committees began to investigate it as we moved into the 1930s. That's where a lot of our information about it comes from.

Public relations is a huge industry. They're spending by now something on the order of a billion dollars a year. All along its commitment was to *controlling the public mind.* In the 1930s, big problems arose again, as they had during the First World War. There was a huge depression and substantial labor organizing. In fact, in 1935 labor won its first major legislative victory, namely, the right to organize, with the Wagner Act. That raised two serious problems. For one thing, democracy was misfunctioning. The bewildered herd was actually winning legislative victories, and it's not supposed to work that way. The other problem was that it was becoming possible for people to organize. People have to be atomized and segregated and alone. They're not supposed to organize, because then they might be something beyond spectators of action. They might actually be participants if many people with limited resources could get together to enter the political arena. That's really threatening. A major response was taken on the part of Business to ensure that this would be the last legislative victory for labor and that it would be the beginning of the end of this democratic deviation of popular organization. It worked. That was the last legislative victory for labor. From that point on—although the number of people in the unions increased for a while during World War II, after which it started dropping—the capacity to act through the unions began to steadily drop. It wasn't by accident. We're now talking about the business community, which spends lots and lots of money, attention, and thought into how to deal with these problems through the public relations industry and other organizations, like the National Association of Manufacturers and the Business Roundtable, and so on. They immediately set to work to try to find a way to counter these democratic deviations.

The first trial was one year later, in 1937. There was a major strike, the Steel strike in western Pennsylvania at Johnstown. Business tried out a new technique of labor destruction, which worked very well. Not through goon squads and breaking knees. That wasn't working very well any more, but through the more subtle and effective means of propaganda. The idea was to figure out ways to turn the public against the strikers, to present the strikers as disruptive, harmful to the public and against the common interests. The common interests are those of "us," the businessman, the worker, the housewife. That's all "us." We want to be together and have things like harmony and Americanism and working together. Then there's those bad strikers out there who are disruptive and causing trouble and breaking harmony and violating Americanism. We've got to stop them so we can all live together. The corporate executive and the guy who cleans the floors all have the same interests. We can all work together and work for Americanism in harmony, liking each other. That was essentially the message. A huge amount of effort was put into presenting it. This is, after all, the business community, so they control the media and have massive resources. And it worked, very effectively. It was later called the "Mohawk Valley formula" and applied over and over again to break strikes. They were called "scientific methods of strike-breaking," and worked very effectively by mobilizing community opinion in favor of vapid, empty concepts like Americanism. Who can be against that? Or harmony. Who can be against that? Or, as in the Persian Gulf War, "Support our troops." Who can be against that? Or yellow ribbons. Who can be against that? Anything that's totally vacuous.

In fact, what does it mean if somebody asks you, Do you support the people in Iowa? Can you say, *Yes, I support them*, or *No, I don't support them*? It's not even a question: It doesn't mean anything. That's the point. The point of public relations slogans like "Support our troops" is that they don't mean anything. They mean as much as whether you support the people in Iowa. Of course, there was an issue. The issue was, *Do you support our policy?* But you don't want people to think about that issue. That's the whole point of good propaganda. You want to create a slogan that nobody's going to be against, and everybody's going to be for. Nobody knows what it means, because it doesn't mean anything. Its crucial value is that it diverts your attention from a question that *does* mean something: *Do you support our policy?* That's the one you're not allowed to talk about. So you have people arguing about support for the troops? "Of course I don't *not* support them." Then they've won. That's like Americanism and harmony. We're all together, empty slogans, let's join in, let's make sure we don't have these bad people around to disrupt our harmony with their talk about class struggle, rights and that sort of business.

That's all very effective. It runs right up to today. And of course it is carefully thought out. The people in the public relations industry aren't there for the fun of it. They're doing work. They're trying to instill the right values. In fact, they have a conception of what democracy ought to be: it ought to be a system in which the specialized class is trained to work in the service of the masters, the people who own the society. The rest of the population ought to be deprived of any form of organization, because organization just causes trouble. They ought to be sitting alone in front of the TV and having drilled into their heads the message, which says, the only value in life is to have more commodities or live like that rich middle class family you're watching and to have nice values like harmony and Americanism. That's all there is in life. You may think in your own head that there's got to be something more in life than this, but since you're watching the tube alone you assume, I must be crazy, because that's all that's going on over there. And since there is no organization permitted—that's absolutely crucial—you never have a way of finding out whether you are crazy, and you just assume it, because it's the natural thing to assume.

So that's the ideal. Great efforts are made in trying to achieve that ideal. Obviously, there is a certain conception behind it. The conception of democracy is the one that I mentioned. The bewildered herd is a problem. We've got to prevent their roar and trampling. We've got to distract them. They should be watching the Superbowl or sitcoms or violent movies. Every once in a while you call on them to chant meaningless slogans like "Support our troops." You've got to keep them pretty scared, because unless they're properly scared and frightened of all kinds of devils that are going to destroy them from outside or inside or somewhere, they may start to think, which is very dangerous, because they're not competent to think. Therefore it's important to distract them and marginalize them.

That's one conception of democracy. In fact, going back to the business community, the last legal victory for labor really was 1935, the Wagner Act. After the war came, the unions declined as did a very rich working class culture that was associated with the unions. That was destroyed. We moved to a business-run society at a remarkable level. This is the only state-capitalist industrial society which doesn't have even the normal social contract that you find in comparable societies. Outside of South Africa, I guess, this is the only industrial society that doesn't have national health care. There's no general commitment to even minimal standards of survival for the parts of the population who can't follow those rules and gain things for themselves individually. Unions are virtually nonexistent. Other forms of popular structure are virtually nonexistent. There are no political parties or organizations. It's a long way toward the ideal, at least structurally. The media are a corporate monopoly. They have the same point of view. The two parties are two factions of the business party. Most of the population doesn't even bother voting because it looks meaningless. They're marginalized and properly distracted. At least that's the goal. The leading figure in the public relations industry, Edward Bernays, actually came out of the Creel Commission. He was part of it, learned his lessons there and went on to develop what he called the "engineering of consent," which he described as "the essence of democracy." The people who are able to engineer consent are the ones who have the resources and the power to do it—the business community—and that's who you work for.

ENGINEERING OPINION

It is also necessary to whip up the population in support of foreign adventures. Usually the population is pacifistic, just like they were during the First World War. The public sees no reason to get involved in foreign adventures, killing, and torture. So you *have* to whip them up.

And to whip them up you have to frighten them. Bernays himself had an important achievement in this respect. He was the person who ran the public relations campaign for the United Fruit Company in 1954, when the United States moved in to overthrow the capitalist-democratic government of Guatemala and installed a murderous death-squad society, which remains that way to the present day with constant infusions of U.S. aid to prevent more than empty-form democratic deviations. It's necessary to constantly ram through domestic programs which the public is opposed to, because there is no reason for the public to be in favor of domestic programs that are harmful to them. *This*, too, takes extensive propaganda. We've seen a lot of this in the last ten years. The Reagan programs were overwhelmingly unpopular. Voters in the 1984 "Reagan landslide," by about three to two, hoped that his policies would not be enacted. If you take particular programs, like armaments, cutting back on social spending, etc., almost every one of them was overwhelmingly opposed by the public. But as long as people are marginalized and distracted and have no way to organize or articulate their sentiments, or even know that others have these sentiments, people who said that they prefer social spending to military spending, who gave that answer on polls, as people overwhelmingly did, assumed that they were the only people with that crazy idea in their heads. They never heard it from anywhere else. Nobody's supposed to think that. Therefore, if you do think it and you answer it in a poll, you just assume that you're sort of weird. Since there's no way to get together with other people who share or reinforce that view and help you articulate it, you feel like an oddity, an oddball. So you just stay on the side and you don't pay any attention to what's going on. You look at something else, like the Superbowl.

To a certain extent, then, that ideal was achieved, but never completely. There are institutions which it has as yet been impossible to destroy. The churches, for example, still exist. A large part of the dissident activity in the United States comes out of the churches, for the simple reason that they're there. So when you go to a European country and give a political talk, it may very likely be in the union hall. Here that won't happen, because unions first of all barely exist, and if they do exist they're not political organizations. But the churches do exist, and therefore you often give a talk in a church. Central American solidarity work mostly grew out of the churches, mainly because they exist.

The bewildered herd never gets properly tamed, so this is a constant battle. In the 1930s they arose again and were put down. In the 1960s there was another wave of dissidence. There was a name for that. It was called by the specialized class "the crisis of democracy." Democracy was regarded as entering into a crisis in the 1960s. The crisis was that large segments of the population were becoming organized and active and trying to participate in the political arena. Here we come back to these two conceptions of democracy. By the dictionary definition, that's an *advance* in democracy. By the prevailing conception that's a *problem*, a crisis that has to be overcome. The population has to be driven back to the apathy, obedience and passivity that is their proper state. We therefore have to do something to overcome the crisis. Efforts were made to achieve that. It hasn't worked. The crisis of democracy is still alive and well, fortunately, but not very effective in changing policy. But it is effective in changing opinion, contrary to what a lot of people believe. Great efforts were made after the 1960s to try to reverse and overcome this malady. One aspect of the malady actually got a technical name. It was called the "Vietnam Syndrome." The Vietnam Syndrome, a term that began to come up around 1970, has actually been defined on occasion. The Reaganite intellectual Norman Podhoretz defined it as "the sickly inhibitions against the use of military force." There were these sickly inhibitions against violence on the part of a large part of the public. People just didn't understand why we should go around torturing people and killing people and carpet-bombing them. It's very dangerous for a population to be overcome by these sickly inhibitions, as Goebbels understood, because then there's a limit on foreign adventures. It's necessary, as the *Washington Post* put it rather proudly during the Gulf War hysteria, to instill in people respect for "martial values." That's important. If you want to have a violent society that uses force around the world to achieve the ends of its own domestic elite, it's necessary to have a proper appreciation of the martial virtues and none of these sickly inhibitions about using violence. So that's the Vietnam Syndrome. It's necessary to overcome that one.

REPRESENTATION AS REALITY

It's also necessary to completely falsify history. That's another way to overcome these sickly inhibitions, to make it look as if when we attack and destroy somebody we're really protecting and defending ourselves against major aggressors and monsters and so on. There has been a *huge* effort since the Vietnam war to reconstruct the history of that. Too many people began to understand what was really going on. Including plenty of soldiers and a lot of young people who were involved with the peace movement and others. That was bad. It was necessary to rearrange those bad thoughts and to restore some form of sanity, namely, a recognition that whatever we do is noble and right. If we're bombing South Vietnam, that's because we're defending South Vietnam against somebody, namely, the South Vietnamese, since nobody else was there. It's what the Kennedy intellectuals called defense against "internal aggression" in South Vietnam. That was the phrase used by Adlai Stevenson and others. It was necessary to make that the official and well-understood picture. That's worked pretty well. When you have total control over the media and the educational system and scholarship is conformist, you can get that across. One indication of it was revealed in a study done at the University of Massachusetts on attitudes toward the current Gulf crisis—a study of beliefs and attitudes in television watching. One of the questions asked in that study was, How many Vietnamese casualties would you estimate that there were during the Vietnam War? The average response on the part of Americans today is about 100,000. The official figure is about two million. The actual figure is probably three to four million. The people who conducted the study raised an appropriate question: What would we think about German political culture if, when you asked people today how many Jews died in the Holocaust, they estimated about 300,000? What would that tell us about German political culture? They leave the question unanswered, but you can pursue it. What does it tell us about our culture? It tells us quite a bit. It is necessary to overcome the sickly inhibitions against the use of military force and other democratic deviations. In this particular case it worked. This is true on every topic. Pick the topic you like: the Middle East, international terrorism, Central America, whatever it is—the picture of the world that's presented to the public has only the remotest relation to reality. The truth of the matter is buried under edifice after edifice of lies upon lies. It's all been a marvelous success from the point of view of deterring the threat of democracy, achieved under conditions of freedom, which is extremely interesting. It's not like a totalitarian state, where it's done by force. These achievements are under conditions of freedom. If we want to understand our own society, we'll have to think about these facts. They are important facts, important for those who care about what kind of society they live in.

DISSIDENT CULTURE

Despite all of this, the dissident culture survived. It's grown quite a lot since the 1960s. In the 1960s the dissident culture first of all was extremely slow in developing. There was no protest against the Indochina war until years after the United States had started bombing South Vietnam. When it did grow it was a very narrow dissident movement, mostly students and young people. By the 1970s that had changed considerably. Major popular movements had developed: the environmental movement, the feminist movement, the antinuclear movement, and others. In the 1980s there was an even greater expansion to the solidarity movements, which is something very new and important in the history of at least American, and maybe even world dissidence. These were movements that not only protested but actually involved themselves, often intimately, in the lives of suffering people elsewhere. They learned a great deal from it and had quite a civilizing effect on mainstream America. All of this has made a very large difference. Anyone who has been involved in this kind of activity for many years must be aware of this. I know myself that the kind of talks I give today in the most reactionary parts of the country—central Georgia, rural Kentucky, etc.—are talks of the kind that I couldn't have given at the peak of the peace movement to the most active peace movement audience. Now you can give them anywhere. People may agree or not agree, but at least they understand what you're talking about and there's some sort of common ground that you can pursue.

These are all signs of the civilizing effect, despite all the propaganda, despite all the efforts to control thought and manufacture consent. Nevertheless, people are acquiring an ability and a willingness to think things through. Skepticism about power has grown, and attitudes have changed on many, many issues. It's kind of slow, maybe even glacial, but perceptible and important. Whether it's fast enough to make a significant difference in what happens in the world is another question. Just to take one familiar example of it: the famous gender gap. In the 1960s attitudes of men and women were approximately the same on such matters as the "martial virtues" and the sickly inhibitions against the use of military force. Nobody, neither men nor women, were suffering from those sickly inhibitions in the early 1960s. The responses were the same. Everybody thought that the use of violence to suppress people out there was just right. Over the years it's changed. The sickly inhibitions have increased all across the board. But meanwhile a gap has been growing, and by now it's a very substantial gap. According to polls, it's something like twenty-five percent. What has happened? What has happened is that there is some form of at least semi-organized popular movement that women are involved in—the feminist movement. Organization has its effects. It means that you discover that you're not alone. Others have the same thoughts that you do. You can reinforce your thoughts and learn more about what you think and believe. These are very informal movements, not like a membership organizations, just a mood that involves interactions among people. It has a very noticeable effect. That's the danger of democracy: If organizations can develop, if people are no longer just glued to the tube, you may have all these funny thoughts arising in their heads, like sickly inhibitions against the use of military force. That has to be overcome, but it hasn't been overcome.

PARADE OF ENEMIES

Instead of talking about the last war, let me talk about the next war, because sometimes it's useful to be prepared instead of just reacting. There is a very characteristic development going on in the United States now. It's not the first country in the world that's done this. There are growing domestic social and economic problems, in fact, maybe catastrophes. Nobody in power has any intention of doing anything about them. If you look at the domestic programs of the administrations of the past ten years—I include here the Democratic opposition—there's really no serious proposal about what to do about the severe problems of health, education, homelessness, joblessness, crime, soaring criminal populations, jails, deterioration in the inner cities—the whole raft of problems. You all know about them, and they're all getting worse. Just in the two years that George Bush has been in office three million more children crossed the poverty line, the debt is zooming, educational standards are declining, real wages are now back to the level of about the late

1950s for much of the population, and nobody's doing anything about it. In such circumstances you've got to divert the bewildered herd, because if they start noticing this they may not like it, since they're the ones suffering from it. Just having them watch the Superbowl and the sitcoms may not be enough. You have to whip them up into fear of enemies. In the 1930s Hitler whipped them into fear of the Jews and Gypsies. You had to crush them to defend yourselves. We have our ways, too. Over the last ten years, every year or two, some major monster is constructed that we have to defend ourselves against. There used to be one that was always readily available: The Russians. You could always defend yourself against the Russians. But they're losing their attractiveness as an enemy, and it's getting harder and harder to use that one, so some new ones have to be conjured up. In fact, people have quite unfairly criticized George Bush for being unable to express or articulate what's really driving us now. That's very unfair. Prior to about the mid-1980s, when you were asleep you would just play the record: the Russians are coming. But he lost that one and he's got to make up new ones, just like the Reaganite public relations apparatus did in the 1980s. So it was international terrorists and narco-traffickers and crazed Arabs and Saddam Hussein, the new Hitler, was going to conquer the world. They've got to keep coming up one after another. You frighten the population, terrorize them, intimidate them so that they're too afraid to travel and cower in fear. Then you have a magnificent victory over Grenada, Panama, or some other defenseless third-world army that you can pulverize before you ever bother to look at them—which is just what happened. That gives relief. We were saved at the last minute. That's one of the ways in which you can keep the bewildered herd from paying attention to what's really going on around them, keep them diverted and controlled. The next one that's coming along, most likely, will be Cuba. That's going to require a continuation of the illegal economic warfare, possibly a revival of the extraordinary international terrorism. The most major international terrorism organized yet has been the Kennedy administration's Operation Mongoose, then the things that followed along, against Cuba. There's been nothing remotely comparable to it except perhaps the war against Nicaragua, if you call that terrorism. The World Court classified it as something more like aggression. There's always an ideological offensive that builds up a chimerical monster, then campaigns to have it crushed. You can't go in if they can fight back. That's much too dangerous. But if you are sure that they will be crushed, maybe we'll knock that one off and heave another sigh of relief.

SELECTIVE PERCEPTION

This has been going on for quite a while. In May 1986, the memoirs of the released Cuban prisoner, Armando Valladares, came out. They quickly became a media sensation. I'll give you a couple of quotes. The media described his revelations as "the definitive account of the vast system of torture and prison by which Castro punishes and obliterates political opposition." It was "an inspiring and unforgettable account" of the "bestial prisons, inhuman torture, [and] record of state violence [under] yet another of this century's mass murderers," who we learn, at last, from this book "has created a new despotism that has institutionalized torture as a mechanism of social control" in "the hell that was the Cuba that [Valladares] lived in." That's the *Washington Post* and *New York Times* in repeated reviews. Castro was described as "a dictatorial goon." His atrocities were revealed in this book so conclusively that "only the most light-headed and cold-blooded Western intellectual will come to the tyrant's defense," said the *Washington Post.* Remember, this is the account of what happened to one man. Let's say it's all true. Let's raise no questions about what happened to the one man who says he was tortured. At a White House ceremony marking Human Rights Day, he was singled out by Ronald Reagan for his courage in enduring the horrors and sadism of this bloody Cuban tyrant. He was then appointed the U.S. representative at the U.N. Human Rights Commission, where he has been able to perform signal services defending the Salvadoran and Guatemalan governments against charges that they conduct atrocities so massive that they make anything he suffered look pretty minor. That's the way things stand.

That was May 1986. It was interesting, and it tells you something about the manufacture of consent. The same month, the surviving members of the Human Rights Group of El Salvador—the leaders had been killed—were arrested and tortured, including Herbert Anaya, who was the director. They were sent to a prison—La Esperanza (hope) Prison. While they were in prison they continued their human rights work. They were lawyers, they continued taking affidavits. There were

432 prisoners in that prison. They got signed affidavits from 430 of them in which they described, under oath, the torture that they had received: electrical torture and other atrocities, including, in one case, torture by a North American U.S. major in uniform, who is described in some detail. This is an unusually explicit and comprehensive testimony, probably unique in its detail about what's going on in a torture chamber. This 160-page report of the prisoners' sworn testimony was sneaked out of prison, along with a videotape which was taken showing people testifying in prison about their torture. It was distributed by the Marin County Interfaith Task Force. *The national press refused to cover it. The TV stations refused to run it.* There was an article in the local Marin County newspaper, the *San Francisco Examiner,* and I think that's all. No one else would touch it. This was a time when there was more than a few "light-headed and cold-blooded Western intellectuals" who were singing the praises of José Napoleón Duarte and of Ronald Reagan. Anaya was not the subject of any tributes. He didn't get on Human Rights Day. He wasn't appointed to anything. He was released in a prisoner exchange and then assassinated, apparently by the U.S.-backed security forces. Very little information about that ever appeared. The media never asked whether exposure of the atrocities—instead of sitting on them and silencing them—might have saved his life.

This tells you something about the way a well-functioning system of consent manufacturing works. In comparison with the revelations of Herbert Anaya in El Salvador, Valladares's memoirs are not even a pea next to the mountain. But you've got your job to do. That takes us toward the next war. I expect, we're going to hear more and more of this, until the next operation takes place.

A few remarks about the last one. Let's turn finally to that. Let me begin with this University of Massachusetts study that I mentioned before. It has some interesting conclusions. In the study people were asked whether they thought that the United States should intervene with force to reverse illegal occupation or serious human rights abuses. By about two to one, people in the United States thought we should. We should use force in the case of illegal occupation of land and *severe* human rights abuses. If the United States was to follow that advice, we would bomb El Salvador, Guatemala, Indonesia, Damascus, Tel Aviv, Capetown, Turkey, Washington, and a whole list of other states. These are all cases of illegal occupation and aggression and severe human rights abuses. If you know the facts about that range of examples, you'll know very well that Saddam Hussein's aggression and atrocities fall well within the range. They're not the most extreme. Why doesn't anybody come to that conclusion? The reason is that nobody knows. In a well-functioning propaganda system, nobody would know what I'm talking about when I list that range of examples. If you bother to look, you find that those examples are quite appropriate.

Take one that was ominously close to being perceived during the Gulf War. In February, right in the middle of the bombing campaign, the government of Lebanon requested Israel to observe U.N. Security Council Resolution 425, which called on it to withdraw immediately and unconditionally from Lebanon. That resolution dates from March 1978. There have since been two subsequent resolutions calling for the immediate and unconditional withdrawal of Israel from Lebanon. Of course it doesn't observe them because the United States backs it in maintaining that occupation. Meanwhile southern Lebanon is terrorized. There are big torture chambers with horrifying things going on. It's used as a base for attacking other parts of Lebanon. Since 1978, Lebanon was invaded, the city of Beirut was bombed, about 20,000 people were killed, about 80 percent of them civilians, hospitals were destroyed, and more terror, looting, and robbery was inflicted. All fine, the United States backed it. That's just one case. You didn't see anything in the media about it or any discussion about whether Israel and the United States should observe U.N. Security Council Resolution 425 or any of the other resolutions, nor did anyone call for the bombing of Tel Aviv, although by the principles upheld by two-thirds of the population, we should. After all, that's illegal occupation and severe human rights abuses. That's just one case. There are much worse ones. The Indonesian invasion of East Timor knocked off about 200,000 people. They all look minor by that one. That was strongly backed by the United States and is *still* going on with major United States diplomatic and military support. We can go on and on.

THE GULF WAR

That tells you how a well-functioning propaganda system works. People can believe that when we use force against Iraq and Kuwait it's because we really observe the principle that illegal occupation and human rights abuses should be met by force. They don't see what it would mean if those principles were applied to U.S. behavior. That's a success of propaganda of quite a spectacular type.

Let's take a look at another case. If you look closely at the coverage of the war since August (1990), you'll notice that there are a couple of striking voices missing. For example, there is an Iraqi democratic opposition, in fact, a very courageous and quite substantial Iraqi democratic opposition. They, of course, function in exile because they couldn't survive in Iraq. They are in Europe primarily. They are bankers, engineers, architects—people like that. They are articulate, they have voices, and they speak. The previous February, when Saddam Hussein was still George Bush's favorite friend and trading partner, they actually came to Washington, according to Iraqi democratic opposition sources, with a plea for some kind of support for a demand of theirs calling for a parliamentary democracy in Iraq. They were totally rebuffed, because the United States had no interest in it. There was no reaction to this in the public record.

Since August it became a little harder to ignore their existence. In August we suddenly turned against Saddam Hussein after having favored him for many years. Here was an Iraqi democratic opposition who ought to have some thoughts about the matter. They would be happy to see Saddam Hussein drawn and quartered. He killed their brothers, tortured their sisters, and drove them out of the country. They have been fighting against his tyranny throughout the whole time that Ronald Reagan and George Bush were cherishing him. What about their voices? Take a look at the national media and see how much you can find about the Iraqi democratic opposition from August through March (1991). You can't find a word. It's not that they're inarticulate. They have statements, proposals, calls, and demands. If you look at them, you find that they're indistinguishable from those of the American peace movement. They're against Saddam Hussein and they're against the war against Iraq. They don't want their country destroyed. What they want is a peaceful resolution, and they knew perfectly well that it might have been achievable. That's the wrong view and therefore they're out. We don't hear a word about the Iraqi democratic opposition. If you want to find out about them, pick up the German press, or the British press. They don't say much about them, but they're less controlled than we are and they say something.

This is a spectacular achievement of propaganda. First, that the voices of the Iraqi democrats are completely excluded, and second, that nobody notices it. That's interesting, too. It takes a really deeply indoctrinated population not to notice that we're not hearing the voices of the Iraqi democratic opposition and not asking the question, *Why?* and finding out the obvious answer: because the Iraqi democrats have their own thoughts; they agree with the international peace movement and therefore they're out.

Let's take the question of the reasons for the war. Reasons were offered for the war. The reasons are: aggressors cannot be rewarded and aggression must be reversed by the quick resort to violence; that was the reason for the war. There was basically no other reason advanced. Can that possibly be the reason for the war? Does the United States uphold those principles, that aggressors cannot be rewarded and that aggression must be reversed by a quick resort to violence? I won't insult your intelligence by running through the facts, but the fact is those arguments could be refuted in two minutes by a literate teenager. However, they never were refuted. Take a look at the media, the liberal commentators and critics, the people who testified in Congress and see whether anybody questioned the assumption that the United States stands up to those principles. Has the United States opposed its own aggression in Panama and insisted on bombing Washington to reverse it? When the South African occupation of Namibia was declared illegal in 1969, did the United States impose sanctions on food and medicine? Did it go to war? Did it bomb Capetown? No, it carried out twenty years of "quiet diplomacy." It wasn't very pretty during those twenty years. In the years of the Reagan-Bush administration alone, about 1.5 million people were killed by South Africa just in the surrounding countries. Forget what was happening in South Africa and Namibia. Somehow that didn't sear our sensitive souls. We continued with "quiet diplomacy" and ended up with ample reward for the aggressors. They were given the major port in Namibia and plenty of advantages that took into account their security concerns. Where is this principle that we uphold? Again, it's child's play to demonstrate that those couldn't possibly have been the reasons for going to war, because we don't uphold these principles.

But nobody did it—that's what's important. And nobody bothered to point out the conclusion that follows: No reason was given for going to war. None. No reason was given for going to war that could not be refuted by a literate teenager in about two minutes. That again is the hallmark of a totalitarian culture. It ought to frighten us, that we are so deeply totalitarian that we can be driven to war without any reason being given for it and without anybody noticing Lebanon's request or caring. It's a very striking fact.

Right before the bombing started, in mid-January, a major *Washington Post*–ABC poll revealed something interesting. People were asked, If Iraq would agree to withdraw from Kuwait in return for Security Council consideration of the problem of Arab-Israeli conflict, would you be in favor of that? By about two-to-one, the population was in favor of that. So was the whole world, including the Iraqi democratic opposition. So it was reported that two-thirds of the American population were in favor of that. Presumably, the people who were in favor of that thought they were the only ones in the world to think so. Certainly nobody in the press had said that it would be a good idea. The orders from Washington have been, *we're supposed to be against "linkage,"* that is, diplomacy, and therefore everybody goose-stepped on command and everybody was against diplomacy. Try to find commentary in the press—you can find a column by Alex Cockburn in the *Los Angeles Times*, who argued that it would be a good idea. The people who were answering that question thought, *I'm alone, but that's what I think.* Suppose they knew that they weren't alone, that other people thought it, like the Iraqi democratic opposition. Suppose that they knew that this was not hypothetical, that in fact Iraq had made exactly such an offer. It had been released by high U.S. officials just eight days earlier. On January 2, these officials had released an Iraqi offer to withdraw totally from Kuwait in return for consideration by the Security Council of the Arab-Israeli conflict and the problem of weapons of mass destruction. The United States had been refusing to negotiate this issue since well before the invasion of Kuwait. Suppose that people had known that the offer was actually on the table and that it was widely supported and that in fact it's exactly the kind of thing that any rational person would do if they were interested in peace, as we do in other cases, in the rare cases that we do want to reverse aggression. Suppose that it had been known. You can make your own guesses, but I would assume that the two-thirds would probably have risen to 98 percent of the population. Here you have the great successes of propaganda. Probably not one person who answered the poll knew any of the things I've just mentioned. The people thought they were alone. Therefore it was possible to proceed with the war policy without opposition.

There was a good deal of discussion about whether sanctions would work. You had the head of the CIA come up and discuss whether sanctions would work. However, there was no discussion of a much more obvious question: Had sanctions already worked? The answer is yes, apparently they had—probably by late August, very likely by late December. It was very hard to think up any other reason for the Iraqi offers of withdrawal, which were authenticated or in some cases released by high U.S. officials, who described them as "serious" and "negotiable." So the real question is: Had sanctions already worked? Was there a way out? Was there a way out in terms quite acceptable to the general population, the world at large and the Iraqi democratic opposition? These questions were not discussed, and it's crucial for a well-functioning propaganda system that they *not* be discussed. That enables the chairman of the Republican National Committee to say that if any Democrat had been in office, Kuwait would not be liberated today. He can say that and no Democrat would get up and say that if I were president it would have been liberated not only today but six months ago, because there were opportunities then that I would have pursued and Kuwait would have been liberated without killing tens of thousands of people and without causing an environmental catastrophe. No Democrat would say that because no Democrat took that position. Henry Gonzalez and Barbara Boxer took that position. But the number of people who took it is so marginal that it's virtually nonexistent. Given the fact that almost no Democratic politician would say that, Clayton Yeutter is free to make his statements.

When Scud missiles hit Israel, nobody in the press applauded. Again, that's an interesting fact about a well-functioning propaganda system. We might ask, why not? After all, Saddam Hussein's arguments were as good as George Bush's arguments. What were they, after all? Let's just take Lebanon. Saddam Hussein says that he can't stand annexation. He can't let Israel annex the Syrian Golan Heights and East Jerusalem, in opposition to the unanimous agreement of the Security Council. He can't stand annexation. He can't stand aggression. Israel has been occupying southern Lebanon since 1978 in violation of Security Council resolutions that it refuses to abide by. In the course of that period it attacked all of Lebanon, and still bombs most of Lebanon at will. He can't stand it. He might have read the Amnesty International report on Israeli atrocities in the West Bank. His heart is bleeding. He can't stand it. Sanctions can't work because the United States vetoes them. Negotiations won't work because the United States blocks them. What's left but force? He's been waiting for years. Thirteen years in the case of Lebanon, twenty years in the case of the West Bank. You've heard that argument before. The only difference between that argument and the one you heard is that Saddam Hussein could truly say sanctions and negotiations can't work because the United States blocks them. But George Bush couldn't say that, because sanctions apparently had worked, and there was every reason to believe that negotiations could work—except that he adamantly refused to pursue them, saying explicitly, there will be no negotiations right through. Did you find anybody in the press who pointed that out? No. It's a triviality. It's something that, again, a literate teenager could figure out in a minute. But nobody pointed it out, no commentator, no editorial writer. That, again, is the sign of a very well-run totalitarian culture. It shows that the manufacture of consent is working.

Last comment about this. We could give many examples, you could make them up as you go along. Take the idea that Saddam Hussein is a monster about to conquer the world—widely believed, in the United States, and not unrealistically. It was drilled into people's heads over and over again: He's about to take everything. We've got to stop him now. How did he get that powerful? This is a small, third-world country without an industrial base. For eight years Iraq had been fighting Iran. That's post-revolutionary Iran, which had decimated its officer corps and most of its military force. Iraq had a little bit of support in that war. It was backed by the Soviet Union, the United States, Europe, the major Arab countries, and the Arab oil producers. It couldn't defeat Iran. But all of a sudden it's ready to conquer the world. Did you find anybody who pointed that out? The fact of the matter is, this was a third-world country with a peasant army. It is now being conceded that there was a ton of disinformation about the fortifications, the chemical weapons, etc. But did you find anybody who pointed it out? No. You found virtually nobody who pointed it out. That's typical. Notice that this was done one year after exactly the same thing was done with Manuel Noriega. Manuel Noriega is a minor thug by comparison with George Bush's friend Saddam Hussein or George Bush's other friends in Beijing or George Bush himself, for that matter. In comparison with them, Manuel Noriega is a pretty minor thug. Bad, but not a world-class thug of the kind we like. He was turned into a creature larger than life. He was going to destroy us, leading the narco-traffickers. We had to quickly move in and smash him, killing a couple hundred or maybe thousand people, restoring to power the tiny, maybe eight percent white oligarchy, and putting U.S. military officers in control at every level of the political system. We had to do all those things because, after all, we had to save ourselves or we were going to be destroyed by this monster. One year later the same thing was done by Saddam Hussein. Did anybody point it out? Did anybody point out what had happened or why? You'll have to look pretty hard for that.

Notice that this is not all that different from what the Creel Commission did when it turned a pacifistic population into raving hysterics who wanted to destroy everything German to save ourselves from Huns who were tearing the arms off Belgian babies. The techniques are maybe more sophisticated, with television and lots of money going into it, but it's pretty traditional.

I think the issue, to come back to my original comment, is not simply disinformation and the Gulf crisis. The issue is much broader. It's whether we want to live in a free society or whether we want to live under what amounts to a form of self-imposed totalitarianism, with the bewildered herd marginalized, directed elsewhere, terrified, screaming patriotic slogans, fearing for their lives and admiring with awe the leader who saved them from destruction, while the educated masses goose-step on command and repeat the slogans they're supposed to repeat and the society deteriorates at home. We end up serving as a mercenary enforcer state, hoping that others are going to pay us to smash up the world. Those are the choices. That's the choice that you have to face. The answer to those questions is very much in the hands of people like *you* and *me.*

More Information

RADIO AND TELEVISION RESOURCES

Alternative Radio Cassette Series

Alternative Radio Cassette Series presents a seminal audio-archive of many of today's most vital scholars, dissidents, historians, and activists. Programs in the series confront issues that are systematically ignored by mainstream media, issues like propaganda, the CIA, U.S. foreign policy, institutional racism and sexism, Native American resistance, the economy, and media bias. Produced by David Barsamian, the series features lectures and interviews with Noam Chomsky, Barbara Ehrenreich, Edward Said, Angela Davis, Howard Zinn, Joanne Landy, Manning Marable, and *many* others. Send a self-addressed stamped envelope for a free catalog listing all available cassettes:
2129 Mapleton, Boulder, CO 80304
Tel. (303) 444-8788

Public Radio Satellite System

The Public Radio Satellite System enables grass roots organizations and individuals to have their own audio-programs uplinked to a communications satellite and made accessible to over 400 public radio stations nationwide. Uplink fees for 1 hour of satellite time are shockingly inexpensive. Free brochure with detailed information available upon request:
2025 M Street, NW, Washington, DC 20036
Tel. (202) 822-2612

Paper Tiger Television

Paper Tiger video programs lift the veil of OZ from the communications, media, and information industries. Their subject catalog ranges from art, women, and information politics to international affairs and business. Send $2 for their superb catalog:
339 Lafayette Street, NY, NY 10012
Tel. (212) 420-9045

Media Network

Media Network is a national membership organization helping concerned individuals use videos for social change. They research and publish 2 directories/year listing new media titles addressing pressing social themes. Write or call:
39 W. 14th Street, Suite 403, NY, NY 10011
Tel. (212) 929-2663

Radio for Peace International

The only short-wave station on UN land (based in Costa Rica) not subject to any national censorship laws. Broadcasting on four frequencies (21.465Kz, 13.360Kz, 7.375Kz and 15.030Kz), in four languages: English, Spanish, German and Creole. A quarterly guide (and $35 membership) can be obtained from:
Box 10689, Eugene, OR 97440
Tel. (503) 741-1794

Video Databank

A non-profit distributor of video by and about contemporary artists in the US. The data bank explores mass media analysis & criticism, feminism, sexuality & gender, censorship, and cultures.
37 S. Wabash, Chicago, IL 60603
Tel. (312) 899-5172

The Video Project

Films and videos for a safe and sustainable world—largest non-profit distributor of

environmental and social issue documentaries. They distribute *A Deadly Deception* and *Building Bombs* (both Academy Award winners). Write for a free catalog.
5322 College Avenue, Oakland, CA 94618
Tel. (800) 4-PLANET

National Federation of Community Broadcasters
A network of public radio stations dedicated to providing noncommercial educational/cultural programing, local access to the airwaves, and consulting and referral services for radio-nauts.
666 11th St., NW, Suite 805, Washington, DC 20001 • Tel. (202) 393-2355

Pacifica Radio Archives
Cassette copies of radio programs going back to 1949 from independent producers like David Barsamian and Helene Rosenbluth and the Pacifica Radio Network stations: WBAI-NY, WPFW-DC, KPFT-Houston, KPFK-LA, KPFA-Berkeley.
3729 Cahuenga Blvd., W., N. Hollywood, CA 91604 • Tel. (800) 735-0230

Television and the Crisis of Democracy
This book by Douglas Kellner examines the relationships among television, the state, corporate ownership, and public power. Kellner traces the history of television broadcasting, emphasizing its malignant socioeconomic impact and its bloated political influence. Throughout, Kellner evaluates the contradictory influence of television, a medium that has clearly served the interests of the powerful but has the potential to serve and enrich public democracy rather than manipulate it. Interesting and accessible reading. Available from:
Westview Press, 5500 Central Avenue, Boulder, CO 80301

ALTERNATIVE BOOK PUBLISHERS

South End Press
A nonprofit publishing house, South End Press presents an invaluable compendium of books addressing the most pressing issues of our times. In every area of radical social change—race, class, gender, economics, media, ecology, national security, activist strategies, and foreign policy, South End Press books are a resource to both the lay reader and the researcher. Readers can order books over the phone, or join their membership program entitling two free books and a 40 percent discount on all titles. Write for a free catalog:
116 St. Botolph Street, Boston, MA 02115
Tel. (617) 266-0629

Common Courage Press
Founded in 1991 as an activist publishing house, Common Courage books present perspectives and strategies for social change. Manning Marable, Noam Chomsky, and Ward Churchill are among the authors Common Courage has recently published. Write for a free catalog of all available titles:
PO Box 702, Corner Route 139 and Jackson Road, Monroe, ME 04951

ALTERNATIVE PRINT MEDIA

Village Voice
The *Village Voice* is the nation's leading weekly newspaper for alternative information and commentary. Despite being an unashamedly commercial paper, the *Voice* consistently publishes some of the most staggering in-depth investigative journalism produced today. Feature stories on the elections, activism, media bias, the Gulf War, October Surprise, Iran-Contra, Clarence Thomas, the savings and loan scams—to name a few—far outlast the one-week shelf life of each issue. A bastion of free thought and uninhibited commentary. Six-month subscription—$28.95
842 Broadway, NY, NY 10003
Tel. (800) 526-4859

The Progressive
With regular columns from social critics Molly Ivins, Peter Dykstra, June Jordan,

Nat Hentoff, and Elayne Rapping, *The Progressive* offers penetrating insights into contemporary U.S. politics. Critical of left and right politics, yet receptive to environmentalist, feminist, and anarchist insights, *The Progressive* provides an essential forum for multicultural, democratic social movements. Subscriptions in the US: $30 for 1 year; $55 for 2 years; Foreign: $36 for 1 Year; $67 for 2 years.
409 East Main Street, Madison, WI 53703
Tel. (608) 257-4626

The Guardian

The Guardian is a lucid source of political opinion and progressive reporting. Published weekly by the Institute for Independent Social Journalism, *The Guardian* features hard-hitting investigative reports, articles on international and domestic affairs, and reviews of new books, music, and events. Always worth much more than the cover price. Sample copy: $1.25. Subscriptions: $33.50/year; $18/6 months.
33 W. 17th Street, NY, NY 10011
Tel. (212) 691-0404

The Nation

Since 1865, *The Nation* has been an uncompromising source of sociopolitical reporting and commentary. Every issue brings together a collection of terse editorials, essays, and political tracts that keeps its readers on the frontlines. The cover price simply can't be beat. Sample copy—$1.50; 24 issue subscription—$15
The Nation, P.O. Box 10791, Des Moines, IA 50340-0791

Z Magazine

Z Magazine presents in-depth assessments of the political, cultural, social, and economic life in the United States. Each issue is packed with articles, essays, reviews, updates, and networking information supporting a diverse range of resistance efforts and projects for social change—a potent source of information and activist contacts. $3.50 an issue. For information:
150 West Canton Street, Boston, MA 02118

THE NATIONAL SECURITY STATE

Covert Action Information Bulletin

Covert Action Bulletin investigates, documents, and exposes many dimensions of secret U.S. intervention and manipulation at home and abroad. Published quarterly, it has featured important research by Jane Hunter, Noam Chomsky, Diana Reynolds, Clarence Lusane, Edward Herman, and many others. Sample copy—$6;. 4-issue subscription—$19.
1500 Massachusetts Avenue, Room 732, Washington, D.C. 20005

C.I.A. BASE

C.I.A.BASE is an easy-to-use IBM-compatible database developed by Ralph McGehee, a 25-year C.I.A. veteran and author of *Deadly Deceits.* The product of over six years of research, C.I.A.BASE consists of over 4 megabytes of annotated entries and is growing all the time. Sources cited in the database include congressional reports, newspapers, magazines, and over 170 books. The database offers subject categories ranging from Death Squads, Domestic Operations, and Media to Biological Warfare, Sex, and Mind Control. Send an SASE for more info to:
P.O. Box 5022, Herndon, VA 22070

MEDIA WATCHDOGS AND RESOURCES

Extra!

Published by Fairness and Accuracy in Reporting (FAIR), *Extra!*'s articles reveal the extent that the profit-motivated mass media bias information and manipulate the public. Many issues are devoted to a single theme, and meticulously cited articles provide strong source material for media research. Essential reading. Sample copy—$2.50; yearly subscription—$30
175 5th Avenue, Suite 2245, NY, NY 10010

Lies of Our Times

Lies of Our Times is a magazine of media criticism that exposes the biases which sys-

tematically shape reporting. *LOOT* is published by the Institute for Media Analysis, Inc., and edited by Ellen Ray, William H. Schaap, Edward S. Herman. Sample copy—$3; Subscription—$24
145 West 4th Street, NY, NY 10012

In These Times
Published weekly by the Institute for Public Affairs, *In These Times* presents alternative analysis and background on a wide range of foreign and domestic issues. One year subscription—$34.95.
2040 North Milwaukee Avenue, Chicago, IL 60647

Quarterly Review of Doublespeak
QRD airs the dirty laundry of lies, doublespeak, misinformation, and propaganda spewed from the mouths of politicians and corporate executives. Subscriptions: $10 per year. Send checks or money orders payable to:
National Council of Teachers of English, 1111 Kenyon Road, Urbana, IL 61801

Adbusters
Adbusters Magazine attacks the various ways that commercial media sell ownership as identity and consumption as a way of life. Each issue decodes the images and illusions generated by advertising and reports on constructive strategies toward the liberation of public space. Sample copy, $4.75; Subscription, $16.
1243 West 7th Avenue, Vancouver, British Columbia V6H 1B7 Canada

COUNTER CULTURE

Situationist Anthology
Edited and translated from the French by Ken Knabb, this 392 page opus makes available in English many of the writings of the insurgent art collective, the Situationist International. Laced with a biting sense of humor and at some points theoretically obtuse, the S.I.'s insurgent cultural critique continues to provide penetrating insight and radical tactics for subverting our "society of the spectacle." Fifteen dollars and well worth it. Write to:
Bureau of Public Secret, P.O. Box 1044, Berkeley, CA 94701

Retrofuturism Journal
Retrofuturism is a xerox-top journal of aggressive criticism, countercultural observations, theory, and reviews of other underground publications, cassettes, and projects. One of the best publications in America's "'zine scene," *Retrofuturism*'s subversive collage of writing and graphics strikes out at the homogeneity of mainstream culture. Always interesting, never predictable. Send three dollars for a sample issue.
P.O. Box 227, Iowa City, IA 52244

Central Park
Central Park Magazine is one of America's most thought-provoking literary journals. Each issue features a wide selection of theory, photography, fiction, poetry, experimental writing, and reviews that touch on everything from new models of perception and learning to scathing critiques of advertising and commodity culture. A veritable think-tank of pioneering and provocative works. Not to be missed at $7.50 a copy.
P.O. Box 1446, NY, NY 10023

Clash
A monthly journal of radical politics and dissident actions covering international resistance (armed and otherwise), racism, fascism, and imperialism. Reports on Squatter's movements, prisoner strikes, union wildcat strikes and other actions. Sample copies are $5. For more info, write:
Stichting Marinus vd Lubbe, Postbus 11149, 1001 GL Amsterdam, Holland

CIVIL RIGHTS ADVOCACY GROUPS

The Center for Democratic Renewal
Formerly known as the National Anti-Klan Network, CDR is dedicated to pro-

moting opposition to hate-group activity and bigoted violence through education, activism, and action for the long term. CDR provides programs in education, research, victim assistance, community organizing, leadership training, and public policy advocacy. The organization is multiracial, multiethnic, interfaith, and nonprofit. For more information and a free copy of CDR's journal, *The Monitor,* write:
P.O. Box 50469, Atlanta, GA 30302-0469
Tel. (404) 221-0025

Martin Luther King, Jr., Center for Nonviolent Social Change
Established in 1968, the center preserves and advances Dr. King's unfinished work through teaching, interpreting, and advocating the nonviolent elimination of poverty, racism, and violence. For free information and literature write:
449 Auburn Avenue, N.E., Atlanta, GA 30322

National Alliance Against Racist and Political Repression
Since 1973, the NAARPR has organized a national multicultural coalition of labor, church, educational, activist, and women's groups. Confronting racism, anti-Semitism, police crime, and the presence of political prisoners in the United States and South Africa are central among the Alliance's concerns. Send a SASE for a complimentary copy of the *Organizer,* the Alliance's newsletter:
11 John Street, Room 702, NY, NY 10038

Southern Organizing Committee for Economic and Social Justice
SOC is an interracial network of southern activists and organizers who work with their local communities against racism and war. The group is involved with community labor coalition building and is presently organizing a major conference devoted to improving human health, safety, and the environment. For a free copy of their newsletter, *Southern Fightback,* write:
P.O. Box 811, Birmingham, AL 35201

National Association for the Advancement of Colored People
The NAACP is the oldest and largest civil rights organization in the United States. They presently have 1,800 branches, 300 youth and college chapters, and a membership of over 500,000 people. For more information write:
4805 Mount Hope Drive, Baltimore, MD 21215

American Civil Liberties Union (ACLU)
A national civil rights advocacy and litigation group that publishes a free bi-weekly newsletter and annual list of cases.
132 W. 43rd. Street, NY, NY 10036
Tel. (212) 944-9800

THE LOS ANGELES REBELLION

Inside the L.A. Riots
Pooling articles from *L.A. Weekly, Village Voice, The Nation, San Francisco Bay Guardian,* and other alternative press sources, *Inside The L.A. Riots* is the first book out on the uprisings in Los Angeles, Las Vegas, and other American cities. Edited by Don Hazon and published by the Institute for Alternative Journalism. $8.95 postpaid from:
100 East 85th Street, NY, NY 10028

Civil Liberties in Crisis: Los Angeles During the Emergency
The first comprehensive report on "assembly-line" justice in the aftermath of L.A. rebellion. Details widespread abuses of the rights of immigrants and homeless. Available from American Civil Liberties Union of Southern California. For more info write:
1616 Beverly Blvd., Los Angeles, CA 90025

Strategy Center Report on Reconstructing Los Angeles
"A progressive antidote to the Ueberroth, corporatist vision of inner city redomina-

tion." Written by Cynthia Hamilton, Eric Mann, Anthony Thigpenn, and other members of the Urban Strategies Group. Send $5 postpaid to:
14540 Haynes Street, Suite 20D, Van Nuys, CA 91411

Illegal Deportation of Immigrants
CARECEN is the unofficial civic center for Los Angeles's Central-American population. It provides legal support for families victimized by INS raids during the L.A. rebellion. Contact Central American Refugee Center:
668 South Bonnie Brae Street, Los Angeles, CA 90057

The Bush Case & Police Abuse in Las Vegas
Chan Kendrick of the ACLU struggles single-handedly to defend civil liberties inside the glitterdome. For more information contact the American Civil Liberties Union of Nevada at:
325 South Third Street, Suite 25, Las Vegas, Nevada 89101

REPRODUCTIVE RIGHTS ADVOCACY GROUPS

Women of Color for Reproductive Freedom
A network of women of color who have come together to share knowledge and support for work in communities of color. The group focuses on health care, reproductive and family rights.
P.O. Box 1200, Boston, MA 02117-1200

Federation of Feminist Women's Health Centers
Association of women's health projects providing health services to women, including abortion, well-women care, birth control; self-help clinic, where women are taught self-examination; they also distribute a video, "No Going Back" which introduces the concept and technique of menstrual extraction.
6221 Wilshire Blvd., Suite 419-A,
Los Angeles, CA 90048 • Tel. (213) 957-4062

National Black Women's Health Project
Self-help and health advocacy organization addressing health issues facing black women and their families; works through its self-help chapters, networking, national and regional conferences; publishes a newsletter, *Vital Signs* and distributes the film, "On Becoming a Woman."
1237 Ralph David Abernathy Drive SW, Atlanta, GA 30310 • Tel. (404)-758-9590

International Women's Health Coalition
A private, nonprofit organization dedicated to improving women's reproductive health in the Third World. It supports health care projects, policy-oriented field research, and public education.
24 East 21st Street, NY, NY 10010
Tel. (212) 979-8500

National Women's Health Network
Works for abortion rights and other women's health issues; maintains national communications about antiabortion legislation, RU 486, and harassment of feminist abortion providers.
1325 G Street NW, Washington, DC 20005
Tel. (202) 347-1140

Women of All Red Nations (WARN)
Native American women's group promoting Native American women's health and reproductive rights; fighting against violence against women; supporting tribal treaty rights; stopping spiritual and cultural exploitation.
4511 North Hermitage, Chicago IL 60640

The Women of Color Partnership Program
Created by RCAR as a way in which African American, Latin American, Asian-Pacific American, Native American, and all women of color in this country can become actively involved in the reproductive choice movement; also addresses reproductive health care concerns from the unique perspectives of women of color. Write for free newsletter.

100 Maryland Avenue, NE, Suite 307, Washington, D.C. 20002 • Tel. (202) 543-7032

Women's Health and Action Mobilization!
WHAM! is a direct action group which escorts women to abortion clinics and fights actively for quality health care for all.
P.O. Box 733, NY, NY 10009
Tel. (212) 713-5966

Students Organizing Students
A multicultural, student-run, student-led reproductive rights organization. Write for more info:
1600 Broadway, Suite 404, NY, NY 10019
Tel. (212) 977-6710

Native American Women's Health Education Resource Center
A reservation-based Native American women's self-help project that works to assist women in the empowerment process. NAWHERC runs programs for AIDS & cancer prevention, health awareness, and the Native Women's Reproductive Health Project. Ask about their health, education and policy materials.
P.O. Box 572, Lake Andes, SD 57356
Tel. (605) 487-7072

The Religious Coalition for Abortion Rights
A coalition of Protestant and Jewish groups who lobby and educate in support of legal abortion. For more info contact:
100 Maryland Avenue, NE, Washington, DC 20002 • Tel. (202) 543-7032

AIDS AWARENESS AND ADVOCACY GROUPS

AIDS Coalition to Unleash Power
"ACTUP is a diverse, non-partisan group of individuals united in anger and committed to direct action to end the AIDS Crisis. We meet with government and health officials; we research and distribute the latest medical information. We protest and demonstrate; we are not silent."

ACT UP Network
POB 190712, Dallas, TX 75219
ACT UP/Chicago
(312)-509-6802
ACT UP/Golden Gate
(415)-252-9200
ACT UP/Kansas City
(816)-753-5930
ACT UP/Los Angeles
(213)-669-7301
ACT UP/Miami
(305)-787-1131
ACT UP/Minneapolis
(612)-823-8526
ACT UP/New York
(212)-564-AIDS
ACT UP/Washington, DC
(202)-328-AIDS
ACT UP/Paris—Europe
011-33-1-43-57-5205
ACT UP/San Francisco
415-563-0724
ACT UP/Sydney (Australia)
612-283-3550

AIDS Treatment Data Network
Provides info, counseling, case management, referral and outreach services on treatments, research and resources for PWAs.
259 West 30th Street, 9th Floor, NY, NY 10001 • Tel. 212-268-4196 (English)
212-643-0870 (Spanish)

Health Education AIDS Liaison
HEAL offers oral and written information on alternative, holistic and complimentary AIDS treatments.
c/o Hillman Health Center, 16 E. 16th Street, NY, NY 10003 • Tel. 212-674-HOPE

National AIDS Brigade
Committed to direct action to stem the tide of HIV, the Brigade distributes needles and condoms and advocates for the homeless. A nationwide group engaged in challenging unjust laws.
192 E. Broadway, Boston, MA 02127
Tel. (617) 269-8236

People with AIDS Coalition
By and for PWAs, PWAC provides a public *Speaker's Bureau*, a *Livingroom* with meals and social events for PWAs, and *PWAC Newsline* (free for PWAs; $35/yr subscription; free sample copy).
31 West 26th Street, NY, NY 10010
Tel. 212-532-0568 or 800-828-3280

Prisoners w/AIDS Rights Advocacy Group
An up-to-date resource on medical care and civil rights abuses of prisoners with AIDS. Free to PWAs. Others send $2.50 handling.
Box 2161, Jonesboro, GA 30237
Tel. 404-946-9346

Direct AIDS Alternative Info Resources
DAAIR is a nonprofit AIDS/HIV buyer's club; sells supplements and herbs; distributes the latest scientific information.
31 E. 30th Street, NY, NY 10016
Tel. 212-689-8140

MIDDLE EAST ISSUES

Journal of Palestinian Studies
An invaluable ongoing documentary of the Palestinian-Israeli conflict. *JPS* features interviews with key people in the Palestinian struggle for self-determination, like Faisal Husseini; scholarly articles from Edward W. Said, Donald Neff, Ann M. Lesch, and Fawaz A. Gerges; and several source documents from the United Nations, the Israeli government, and the PLO. Write to:
University of California Press, 2120 Berkeley Way, Berkeley, CA 94720

Middle East Report (MERIP)
Middle East Report is a bi-monthly journal of Middle Eastern political economy, regional struggles, and commentary. The breadth and substance of its coverage are exemplary.
Dept. A, Suite 119, 1500 Massachusetts Avenue NW, Washington, DC 20005

Palestinian Human Rights Info Center
Publishing a monthly newsletter, the Palestinian Human Rights Information Center documents the Israeli government's ongoing violations of Palestinian human rights. Write to:
4753 North Broadway, Suite 930, Chicago, IL 10010

Al-Fajr Weekly Edition
The *Al-Fajr Weekly* is the English edition of a Jerusalem-based Arabic newspaper. Highly recommended for up-to-date information on life for Palestinians under occupation. Write to:
2025 I Street NW, Washington, DC 20006

COUNTER-QUINCENTENNIAL

Alliance for Cultural Democracy
National network of artists, educators, and organizers committed to grass roots cultural expression. The Alliance has been working on counter-Quincentennial projects since 1988 and publishes a newspaper that is available free by writing to:
P.O. Box 7591, Minneapolis, MN 55407

Clergy and Laity Concerned
CALC is an interdenominational peace and social justice group that works with counter-Quincentennial projects and publishes a free newsletter, *CALC Report.* Write to:
P.O. Box 1987, Decatur, GA 30031

Dangerous Memories: Invasion and Resistance Since 1492
Dangerous Memories is a comprehensive collection of networking info, historical tracts, and source documents compiled to assist and inform teachers, activists, and readers.
59 E. Van Buren, Suite 1400, Chicago, IL 60605
Tel. (312) 663-4398

ECOLOGY INFORMATION

Worldwatch—State of the World Report
The primary environmental intelligence report for many countries, the *State of the*

World Report is an excellent source of environmental data and analyses. Send a check for $10.95 to:
1776 Massachusetts Avenue, Washington, DC 20036 • Tel. (202) 452-1999

Ecodefense
Committed to environmental preservation, this book guides readers through an array of step-by-step tactics that involve direct action, civil disobedience, and nonviolent sabotage. Topics cover everything from billboard removal to disabling logging and earthmoving equipment. Available for $12.
Ned Ludd Books, P.O. Box 5871, Tucson, AZ 85703

Green Letter
Green Letter is a national quarterly newspaper reporting on the development of the Green movement in the United States and abroad. Each issue covers international, national, and indigenous organizing with news, analysis and resources linking social justice and environmental movements. $5 per issue; $20 per year.
P.O. Box 14141, San Francisco, CA 94110

Left Green Network
The Left Green Network is a continental organization devoted to "Greening the Left and Radicalizing the Greens." The principles of the Left Green Network and info on how to participate in the network are available from:
P.O. Box 366, Iowa City, IA 52244
$10/year subscriptions to Left Green Notes *are available from:*
825 East Roosevelt, Suite178, Lombard, IL 60148

Green Perspectives
Green Perspectives is a collective, eco-anarchist, social ecology newsletter, edited by Janet Beihl, Murray Bookchin, Chuck Morse, and Gary Sisco. Covers issues of radical ecology, social ecology, communities and natural ecologies. 10 issues for $10.
Box 111, Burlington, VT 05402

Rocky Mountain Institute
Considered to be the world's leading energy analysts, Amory and Hunter Lovins founded (1982) and continue to run RMI. A nonprofit resource policy center, RMI's eco-wisdom is sought by corporations and governments world wide. *Least-Cost Energy* (US $15 ppd., add $7.53 postage for foreign orders), as well as a catalog of related materials, can be obtained from:
1739 Snowmass Creek Road, Snowmass, CO 81654-9199 • Tel. (303) 927-3851

Nuclear Times
"Issues and Activism for Global Survival" is this magazine's motto. Published by the Winston Foundation For World Peace, *Nuclear Times* is an activist-oriented journal that features articles, interviews and dispatches on foreign affairs, disarmament, the environment, peace strategies, and networking information. Published quarterly. Cover price: $4.50. Four issue subscription: $15.
P.O. Box 351, Kenmore Station, Boston, MA 02215

Peacenet Computer Network
Through computer modems, Peacenet links together media, environmental, and human rights activists in over 70 countries. The net opens access to more than 600 electronic conferences that provide everything from timely information on world events to open discussions, activist tactics, and media strategies. Initial set-up fee is $15; monthly subscription fee is $10; online rates $5-$10/hr.; Internet access from universities—$3/hr.
18 De Boom Street, San Francisco, CA 94107 • Tel. (415) 442-0220
Fax (415) 546-1794